Sport Coaches' Handbook

International Council for Coaching Excellence

Dan Gould
Cliff Mallett
Editors

HUMAN KINETICS

Library of Congress Cataloging-in-Publication Data

Names: International Council for Coaching Excellence, author. | Gould, Daniel, 1952- editor. | Mallett, Clifford J., 1958- editor.

Title: Sport coaches' handbook / Dan Gould, Editor, Cliff Mallett, Editor.

Description: Champaign, IL : Human Kinetics, [2021] | Includes bibliographical references and index.

Identifiers: LCCN 2020014642 (print) | LCCN 2020014643 (ebook) | ISBN 9781492515807 (paperback) | ISBN 9781718200999 (epub) | ISBN 9781718201002 (pdf)

Subjects: LCSH: Coaching (Athletics) | Athletes--Training of.

Classification: LCC GV711 .I53 2021 (print) | LCC GV711 (ebook) | DDC 796.077--dc23

LC record available at https://lccn.loc.gov/2020014642

LC ebook record available at https://lccn.loc.gov/2020014643

ISBN: 978-1-4925-1580-7 (print)

Copyright © 2021 by International Council for Coaching Excellence

Managing Editor: Hannah Werner; **Copyeditor:** Tom Tiller; **Indexer:** Andrea J. Hepner; **Permissions Manager:** Martha Gullo; **Graphic Designer:** Denise Lowry; **Cover Designer:** Keri Evans; **Cover Design Specialist:** Susan Rothermel Allen; **Photographs (cover):** Robert B. Stanton/NFLPhotoLibrary/Getty Images; ANP Sport via Getty Images; FRANCOIS XAVIER MARIT/AFP via Getty Images; Icon Sportswire/Getty Images; **Photographs (interior):** Photo on page vii © ICCE. Photo on page xi © Rich Clarkson/NCAA Photos via Getty Images. Photo on page 8 © Robert W. Kelley/The LIFE Picture Collection via Getty Images. Photo on page 11 © DANIEL MIHAILESCU/AFP via Getty Images. Photo on page 21 © Stephen Dunn/Getty Images. Photo on page 25 © ERIC FEFERBERG/AFP via Getty Images. Photo on page 38 © VCG/VCG via Getty Images. Photo on page 46 © LUCY NICHOLSON/AFP via Getty Images. Photo on page 59 © Sara D. Davis/Getty Images. Photo on page 65 © Vaughn Ridley/Getty Images. Photo on page 80 © LUIS ROBAYO/AFP via Getty Images. Photo on page 89 courtesy of University of St. Francis (Ill.). Photo on page 100 © Michael Steele/Getty Images. Photo on page 108 © Dave Sandford/Getty Images/NHLI. Photo on page 125 courtesy of USA Hockey. Photos on pages 129 and 187 © TPN/Getty Images. Photo on page 137 © Feng Li/Getty Images. Photo on page 143 © Phil Walter/Getty Images. Photo on page 149 © Michael Regan/Getty Images. Photo on page 160 © Hunter Martin/Getty Images. Photo on page 172 © Jim Barcus/Kansas City Star/Tribune News Service via Getty Images. Photos on page 184 courtesy of Georgia Giblin. Photo on page 188 © Damian Farrow. Photo on page 189 © Waco Tribune-Herald/Rod Aydelotte. Photo on page 194 © FRANCOIS XAVIER MARIT/AFP via Getty Images. Photo on page 211 © John Tlumacki/The Boston Globe via Getty Images. Photo on page 219 © Abbie Parr/Getty Images. Photo on page 231 © Katharine Lotze/Getty Images. Photo on page 243 courtesy of UEFA. Photo on page 246 courtesy of FSU Sports Information. Photo on page 253 © Dima Korotayev/Bongarts/Getty Images; **Photo Asset Manager:** Laura Fitch; **Photo Production Manager:** Jason Allen; **Senior Art Manager:** Kelly Hendren; **Illustrations:** © Human Kinetics, unless otherwise noted; **Printer:** Versa Press

Printed in the United States of America   10 9 8 7 6 5 4 3 2 1

The paper in this book is certified under a sustainable forestry program.

Human Kinetics
1607 N. Market Street
Champaign, IL 61820
USA

United States and International
Website: **US.HumanKinetics.com**
Email: info@hkusa.com
Phone: 1-800-747-4457

Canada
Website: **Canada.HumanKinetics.com**
Email: info@hkcanada.com

E6648

Tell us what you think!
Human Kinetics would love to hear what we can do to improve the customer experience. Use this QR code to take our brief survey.

Sport Coaches' Handbook

CONTENTS

TRIBUTE TO PAT DUFFY

The *Sport Coaches' Handbook* was the brainchild of professor Pat Duffy, a prominent figure in the world of coaching. Pat served as vice president for strategy and development at the International Council for Coaching Excellence (ICCE), chair of the European Coaching Council, professor of sport coaching at Leeds Beckett University (UK), and cochair of the ICCE–Association of Summer Olympic International Federations project group that developed the *International Sport Coaching Framework*. He was also a key figure in developing coaching in his native Ireland as head of the National Coaching and Training Centre (now Sport Ireland Coaching).

Pat brought visionary leadership and passion to his work in coaching and coach development. Indeed, he was the driving force in the conception of this book in 2012 as part of a broader publishing plan agreed to by the ICCE and Human Kinetics.

That plan also included the *International Sport Coaching Framework* and the *International Sport Coaching Journal*. The framework, now a version advanced from the original, has profoundly influenced coach education and coaching around the world, as many sport federations and organizations have adopted or adapted it to best serve their needs and aims. The journal has also developed beautifully, thanks in large part to the splendid, dedicated stewardship of Wade Gilbert, who served as editor in chief from 2014-2019. No doubt, Pat would be pleased with the quality and progress of these publications in serving their intended purposes.

Pat might be less pleased that it took so long for the third piece of the plan—the handbook he envisioned as the link between the framework's concepts and principles and front-line coaching practices—to be completed. But here it is, solely due to the inspiration that Pat still provides for all whom he taught, advised, and addressed in presentations; all with whom he worked, joked, collaborated, and shared a pint; and all who admired and respected such a learned and accomplished leader in his field who could be so humble, caring, and inspired to do better and do more.

We agreed to edit this book not only because it was needed but also because the project was so important to Pat. We each considered Pat a friend and a great guy and respected his efforts to professionalize coaching and promote its scientific bases. We hope that this work advances the field of coaching as he believed it would.

Though he passed far too early at the age of 55, Pat's positive influence will be felt for many generations. Thus, we dedicate this book to that inspirational figure and trust that it will make a valuable addition to his legacy in coaching.

Dan Gould and Cliff Mallett

INTRODUCTION

Coaching and Its Development as a Profession

Wade Gilbert

Several years ago, an influential business leader asked if I knew the origin of the word *coach*. Somewhat embarrassed, I admitted that I did not, despite dedicating my career to studying and teaching coaches. He explained that the word was originally used to describe a carriage—that is, a horse-drawn wheeled vehicle for transporting people. In time, the term was also used to refer to private tutors hired for children in the privileged families who rode in such carriages.

Only later, when organized sport competitions began to emerge during the 19th century, did *coach* become associated with athletic training, in particular in the sport of boxing.[1] Beyond the history of the term, coaching as a legitimate and full-time profession goes back to the Olympic movement that achieved global significance in the mid-20th century. Whereas only 14 nations competed in the first Summer Olympics in 1896, the number exceeded 80, representing all inhabited continents, at the 1960 Summer Games.[2, 3] This historical perspective illustrates two important points about sport coaching: The purpose of coaching has always been to teach, and coaching as a formal profession is relatively young.

Much of what we know about high-quality teaching in sport can be traced back to a fateful game of pickup basketball played in 1973 in Los Angeles by two young social psychologists, Roland Tharp and Ronald Gallimore. They were in the early stages of building distinguished careers in psychology and education through their studies of human behavior and learning. Coincidentally, they happened to be working at the same university where one of the world's great teachers held class every day in a gymnasium. His name was John Wooden, and he was nearing the end of a legendary coaching career that would soon culminate in his men's basketball team winning a record 10th national championship.

Fortunately for the rest of us, Tharp and Gallimore were basketball fans who wondered what made Coach Wooden so effective. To find out, they asked to observe his practices, and he gladly agreed. Assuming that a formal body of scientific literature had been established on effective coaching, Tharp and Gallimore searched for a coach observation tool. After learning that none existed, they adapted one from teaching. Hence the first coach observation instrument was created. Over the course of 14 practices during the 1974-1975 season—Coach Wooden's last—they used pen and paper to meticulously chart his teaching behaviors on their observation sheet. Little did they know that what began as a fun diversion from their primary research would help spark the coaching science movement and become a seminal study that is still cited frequently in the coaching literature.[4, 5]

Their results, and a follow-up interview with Coach Wooden 30 years later, show that high-quality teaching in sport rests on the following factors: the coach's understanding of the sport; meticulously prepared practice plans that align with the principles of athlete skill development and learning; awareness of individual athletes' needs, identities, and learning styles; and eagerness to constantly reflect and evolve as a coach.[6-8] These findings have since been supported by numerous studies involving a wide range of coaches and are consistent with recognized theories of teaching and learning.[9-13] Indeed, current views of coaching are underpinned by the very elements observed in Wooden's coaching practice: knowledge of one's sport and how to teach it, knowledge of one's athletes and how to tailor one's teaching to meet their unique needs and profiles, and knowing one's strengths and weaknesses as a teacher.[14-16]

Coaches now have access to a deep body of literature, as well as established principles, to inform high-quality teaching in sport. Even so, the emergence of coaching as a formal and well-organized profession remains a work in progress. Despite the global spread of organized sport and the accompanying need for effective coaches, we have yet to establish a universally agreed-on path for becoming a coach or a universal set of coaching standards or principles for credentialing coaches.[17-19] Although in many countries around the world coach education has become more standardized and coaches go through exhaustive programs, there are still instances where the requirements for coaches involve no more than (at best) a few hours of attending a coaching course—and sometimes as little as a criminal background check and a willingness to coach.

Efforts to develop professional standards and principles of practice for coaches have long been led by individual sport federations around the world. Comprehensive, evidence-based examples include the multitiered and interdisciplinary coach education programs developed by England's Football (Soccer) Association[20] and USA Hockey's American Development Model.[21] In some countries, including the United States, sport coaching coalitions have also created generic coaching standards that can be used to inform sport-specific coaching guidelines.[22, 23]

COACHING SNAPSHOT

John Wooden is remembered and respected as much for his contributions to coaching as his amazing coaching record. His Pyramid of Success, thoughtful truisms, and writings have provided coaches many insights and teaching points to apply in their careers, such as his definition of success: *"Success is peace of mind, which is a direct result of self-satisfaction in knowing you made the effort to become the best you are capable of becoming."*

Until fairly recently, however, the professionalization efforts made by individual sport federations were not informed by a globally recognized, evidence-based coaching framework. That changed in 2013, when a consortium led by the International Council for Coaching Excellence (ICCE) created an updated and expanded version of the *International Sport Coaching Framework* (ISCF).[24] The ISCF provides a blueprint for coaching competence and coach development based on six primary tasks undertaken by sport coaches:

1. Setting vision and strategy
2. Shaping the environment
3. Building relationships
4. Conducting practices and preparing for competitions
5. Reading and reacting to the field
6. Learning and reflecting

Helping coaches learn how to effectively perform—and continually refine—these six core competencies will empower our continuing progress toward the professionalization of coaching.

Growing evidence shows that the ISCF is being adopted as a guiding framework for creating sport-specific and culturally relevant standards for coaching practice and ongoing coach development. For example, since its launch in 2014, every issue of the *International Sport Coaching Journal* features an article profiling the status of coaching and coach education in a different country. These articles make clear that the ISCF is increasingly being used by national sport and coaching organizations to define and shape the development of coaching.[25, 26] Thus it appears that the ISCF is slowly realizing its goals of bringing coherence to the global efforts to raise the status of coaching as a profession. Moreover, based on my interactions with national sport and coaching leaders around the world, I have no doubt that the ISCF will play an ever more prominent role in shaping coaching and coach education.

Even as coaching matures as an occupation, some have argued that it is ill-suited to becoming more professionalized. As one group has noted,[27] the motives for professionalizing coaching in today's world—marked by decentralized control, open access to knowledge, and interdisciplinary collaboration and reliance—differ vastly from the purposes and needs that drove professionalization in occupations such as medicine and psychology in the 19th century. In addition, coaching is characterized by a degree of variation—ranging from volunteer coaches in participation-oriented settings to paid coaches in performance-oriented settings—that other professions have not had to address. For instance, there is no need to create standards of practice and credentialing guidelines for both professionals and volunteers among doctors or lawyers. Thus sport coaching is often referred to as a blended profession.[28]

These tensions, both within and across sports and countries, are evident in current efforts to professionalize coaching. Moreover, this mixed reality may constitute a necessary and normal state of affairs as we work to ensure that coaching continues to mature both as an occupation and as an area of scientific inquiry. As a blended profession, coaching itself is messy and complex, so why would we expect efforts to professionalize it to be any different? Furthermore, as a relatively young and emerging profession, the field may simply be experiencing the typical growing pains that more established professions also experienced during their journeys.[29]

A few years ago, some thoughts on the challenges faced by coaching and coach education were offered through a collaboration between Paul Roetert, now director of education and strategic engagement for the Sport Science Institute of the National Collegiate Athletic Association, and John Bales, president of the ICCE.[28] Their insights, based on decades of leading influential coaching and coach education organizations as well as their own coaching experiences, serve as a call to action by illuminating the most pressing needs of the coaching and coach education community. Here are some of the challenges they identified:[28 (p. 3)]

- Providing a greater body of knowledge in the fields related to coaching education
- Sharing practical applications in a user-friendly manner based on solid research as well as best practices
- Developing an age-appropriate body of knowledge to coach educators of all levels
- Deciding the role of physical literacy in coaching education
- Gender-related coaching strategies
- Aligning, implementing, and evaluating international frameworks for coaching education and coach development
- Conducting research that further identifies the implications of coaching knowledge and ability on athlete development

We must focus our collective efforts on resolving these challenges because it is clear that the need for effective sport coaches will continue to grow along with the expansion and professionalization of sport in general. For example, in the United States, employment of sport coaches is projected to grow by 11 percent per year through 2028 in order to meet growing demand.[30] This growth rate more than doubles the rate for all other occupations, and it doesn't even account for unpaid sport coaches who traditionally make up the vast majority of sport coaches in most countries around the world.

Although the challenges for coaching and coach education are many and complex, those of us who work in these areas feel great optimism about our ability to resolve these challenges. A robust and deep body of coaching science now exists, along with an active and interconnected global network of coaching scientists and coach educators. More specifically, the emergence of national and international conferences, as well as academic journals dedicated to coaching and coach education, offer sure signs that the field is maturing and point to a bright future.

Yet another reason to be optimistic can be found in the publication of this *Sport Coaches' Handbook*, which should serve as a valued resource for all who share a passion for coaching and coach education. It provides a timely and much-needed resource for meeting the challenges we face as a profession. It brings clarity to what we have learned through our collective efforts to professionalize sport coaching and points the way to continue advancing these efforts and raising the quality of coaching around the world. I am honored to have had the opportunity to introduce you to this text, and I look forward to sharing the valuable information compiled by this group of distinguished contributors with members of my coaching communities of practice.

Chapter 1

The Coaching Role

Dan Gould and Cliff Mallett

People coach for many reasons. Perhaps you simply love the game and want to continue competing after your playing days are over. Or you may want to emulate the great coaches you've known and make a difference in players' lives—or counter the negative influence of poor coaches. Whatever your motives, you can be effective only if you deeply understand what the role of a coach involves.

Yet doing so is not as simple as it may seem. Indeed, *coaching* is one of those terms that is used every day but seldom defined or examined. Therefore, this first chapter clarifies what it means to be a sport coach. Specifically, it provides an overview of the coaching process; briefly traces the historical roots of coaching; lays out the key aims, expectations, and duties of sport coaches; and addresses sport coaching as a career.

The Coaching Process

Wikipedia defines coaching as the "training or development in which a person called a *coach* supports a learner in achieving a specific personal or professional goal."[1] The earliest uses of the term can be traced to the Hungarian word *kocsi*,[2] which referred to a carriage for transporting passengers over rough terrain. Although the word *coaching* was once associated almost exclusively with sport, it is used today in many other ways—for instance, in life coaching and in business and executive coaching.

Here, given our focus on sport coaching, we adopt the definition provided by the International Council for Coaching Excellence: "a process of guided (athlete and/or team) improvement and development in a single sport at identifiable stages of development."[3 (p. 14)] Thus sport coaching involves structuring both practice and competition activities to produce desired outcomes for athletes and teams. This definition also suggests that coaching is context specific. Consider, for instance, the difference between coaching elite athletes in a professional setting and coaching entry-level athletes in a recreational program. In addition, coaching is a process that unfolds over time through the interaction of coaches' knowledge, athlete outcomes, and specific sport contexts.[4]

Coaches' Knowledge

Coaches must possess many types of knowledge, which can be categorized into three main areas:

1. Professional knowledge, which includes sport science as well as sport-specific and pedagogical information (technique and tactics, or the Xs and Os of coaching)
2. Interpersonal knowledge, which enables successful interaction with others (e.g., athletes, officials, parents, administrators)
3. Intrapersonal knowledge, which encompasses self-reflection and self-understanding and is especially important for master coaches, who critically and continually examine their coaching practices in search of ways to improve[4]

These types of knowledge do not exist in isolation; rather, coaches integrate them with each other and with their personal experiences.

Athlete Outcomes

A review of the coaching literature[5] suggested that outcomes associated with coaching fall into one of four categories known as the 4 Cs: competence, confidence, connection, and character/caring. The first C, *competence*, may seem obvious, since one main objective of coaching is to help athletes improve their performance. Yet coaches also help athletes become competent in more general terms by developing their independence and improving their health and fitness. Coaches can also help athletes to become more *confident*, both on and off the field, and to develop relationships that enable them to become more *connected* to their teams and communities. Finally, research shows that coaches can help athletes become better people by doing things that help develop their *character*. Specifically, athletes who develop character learn to be empathetic, develop personal and social responsibility, and exhibit respect for their chosen sport and for other people.

Specific Sport Contexts

Coaches carry out their duties in a wide variety of contexts, ranging from local recreational leagues for very young children to professional sports for adults. These varied settings have been categorized into three general coaching contexts: recreational, developmental, and elite.[6] Similarly, the

ICCE has distinguished between participation-focused coaching (geared primarily toward participant enjoyment) and performance coaching (geared toward skill development and competitive success); in either of these domains, coaching may focus on children, adolescents, or adults.[3]

So, how do we judge coaching effectiveness? One answer integrates the types of coaching knowledge, the 4 Cs, and the various types of coaching contexts. In this model, effective coaching involves consistently applying "integrated professional, interpersonal, and intrapersonal knowledge to improve athletes' competence, confidence, connection, and character in specific coaching contexts."[4 (p. 316)] In other words, effective coaches integrate the three forms of coaching knowledge to help their athletes develop some combination of the 4 Cs in a way that makes sense for the specific context in which they coach.

Historical Perspective on Coaching

Sport coaching has a long, rich history dating back to the ancient Olympic Games, for which athletes employed coaches who in many cases were former athletes themselves.[7] It has also been reported that former gladiators served as coaches in ancient Rome[8] and that archers received coaching on the use of the English longbow during the Hundred Years' War.[9] Despite these historical examples, the modern coaching era did not begin until the 20th century,[10] when the development of coaching as a profession paralleled increases in leisure time, the growth of children's and school sports, and the development of the modern Olympic Games.

As sport has become more popular and more professionalized, practitioners have worked to make coaching more professionalized as well. Professionalization involves more than simply paying coaches a stipend or salary. It also requires—in the sense used in medicine, law, and teaching—meeting specific criteria to establish coaching as a profession rather than merely a vocation or job. These criteria include

1. being service oriented,
2. evaluating performance based on intellectual techniques,
3. demonstrating a strong commitment to the profession and full-time positions,
4. basing practice on a common body of knowledge,
5. providing services offered only by members of the profession,
6. requiring specialized formal training,
7. requiring members to demonstrate minimum competencies assessed by examination or supervision, and
8. achieving legal recognition for the field (as in the requirement for a medical doctor to be licensed).[11]

Over the last 50 years, people in the field of coaching have tried to professionalize their work by developing it in line with some of these criteria. For example, efforts have been made to identify the body of knowledge that one needs to possess in order to be a coach. In the United States, SHAPE America has developed 42 knowledge standards that all coaches should meet;[12] see table 1.1. As alluded to earlier, the ICCE has also been working to delineate the knowledge that coaches need by distinguishing between professional knowledge (about the sport, athletes, sport science, coaching theory and methodology, and foundational skills), interpersonal knowledge (about relationships and the social contexts of sport), and intrapersonal knowledge (about one's coaching philosophy and lifelong learning orientation).[3]

Efforts to professionalize coaching have also focused on identifying key competencies for coaches. Specifically, the ICCE has suggested that effective coaches fulfill six major functions:[3]

1. set the vision and strategy for the team or program (e.g., analyze needs, understand the big picture),
2. shape the environment (e.g., organize the setting and personnel; identify and pursue athletes, staff, and resources; develop progress markers),
3. build relationships (e.g., lead, manage, educate),
4. conduct practices and structure competitions (e.g., guide practice, employ appropriate pedagogy, manage competitions),
5. read and reflect on the field (e.g., observe, make decisions and adjustments), and
6. reflect on and learn from one's own actions (e.g., self-monitor, evaluate the program, engage in professional development).

In another move toward professionalization, some organizations have put forth ethical guidelines for coaching. For example, guidelines established by the United States Olympic and Paralympic Committee focus on general standards of behavior,[13] such as professional conduct and competence (e.g., coaching only in activities for which one has developed competence); demonstrating integrity by playing within the rules; respecting all sport participants and showing concern for the welfare of others; and acting responsibly both in and out of the sport context.

Over the last 40 years, sport organizations and governing bodies have also developed coaching education schemes that require coaches to obtain and demonstrate certain types of knowledge and experience in order to be certified to coach. For instance, one of the most developed coaching education systems is found in Canada.[14] Typically such programs require coaches to progress through various levels (e.g., in training, trained, certified, advanced, master) of increasingly comprehensive courses in sport science, techniques, and tactics. As a result, the field has witnessed a shift in the coaching knowledge base from mere physical education to a science of sport and coaching.

In recent years, coaching has also been examined in terms of workforce issues, especially in Europe,[15] with a key aim of building practitioners' capabilities. As part of these efforts, governments are examining the economic impact of coaching, such as the implications of many coaches being volunteers and not paid workers, and how coaching relates to employment issues. A key employment issue is related to the globalization of coaches and coaching work. This globalization of coaches necessitates consideration of the transferability of registration and accreditation of coaches to practice for ethical and legal reasons, among others.

Overall, then, considerable work has been done around the world to advance coaching as a profession. Even so, most of these efforts have been sporadic and inconsistent. The fact remains that many more coaches are untrained than trained, few make a full-time living from coaching, and in many countries and organizations one can become a coach simply by getting a hat and a whistle. Thus coaching remains far from meeting the criteria for becoming a profession. However, recent efforts to continue professionalizing the field are encouraging (in some countries, such as Brazil, coaching now requires a university education!), and this work should be continued so that coaching can achieve professional status.

Primary Aims, Expectations, and Duties of Sport Coaches

Coaches are trusted with carrying out a number of important duties—for instance, helping athletes and teams learn sport skills, tactics, and strategies and achieve peak performance. Fulfilling these duties requires that coaches be developed and supported. In fact, one study found that coaching development and support were correlated with the number of Olympic medals won by a country.[16]

As discussed earlier, another major duty of coaches is to facilitate athletes' personal growth and development through the 4 Cs. This duty is not limited to coaches in school and developmental youth settings. To the contrary, many top coaches of elite athletes have been known for developing not only great performers but also individuals of high character and morals. Think, for example, of swimming coach James "Doc" Counsilman and UCLA basketball guru John Wooden.

TABLE 1.1 National Standards for Sport Coaches

Set Vision, Goals and Standards for Sport Program

Standard 1. Develop and enact an athlete-centered coaching philosophy.

Standard 2. Use long-term athlete development with the intent to develop athletic potential, enhance physical literacy, and encourage lifelong physical activity.

Standard 3. Create a unified vision using strategic planning and goal-setting principles.

Standard 4. Align program with all rules and regulations and needs of the community and individual athletes.

Standard 5. Manage program resources in a responsible manner.

Engage in and Support Ethical Practices

Standard 6. Abide by the code of conduct within their coaching context.

Standard 7. Model, teach and reinforce ethical behavior with program participants.

Standard 8. Develop an ethical decision-making process based on ethical standards.

Build Relationships

Standard 9. Acquire and utilize interpersonal and communication skills.

Standard 10. Develop competencies to work with a diverse group of individuals.

Standard 11. Demonstrate professionalism and leadership with all stakeholders.

Develop a Safe Sport Environment

Standard 12. Create a respectful and safe environment which is free from harassment and abuse.

Standard 13. Collaborate with program directors to fulfill all legal responsibilities and risk management procedures associated with coaching.

Standard 14. Identify and mitigate physical, psychological and sociocultural conditions that predispose athletes to injuries.

Standard 15. Monitor environmental conditions and modify participation as needed to ensure the health and safety of participants.

Standard 16. Reduce potential injuries by instituting safe and proper training principles and procedures.

Standard 17. Develop awareness of common injuries in sport and provide immediate and appropriate care within scope of practice.

Standard 18. Support the decisions of sports medicine professionals to help athletes have a healthy return to participation following an injury.

Standard 19. Model and encourage nutritional practices that ensure the health and safety of athletes.

Standard 20. Provide accurate information about drugs and supplements to athletes and advocate for drug-free sport participation.

Create a Positive and Inclusive Sport Environment

Standard 21. Implement a positive and enjoyable sport climate based on best practices for psychosocial and motivational principles to maximize athlete and team well-being and performance.

Standard 22. Build inclusive practices into the program for all groups (e.g., race/ethnicity, gender/gender identity/gender expression, religion, socioeconomic status, sexual orientation, nationality, etc.) which are aligned with current legal and ethical guidelines.

Standard 23. Understand the importance of including athletes with disabilities in meaningful participation in established sport programs and consider options for athletes who cannot participate in traditional sport opportunities.

Conduct Practices and Prepare for Competition

Plan

Standard 24. Create seasonal and/or annual plans that incorporate developmentally appropriate progressions for instructing sport-specific skills based on best practices in motor development, biomechanics, and motor learning.

Standard 25. Design appropriate progressions for improving sport-specific physiological systems throughout all phases of the sport season using essential principles of exercise physiology and nutritional knowledge.

Standard 26. Plan practices to incorporate appropriate competition strategies, tactics and scouting information.

Standard 27. Incorporate mental skills into practice and competition to enhance performance and athlete well-being.

Standard 28. Create intentional strategies to develop life skills and promote their transfer to other life domains.

Standard 29. Understand components of effective contest management.

Teach

Standard 30. Know the skills, elements of skill combinations and techniques, competition strategies and tactics, and the rules associated with the sport being coached.

Standard 31. Develop and utilize pedagogical strategies in daily practices.

Standard 32. Craft daily practice plans based on sound teaching and learning principles to promote athlete development and optimize competitive performance.

Standard 33. Use appropriate motivational techniques to enhance performance and athlete engagement during practices and competitions.

Assess

Standard 34. Implement appropriate strategies for evaluating athlete training, development and performance.

Standard 35. Engage athletes in a process of continuous self-assessment and reflection to foster responsibility for their own learning and development.

Adapt

Standard 36. Adjust training and competition plans based on athlete needs and assessment practices.

Standard 37. Use strategic decision-making skills to make adjustments or improvements or change course throughout a competition.

Strive for Continuous Improvement

Standard 38. Regularly engage in self-reflection or peer-reflection to deeply examine situations, generate potential solutions, and think through those solutions.

Standard 39. Develop an evaluation strategy to monitor and improve staff and team performance.

Standard 40. Improve coaching effectiveness by seeking to learn the latest information on coaching through various avenues of coach development.

Standard 41. Engage in mentoring and communities of practice to promote a learning culture and continual improvement.

Standard 42. Maintain work-life harmony and practice self-care to manage stress and burnout.

From L. Gano-Overway, M. Thompson, and P. Van Mullem, *National Standards for Sport Coaches: Quality Coaches, Quality Sports,* 3rd ed. (Burlington, MA: Jones & Bartlett Learning, 2021). www.jblearning.com. Reprinted with permission.

COACHING SNAPSHOT

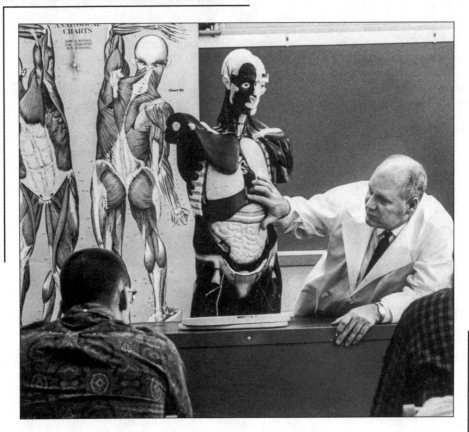

James Counsilman demonstrated his leadership and courage as a World War II pilot, earning the Distinguished Flying Cross. After the war, he resumed his swimming career and became absorbed in the science behind the sport. After earning his PhD in physiology, he became a head coach and professor at the college level and would forever more be known as "Doc" Counsilman. His book *Science of Swimming* is still considered the gold standard in translating complex scientific principles to coaching practice, and his innovative and winning methods (six NCAA and two Olympic championship teams) set him apart from his peers.

Coaches also help athletes achieve optimal fitness by designing well-conceived training and conditioning programs. This role involves helping athletes not only improve their fitness but also learn positive health habits (e.g., optimal weight management, good nutritional practices) and understand that doping has no proper place in sport.

Finally, coaches also have a duty to protect their athletes. They do so, for example, by structuring practice and competitive environments to minimize the chances of physical injury. And when athletes are injured, effective coaches allow them to return to play only when they are medically certified to be truly ready.

In addition to playing these roles, in many countries, individuals who accept a coaching position (volunteer or paid) also take on certain legal duties. In the United States, for example, coaches carry nine legal duties:[17]

1. Properly plan activities (e.g., proper skill progressions)
2. Provide proper instruction (e.g., proper conditioning for learning new skills)
3. Warn of inherent risks (e.g., dangers of headfirst sliding in baseball and softball)
4. Provide a safe physical environment (e.g., playing field free of broken glass, seating far enough from playing area)
5. Provide adequate and proper equipment (e.g., stable goalposts)
6. Match athletes appropriately (e.g., pairing of evenly matched and evenly experienced participants in contact sports)
7. Evaluate athletes for injury or incapacity (e.g., medical clearance for an injured athlete's return)
8. Supervise the activity (e.g., no practice without supervision by coaching staff)
9. Provide adequate emergency assistance (e.g., well-defined plan for handling major injury)

If a coach fails to fulfill any of these duties and an athlete is injured, the coach can be held legally liable. Such legal standards vary across countries, and some countries do not hold coaches to any legal standards. Ultimately, regardless of legal liability, coaches have an ethical duty to provide safe and healthy environments for their athletes.

Coaching as a Career

Coaches may work in a variety of positions. Some act as sport teachers who introduce novices to the basics and focus on instruction—for example, teaching a basic skills class in gymnastics, tennis, soccer, or swimming. Others coach in participation sport settings where they help athletes learn skills and prepare for competition with a focus on fun and enjoyment. Still others, of course, coach in performance settings where athletes focus on developing their talent and succeeding in competition. In any of these domains, a coach may occupy either a paid or an unpaid position; even at the highest levels, some coaches work part-time or as volunteers.

Coaches also work at different levels of responsibility and mastery. For example, one might serve as an apprentice, an assistant coach, an assistant head coach, or a head coach. In some countries and programs, coaches may hold other distinctions. For instance, one might earn the designation of master coach by accumulating a certain level of experience or specialized training (e.g., advanced or graduate degree). In addition, although the coaching field has yet to meet all of the criteria for becoming a profession, anyone who chooses to coach should act as a professional. Indeed, coaches are generally expected to meet the professional standards, duties, and responsibilities discussed in this chapter.

In particular, coaches should develop a well-thought-out philosophy and adopt robust ethical standards in order to navigate the intense pressure to win. Too many coaches have advocated unethical behaviors, such as doping and other forms of cheating, to gain a competitive advantage; in addition, in recent years, another major ethical issue has come to light in the form of sexual abuse of athletes by coaches. It may be easy to think that behaviors such as cheating are exhibited only by "bad people," but many good and well-intentioned coaches have been drawn into ethical transgressions in the heat of the moment or when "just trying to keep up" with competing coaches who are behaving unethically.

Studies of experienced coaches show that they continue to develop over time. When one highly successful coach was asked if he coached differently now than 20 years ago, he said, "I better coach differently now, because if I am not, I have wasted the last 20 years." How do coaches continue to grow and develop? We know that highly successful coaches engage regularly in self-evaluation. They consistently reflect on practices, competitions, and complete seasons. They look at what went right with their team or athletes and their coaching, as well as what went wrong. They think about how they can continue to improve. Many coaches also solicit feedback from key stakeholders in their programs, including administrators, coaches, and athletes. In addition, they network by getting involved in professional coaching associations as both presenters and participants. Finally, they read books about great coaches and leaders. What strategies will you use to stay current and grow as a coach?

Life as a Coach

Coaching offers many benefits: involvement in the game you love, influence in the lives of athletes, winning, status, respect, and perhaps considerable money. It also comes with costs. Only a few coaches enjoy the lucrative salaries we hear about in the media, but coaching is always anything but a typical 9-to-5 job. Coaches also face tremendous pressure to win, to play certain athletes, and to meet their own expectations. In fact, a recent study of elite coaches in England showed that they experienced a wide range of stressors beyond pressure and expectations—for instance, conflict, preparation for competition, isolation, athlete concerns

COACHING SNAPSHOT

Pia Sundhage is the definition of a coach who seeks new challenges and continues to add to her coaching arsenal. After enjoying a long and distinguished playing career both professionally and on the Swedish national team, Sundhage took a player/manager position and would, over the course of the next 28 years, serve as a scout, assistant coach, and head coach for teams in her native country of Sweden, China, the United States, and Brazil, leading the U.S. women to two Olympic gold medals (2008 and 2012) and collecting FIFA World Coach of the Year honors along the way.

such as a lack of commitment and having distractions disrupt their focus, and dealing with sponsoring organizations.[18]

These stressors are exacerbated by the complex, chaotic, and often unpredictable nature of coaching.[19] In fact, especially in high-performance contexts, coaches should be viewed as performers in their own right.[20, 21] As a result, another key issue for professional coaches involves the volatility of their employment, which typically hinges on competitive outcomes for their athletes or team—that is, on winning.[21]

Faced with such intense stressors, coaches need to develop ways to manage them. For instance, in the Serial Winning Coaches (SWC) project,[21] both coaches and athletes reported coaches' obsessive pursuit of performance success for themselves and their athletes. However, they also indicated that this obsessive pursuit was balanced with genuine care and compassion for their athletes, and this defining characteristic of highly successful coaches was termed *driven benevolence*.[22] This orientation of caring for others helps coaches to be more focused on athlete outcomes, such as developing a stronger sense of connection and belonging through these coaches demonstrating genuine care. Indeed, the SWC's relentless pursuit of excellence was balanced with a genuine desire to compassionately support athletes and oneself; in other words, the SWC created an environment characterized by high challenge that was matched with high social and emotional support.

One hidden cost of coaching is the toll it can take on a coach's family. Some coaches spend so much time with their team that their marriage ends. Others spend so much time looking after their athletes that they neglect their own health and well-being. Such neglect can lead to exhaustion and even burnout, in which a once-enjoyable activity becomes a burden.[23] Ultimately, then, coaching at any level of play involves a balancing act. Coaches must commit to their athletes while also tending to their own health, well-being, and personal relationships.

Exercise: Assessing Your Coaching Role

Directions: Complete the following.

In what context do you coach or desire to coach? (Check one.)

_____ Participation-focused coaching

_____ Performance coaching

What is your coaching status?

_____ Apprentice coach

_____ Assistant coach

_____ Assistant head coach

_____ Head coach

What age range and gender of athletes do you coach?

Age range: _____

Gender: _____

Given your current or projected coaching position, identify the expected pluses (benefits) and minuses (negatives).

Benefits:

_____

_____

_____

_____

_____

_____

Negatives:

_____

_____

_____

_____

_____

_____

From International Council for Coaching Excellence, *Sport Coaches' Handbook*, eds. D. Gould and C. Mallett. (Champaign, IL: Human Kinetics, 2021).

Chapter 2

Coaching Ethics

Andy Driska, Laurie Patterson, and Sue Backhouse

As the saying goes, sport may not build character as much as reveal it. As a result, coaches are likely to face many and varied ethical issues even in the course of a single season.[1] Coaches' ethics are expressed in the form of daily decisions and actions related to competitive fairness, personal morals, and athletes' well-being. Our conceptions of ethical behavior are guided by our beliefs about the nature of human behavior and its origin, and understanding this causal relationship can help us appreciate the nature of ethical (and unethical) coaching behaviors. It can also provide us with a framework for intervention.

Ethical mindsets are persistent or habitual ways of thinking that create behavioral intentions (plans) and, to a lesser degree, drive actual behaviors. For our purposes here, a mindset consists of a psychological makeup that leads a coach to think persistently or habitually in a certain way. This makeup includes all of the factors that shape the coach's worldview: dispositional personality traits, moral knowledge, moral reasoning skills, reflections on previous moral decisions and actions, attitudes about the persons involved in a given situation, and emotional attachments. Altogether, this makeup constitutes the coach's sense of right and wrong.

Ethical behaviors, on the other hand, are observable actions that fall within the bounds of a code of conduct that the coach has agreed to honor. Examples of ethical coaching behaviors include adhering to training rules; treating players, officials, and other coaches respectfully; and recruiting athletes honestly and properly. Codes of conduct are not inherently involved in shaping ethical mindsets; instead, their purpose is to constrain and direct behavior. That is, they exist to help ensure that coaches adhere to agreed-on ethical behaviors.

Ethical mindsets, ethical behaviors, and good decision-making skills are generally learned, and any candidate for a coaching position should possess a good moral track record. However, these factors are also shaped by environmental pressures, and a candidate who is found to be morally upstanding is not necessarily immune to the pressure to cheat in certain circumstances.

Consider the case of Jim Tressel, who was viewed as one of the most morally upstanding coaches in the United States when he accepted the prestigious position of head football coach at Ohio State University. The school promoted Tressel's integrity and honesty, boasting that "what you see is what you get." What Buckeye fans saw for a decade was an exceedingly successful football program that won a national championship and competed for multiple others while compiling a 106-22 record. Tressel was lauded for winning in a highly ethical manner, until it was revealed that many of his players were selling OSU equipment and memorabilia, and had been doing so for years—a clear violation of NCAA rules. As documented in a long sequence of emails, Tressel had been informed of the transgressions but done nothing about them and then lied when confronted by university and NCAA officials. As a result, he was fined and essentially banned from coaching at the college level for five years by a "show-cause" order requiring any school that hired him to be penalized unless it could make a convincing case for doing so.

The Tressel case illustrates how coaches with a good ethical history and reputation—trustworthy, principled people by most any measure—can stray from their moral compass and commit ethical transgressions. It also points to the need for coaches to reflect frequently on their moral mindset and do what they know is right regardless of environmental pressures.

Personal Standards for Ethical Behavior

The link between a coach's ethical mindset and ethical behavior is difficult to assess and depends on both situation and context. We all possess values—deeply held beliefs, ideologies, or unquestioned assumptions—that have been learned and reinforced throughout life. These values derive from our unique contexts and experiences as we grow and develop. The relationship between our values and our behaviors may be intentional or may remain unconscious. Some values are learned early and go unchallenged throughout life, whereas others are questioned and may evolve. All of our values ultimately influence our behavior. In sport settings, a coach's behavior is affected both by sport-related values and by more general, or existential, concerns. Here are some examples:

Sport-Related Values

- Views about the nature and purpose of sport, such as demonstrating superiority over an opponent or developing prosocial behaviors in children

- Attitudes toward motivational enhancers, such as rewards for performance or skill mastery
- Conceptions of effective learning by young athletes, perhaps through direct teaching or deliberate engagement with their environment
- Notions of sport as a fun experience, as when an athlete or team enjoys a particularly good practice

Existential Values

- Spiritual beliefs, as reflected in honoring a deity through competition or pursuit of personal excellence
- Religious beliefs, as in using sport to demonstrate moral behavior prescribed by a religious code
- Conceptions of justice, as in believing that those who break rules will be punished in due course
- Notions of equity and fairness and attitudes about the role of a coach as arbiter in situations involving inequity

These examples illustrate the fact that deeply held values can shape coaching behaviors. For help in identifying the values that form the base of your coaching philosophy, see the exercises provided in chapter 3 (Coaching Philosophy).

Personal Standards for Ethical Decision Making

Just as our values are learned and developed, so too is our concept of the moral self.[2] In this process, we develop standards of right and wrong that guide our behavior. We can develop moral reasoning through direct instruction, but this process also occurs through encountering situations that require us to make moral decisions and experiencing the consequences of our actions (or inactions). However, moral reasoning capacity does not serve as the only driver of behavior; to the contrary, behavior is often shaped by interaction between a person and environmental influences.[2] Moreover, as we have seen, a coach who develops the capacity for moral reasoning and ethical decision making remains subject to—and perhaps susceptible to—external pressures.

In a recent example, the pressure to win a championship led the Houston Astros coaching staff to develop a video-based system for sign stealing that allowed their players to take the guesswork out of hitting. Knowing what pitches the opponent is going to throw gives hitters a tremendous advantage. During the 2017 season, this advantage was exploited by manager A.J. Hinch and bench coach Alex Cora, along with the club's general manager and assistant general manager, on their way to a World Series title. After the scheme was revealed in 2019, the coaches and staffers involved were fired by the organization, and Major League Baseball suspended them for a year and levied penalties against the Astros organization. Prior to this episode, Hinch and Cora had not been viewed as cheaters, but, with the apparent approval and support of their bosses, they chose a course of conduct that clearly violated the rules.

As this situation illustrates, any attempt to assess or improve coaches' moral behavior must address both the personal and the environmental factors that influence behavior. This example also suggests that coaches must not only be aware of their personal moral standards but also periodically take stock of the external pressures they face and how those pressures might influence their actions.

Coaches are often forced to make instant decisions, which increases their risk of making a choice they would not have made if allowed more time to evaluate and reflect on all factors. In addition, their decisions often play out in a public arena. Operating under such rushed and vulnerable conditions, coaches must develop a strong moral compass to ensure that their actions are ethical.

Of course, some coaching decisions can be made after considerable deliberation, thus enabling coaches to carefully apply effective decision-making practices. Over time, the guiding principles that coaches learn from this deliberate process will pervade their mindset and drive habitual decisions that must be made quickly, with little or no opportunity to contemplate.

To help you make ethical decisions in your own coaching, here are seven key steps.

1. *Recognize that ethical decisions must be made and that choosing to make no decision constitutes a decision in itself.* Choosing not to act—as when a teacher-coach chooses not to report a failing grade that would make a star player ineligible—is not only a decision but also an abdication of moral responsibility. In contrast, great coaches exhibit the moral courage to accept that difficult ethical decisions must be made, and they are willing to bear the consequences.

2. *Conduct a "before-the-fact" analysis of difficult ethical decisions that you can reasonably anticipate needing to make in the near future.* By identifying such situations and creating virtual test cases, you can think through the implications of various possible responses. For instance, coaches must often decide whether to cut a player from the roster. Before-the-fact analysis enables the coach to detect any potential bias (e.g., favoritism toward the son or daughter of a school board member), rehearse how to handle the meeting with the athlete, and consider alternatives, such as splitting the final roster spot between two athletes over the course of the season.

3. *Assess the context fully and carefully.* Begin by writing down the facts of the situation. Next, determine the most appropriate set of values for the context in which you coach. Then make sure that these values are understood and accepted by the rest of the coaching staff, by athletes, and by their families. Occasionally, your analysis may reveal that the context itself dictates the appropriate course of action, thereby saving you from the need to conduct a prolonged process of ethical decision making. For instance, if a youth sport league's code of conduct indicates that participation is paramount, then cutting a player for lack of ability would contradict the league's principles. Therefore, the code makes the decision for you.

4. *Distinguish emotional judgments from facts and logic.* Coaches form emotional judgments about players, other coaches, and referees. To varying degrees, such judgments are based on facts, but an ethical decision-making process requires us to differentiate judgments from facts. For example, a swimmer's recent time in the 50-meter freestyle is a fact, whereas a coach's interpretation that the swimmer failed to meet full potential is a judgment. Facts and judgments both play a role in ethical decision making, but they must be separated and weighted appropriately.

5. *Make sure that the means are not compromised to achieve desirable ends.* To avoid this pitfall, examine whether a given decision would align with the stated values of your program or coaching staff. For instance, suppose that a coach professes a democratic leadership style and espouses the democratic process, then makes an autocratic decision. This action defies the democratic process that the coach claims to value, thus creating doubt, and perhaps discord, in the program.

6. *Consider the history of the issue.* In addition to the current context, preceding events may also be important. Consideration of prior, related incidents or similar instances may help you grasp what is happening now and why the issue of the moment has arisen. For instance, let's say that a player responds to a taunt by grabbing an opponent's wrists and warning her not to start anything. You bench and scold your player but then learn that she received a similar taunt along with a black eye from the same opponent during summer league competition. Thus you realize that she was merely trying to avoid a recurrence of that episode.

7. *Make the decision.* Finally, the moment of truth arrives. It's time to step up, make the call, and own it. In terms of both leadership and ethics, it is critical that you announce your decision clearly to all affected parties and accept full responsibility for it.

This deliberative decision-making process isn't always feasible when circumstances dictate immediate action. Therefore, it is imperative that you try to anticipate difficult decisions that you may need to make quickly during the course of a season. In addition, identify which steps in the ethical decision-making process you believe will be most helpful in guiding you to an ethical decision in each stressful situation, thereby enabling you to make a choice quickly when necessary.

To reiterate, in order to make ethical decisions in high-pressure situations, coaches must be unfazed by environmental distractions (e.g., emotional triggers, pressure to win) that might lead to unethical choices. If coaches are to serve as moral agents, then their behavior must be driven not by environmental pressures but by their ethical mindset.

Ethics Expected of Coaches

The *International Sport Coaching Framework* (ISCF) states a "clear expectation that coaches will perform their duties in an ethically responsible way, play by the rules at all times, and protect the integrity of sport."[3] [(p. 17)] More specifically, the framework stresses that coaches should develop competence not only in safeguarding and protecting athletes but also in constructively leading and influencing them. The ISCF also indicates that coaches should develop both professional knowledge (of governance, rules, and regulations) and intrapersonal knowledge (related to identity, ethical mindset, philosophy, values, and beliefs). Thus it places the onus on coaches to develop a moral mindset and ethical decision-making skills.

Beyond this type of framework, professional expectations have traditionally been communicated to members of sport organizations through the development of ethical codes, or codes of conduct. Such a code lays out for members the shared ethical values of the organization. Key themes from codes of conduct around the world have been synthesized by the International Council for Coaching Excellence to guide sport organizations in creating their own codes.[4] This analysis has identified the following seven ethical principles:

1. Competence
2. Trustworthiness
3. Respect
4. Fairness
5. Caring
6. Integrity
7. Responsibility

COACHING SNAPSHOT

Few coaches have been as respected as **Eddie Robinson**, and for good reason. A gentleman, patriot, and educator, Coach Robinson used football as a means of developing young mens' character and their ability to succeed outside of sports while also winning a record-setting number of games (408). Though racial injustice prevailed during much of his life, Robinson answered very favorably his own question: *"How else can you judge me except by what I accomplish?"*

Any organization hiring a coach should define each of these principles and indicate how they apply to the organizational context. For instance, an organization's focus on fairness might emphasize that the coach must uphold fair-play standards in competition and provide equal opportunities for all athletes. In terms of responsibility, the organization might stress that coaches must avoid sexual relationships with athletes, promote good sporting behavior on and off the field, and contribute to the holistic development of athletes (beyond performance-related outcomes). If a coach is hired into an organization that lacks an ethical code, then the coach should initiate a discussion with supervisors to gain clarity about each of these seven issues.

A code of conduct may be presented to coaches in a variety of ways. Some institutions and organizations simply share the code through written or electronic correspondence—for instance, posting it on the organization's website. More proactive organizations go a step further by directly training and educating coaches and requiring them to sign an agreement to abide by the code.

It remains to be determined whether codes of conduct are effective in shaping ethical behavior and ethical decision making by coaches. In fact, little research is available to demonstrate that such codes constrain and guide coaches' behavior. However, many highly successful sport programs have found success in developing such codes.[5, 6] In addition to codes developed by coaching organizations (e.g., National Wrestling Coaches Association) and sport organizations (e.g., NCAA), many individual institutions also provide coaches with codes and rules of conduct to follow—both morally and legally. For instance, some institutions require that coaches report any possible sexual harassment or abuse, and others require coaches to immediately inform the athletic administration of any ethical transgression by an athlete. In many places, coaches are no longer expected or welcome to handle ethical matters informally, and some who have tried to do so have lost their jobs. The key, then, is not only for coaches to understand and adhere to general ethical principles but also to understand the specific rules and standards laid out by their institution or sponsoring agency.

As with all human endeavors, codes of conduct can also go awry. A prime example of a code of conduct run amok can be found in the NCAA's lengthy conduct manual for Division I coaches.[7] The 2016 edition of the manual nicely includes three pages devoted to laying out ethical principles (i.e., virtues) for intercollegiate athletics. However, the entire manual, which is rather proscriptive (i.e., focused on "thou shalt not" statements), numbers 420 pages and includes a 58-page chapter devoted entirely to policies about recruiting (which is also a primary focus of an annual certifying exam that must be passed by all NCAA coaches). The NCAA enforces adherence to these rules through a compliance infrastructure staffed by employees whose responsibility is to ensure that coaches follow the code.

The code includes many rules created in direct response to ethically dubious behaviors by coaches and athletic departments that revealed loopholes in the manual. For example, it is not unusual for major college powers in men's basketball to hire the father or high school coach of a very promising recruit as an assistant coach. The new hire may be qualified by some standards but seemingly much less so than many other candidates for the position. Such behaviors have been deemed after the fact to violate the spirit of the principles of intercollegiate athletics. As a result, rules have been added to the code in a piecemeal fashion, thus generating a lengthy and confusing procedures manual and necessitating the large and costly compliance infrastructure.

Ethical Climates

Building on our discussion of personal standards and professional expectations, we turn our attention to the complex interaction between these two factors and consider ethical climates. In order to fully understand ethical dilemmas and moral judgments in sport, we must move beyond considering only individual factors. This need is reflected in the *International Sport Coaching Framework*,[3] which posits that coaches are influenced not only by their expertise and competence but also by their coaching domain (e.g., participation or performance), status (i.e., terms of employment), and specific role (e.g., level of responsibility).

The importance of ethical climate is also emphasized by those who point to the influence of social interactions and cultural context on coaches' moral behavior.[8 (p. 36)] For example, a coach might stray from her moral mindset that it is not appropriate to cheat if she feels that her team is disadvantaged due to cheating by other coaches. A coach's ethical climate can also be affected by the type of organization or context in which he is operating—for instance, a sport club, a national governing body, or an international federation.[9]

In one model, ethical climates have been represented in terms of three ethical approaches:[9]

1. Egoism (maximizing self-interest)
2. Benevolence (maximizing joint interests)
3. Principle

When faced with an ethical dilemma, coaches operating in a climate of egoism focus on their self-interest, coaches in a benevolence-oriented climate consider the welfare of others, and coaches in a principle-based climate seek to apply rules or laws.

This model also posits that ethical climates are defined by ethical referents, which can be individual, local, or cosmopolitan.[9] When using an individual referent, a coach's ethical decision making comes from within, based on personal values and moral beliefs. In contrast, with a local referent, the ethical basis for making a decision comes from the coaching context, such as a team's code of conduct. Finally, a cosmopolitan referent goes beyond both the individual and the immediate coaching context; one example would be a set of guidelines presented in a popular book on leadership by a famous coach.

When these two dimensions—ethical climate and ethical referent[9]—are cross-tabulated, the model produces nine theoretical types of ethical climate (table 2.1). Each of these types foregrounds certain criteria that guide the decision-making process.[10]

TABLE 2.1 Theoretical Types of Ethical Climate

ETHICAL CLIMATE	ETHICAL REFERENT (LOCUS OF ANALYSIS)		
	Individual	Local	Cosmopolitan
Egoism	Self-interest	Major championship success	Efficiency
Benevolence	Coach–athlete relationship	Team interest	Social responsibility
Principle	Personal morality	Team code of conduct	World Anti-Doping Agency code

Adapted from B. Victor and J.B. Cullen, "The Organizational Bases of Ethical Work Climates," *Administrative Science Quarterly* 33, no. 1 (1988): 101-125.

Thus, when making a decision, it can be valuable to consider the prevailing environmental and internal factors that may influence our inclinations. For example, a coach might reflect on the basis for leaving starting players in a game long after victory was certain, and this analysis might lead her to take a different approach in the future.

Coaching Ethics and Doping in Sport

As you might imagine, sport coaches must prepare to respond effectively to a wide range of ethical issues. To illustrate this need, we will examine the issue of doping in sport as an ethical matter that greatly affects coaches, athletes, and administrators. Indeed, the *International Sport Coaching Framework* states that "coaches must abide by the international and national rules relating to anti-doping."[3 (p. 17)]

In terms of international rules, the World Anti-Doping Code (see the appendix on pages 287-288) formally assigns responsibility to "athlete support personnel," including coaches.[11] Specifically, the code states that coaches should (a) be knowledgeable of and comply with all anti-doping policies and rules applicable to them or to athletes, (b) cooperate with the athlete testing program enacted by the relevant anti-doping organization,[11 (p. 12)] (c) cooperate with anti-doping organization investigations, (d) disclose details of any anti-doping rule violation (ADRV) that they have committed in the past 10 years, (e) avoid personal use or possession of any prohibited substance or method without valid justification, and (f) use their influence on athletes' values and behavior to foster anti-doping attitudes.

COACHING SNAPSHOT

Octavian Bellu, regarded by many as one of greatest gymnastics coaches of all time, led the Romanian national team to two Olympic golds and five world championships. But at what price? Bellu and coaching partner Mariana Bitang were tough on their athletes. Later in his career, Bellu expressed dissatisfaction with having to coach *"a bunch of girls that made the national team just because they were eligible."* Former world-champion Romanian gymnast Maria Olaru accused Bellu and other coaches of physical and verbal abuse in her autobiography.

Coaches are subject to sanctions if they are found to have committed an ADRV—for example, possession, trafficking, or administration of a prohibited substance or method; tampering (or attempted tampering) with any part of doping control (the testing process); complicity (i.e., assisting, encouraging, aiding, abetting, conspiring, or covering up an ADRV); prohibited association (i.e., associating with a person found guilty of a criminal or disciplinary offense equivalent to a doping violation);

and retaliation against anyone who reports doping (i.e., a whistleblower). Unfortunately, despite the potential for sanctions, many coaches have committed ADRVs, such as condoning (and even modeling) doping behavior and supplying and administering prohibited substances.

One of the most well-known doping cases involving coaches emerged from the systematic doping regimes of the German Democratic Republic (GDR) during the 1970s and 1980s. GDR coaches surreptitiously administered banned substances to athletes by claiming that the tablets were dietary supplements.[12] Although some GDR athletes felt victimized and intimidated, many continued to place "unconditional trust" or "blind faith" in their coaches due to a belief that coaches would always act in their best interests and "look after" them.[12 (p. 109)] At a deeper level, athletes described the athlete–coach relationship as a "special bond," spoke of their "love" and "respect" for their coaches, and described individual coaches as a "very close personal friend," a "surrogate parent," and "like a father."[12 (p. 101)]

Clearly, these coaches failed to live up to that high regard when they provided unsuspecting athletes with banned substances. At the same time, both anecdotal evidence and supporting documentation indicate that the coaches had little, if any, autonomous power in relation to the doping regime.[12] In fact, they were put under duress by the Ministry for State Security (known as the Stasi, or secret police), who reportedly abused coaches if they refused to be involved.[12] Even so, these coaches condoned cheating, which not only was morally wrong but also created major health risks for the athletes who trusted them.

In another example from the 1980s, Canadian coach Charlie Francis facilitated his athletes' doping by both encouraging and abetting it. When one of his athletes, Ben Johnson, tested positive for doping at the 1988 Seoul Olympics, an investigation ensued. Francis then attempted to justify his actions by stating that he believed a large proportion of world-record-holding sprinters were taking prohibited substances. In other words, drawing on Bandura's theory of moral thought and action,[13] Francis "morally disengaged" from his actions by claiming that the actions of others (diffusion of responsibility) led to his own behavior, which was necessary to level the playing field.[14] In a striking difference from the GDR coaches, reports suggest that Francis openly communicated his pro-doping beliefs to his athletes and engaged in regular monitoring for the purpose of minimizing harm.[14] Ultimately, he normalized doping by convincing his athletes that it was both necessary and acceptable.

More recently, an investigation of doping in Russia found that involvement on the part of coaches is as much of an issue now as it has ever been.[15] In this case, a number of highly ranked coaches from the Russian Athletics Federation supplied and administered banned substances to athletes. Coaches also forewarned athletes of imminent drug tests and helped them conceal positive findings. Although this latter move might appear to be somewhat protective of athletes, the investigation found evidence that coaches (and other support personnel) received payment from athletes for this "service" and felt little if any concern about the consequences for athletes. Moreover, many coaches implicated in this systematic doping regime explicitly denied their involvement in aiding, abetting, or covering up doping. At the very least, however, clear evidence indicates that they stood by and allowed doping to occur rather than reporting it to relevant anti-doping authorities.

Although these historical events paint a relatively negative picture of coaches in the context of doping, most coaches consider the problem to be serious,[16, 17] and many agree that doping constitutes cheating.[18, 19] Furthermore, coaches generally acknowledge that they have a role to play in preventing doping in sport because they hold positions of influence in athletes' lives.[20] To that end, coaches have reported monitoring athletes for changes in performance or mannerisms, as well as giving advice when athletes initiate a conversation about doping.[20, 21] Increasingly, coaches have also come to recognize that the moral atmosphere they create can influence morality-related behaviors by athletes, including behaviors related to doping.[22] Indeed, both theory[23] and research[24] illustrate the power of coach-created climates to prompt adaptive behaviors by athletes—especially climates that are task-focused and autonomy-supportive in which coaches encourage athletes to make their own moral choices by providing an environment in which the proper decisions are more apparent.

More specifically, drug use prevention efforts in sport are affected by the ways in which coaches communicate with their athletes and the behaviors that they encourage through their own coaching practice. In fact, the very nature of coaching means that coaches guide their athletes' decisions and behaviors both directly and indirectly on a daily basis. Therefore, it is vital for coaches to be well aware of what is prioritized in their coaching environment, whether by themselves or by others. Given the risks of doping, this awareness is especially crucial in relation to strategies for performance enhancement—for instance, use of nutritional supplements versus a food-first approach. Thus coaches should explain their own decision making and take time to listen to and consider their athletes' perspectives, opinions, and feelings.[25]

Some coaches oppose doping but take a relatively passive approach to doping prevention.[20, 21] This stance may result from a felt lack of knowledge, concerns about causing more harm than good (e.g., misinforming athletes or making them curious about doping), or a perception that the issue is irrelevant in their coaching context (e.g., in their sport, at their level, or with their particular athletes).[20, 21, 26] Coaches may also struggle to muster the confidence to confront athletes who are doping,[27] and research suggests that this issue causes some coaches to ignore unethical behavior[28] or to indicate that they would not report a doping-related incident.[20] This decision makes them vulnerable because they are in effect choosing to violate anti-doping rules through complicity. Therefore, we must work to ensure that coaches develop the confidence to speak to their athletes about doping-related matters, especially when they believe an athlete might be involved in something untoward.

In order to help coaches feel confident about speaking out, and to prevent doping in sport over the long term, we must remove the code of silence that often shrouds this behavior. Doing so requires us to create sport climates that distinctly emphasize principle and benevolence at the individual, local, and cosmopolitan levels. For example, the U.S. Anti-Doping Agency (USADA) has called for changing the culture of sport from one of winning at all costs to one focused on positive values and life lessons learned through sport.[29] To pursue this goal, USADA has introduced TrueSport, a grassroots initiative designed to produce a cultural shift in children's sport that emphasizes the lifelong benefits of playing, training, and competing. The initiative seeks to accomplish these goals through educational programs for athletes, parents, and coaches.

Such educational initiatives would seem to be a step in the right direction, given that coaches have reported inadequate opportunities to learn about anti-doping topics[21, 30, 31] and called for further training.[32] Thus, even as we need further research, we can suggest now that learning opportunities should enable coaches to learn from others and develop their capacity for ethical decision making through case studies, role playing, and group discussion.[31] These programs should be delivered in a variety of modes (e.g., mediated or unmediated, formal or informal) and through coordinated efforts by various types of organizations (e.g., national and international federations, anti-doping organizations, coaching organizations).[31] Where possible, anti-doping content should also be integrated into general pathways for coach education and development to allow for regular reinforcement and progressive development. Anti-doping expectations for coaches can also be addressed in a code of conduct integrated into employment agreements; as discussed earlier, such expectations and learning opportunities should be tailored to a coach's working environment (e.g., specific sport, coaching domain, and staffing structure).

An Ethical Coaching Base

Up to this point, we have examined coaching ethics in a rather analytical, research-based manner. That dispassionate, objective approach is essential for identifying and understanding the factors that affect the ethical mindsets and behaviors of coaches, as well as the climates in which they work. Given this necessity, the United States Olympic and Paralympic Committee (USOPC) has specified five fundamental ethical principles for coaching: competence, integrity, professional responsibility, respect for participants and dignity, and concern for others' welfare. Yet we continue to see glaring breaches of coaching ethics by individuals who are associated with national sport governing bodies within the USOPC. The same is true for most other sport federations, coaching associations, and even conference and league administrations. Furthermore, enforcement efforts based on a code of conduct too often come only after a transgression has occurred.

Clearly, then, oversight and governance alone will never ensure that all coaches adhere to ethical standards. At the most basic level, ethical coaching hinges on the values that each coach brings to the job and the extent to which each individual adheres to those principles. Thus we are faced with a question: Can coaches who lack an effective moral compass be educated and encouraged in a way that helps them form a proper ethical mindset and conform their behavior to it? Given the high stakes, what alternative is there? If you are a coach (or aspiring coach), reflect on what you value and how those values guide (or will guide) your coaching decisions and actions. Unethical coaching covers a wide spectrum of misbehaviors, ranging from teaching athletes illegal tactics to taking bribes in return for certain favors. The one thing such misdeeds have in common is that they do not serve the best interest of the individuals under the coach's guidance. Instead, you can focus on developing and adhering to values and ethical standards based on an athlete-centered approach to coaching. This solution may not prevent all coaching misconduct, but it provides a solid place to start.

Exercise: Evaluating Your Ethical Stances

Imagine that one of your athletes approaches you after a training session and acts a little out of character. Hesitantly, the athlete tells you that there is a problem—namely, that another athlete may be taking performance-enhancing substances that are banned in your sport.

- What emotional triggers are likely to be set off?

  _____

  _____

  _____

  _____

  _____

- What facts would you want to gather?

  _____

  _____

  _____

  _____

  _____

- What factors or people could influence how you handle this situation?

  _____

  _____

  _____

  _____

  _____

- What are the possible courses of action? Which are you most likely to choose, and why?

  _____

  _____

  _____

  _____

  _____

- What factors could help you carry out this decision, given that you anticipate some resistance?

  _____

  _____

  _____

  _____

  _____

From International Council for Coaching Excellence, *Sport Coaches' Handbook*, eds. D. Gould and C. Mallett. (Champaign, IL: Human Kinetics, 2021).

Chapter 3

Coaching Philosophy

Karen Collins

A sound coaching philosophy provides the foundation for coaching success; some would even say it serves as the key to success. However, even the best coaching philosophy can be only as good as the ethical mindset that underlies it—that is, the persistent, habitual way in which the coach thinks about the world and others. That mindset creates behavioral intentions, or plans, and (to a lesser degree) drives actual behaviors.

Beyond coaching, a philosophy is important in all aspects of our lives. It consists of the basic beliefs and principles that influence and guide our everyday actions. These personal beliefs go a long way toward determining both our credibility and our success in life. In coaching, a philosophy is the most critical factor that enables us to help athletes build the physical and mental skills of success;[1] it also imparts meaning and direction to our work as coaches.

A coaching philosophy can be described as a way of thinking about coaching based on personal values and beliefs about the role of a coach and, more specifically, the coach's role in relation to the lives of athletes.[2] Developing and maintaining a coaching philosophy can be challenging because it not only changes over time but also needs to be congruent with the context in which one is coaching. For example, would the same philosophy work for a recreational town team and a varsity high school team?

The importance of a coaching philosophy is easy to observe by considering great coaches in sport history—for instance, John Wooden (men's college basketball), Jill Ellis (U.S. women's soccer), Muffet McGraw (women's college basketball), Kim Tortolani (U.S. U19 lacrosse, high school field hockey), Charlean Crowell (youth basketball and softball), David Belisle (Little League), and Bob Ladouceur (high school football). Regardless of how recognizable their names are, these coaches share a common trait—each one has developed a clearly articulated philosophy. Even more important, they have practiced what they have preached by putting their philosophy into action every day. Here is World Cup winner Jill Ellis:

> I think part of my coaching philosophy is creating a connection. I think having an understanding of . . . the players and knowing them on and off the field will definitely help me navigate being the full team coach. The players at this level are very professional and really know that whoever the coach is, they're going to need to perform. But I think knowing me will help build that bridge quicker.[3]

At the high school level, Bob Ladouceur views success as a byproduct of putting his philosophy into action. In fact, he sees football as a vehicle for teaching life skills, such as respect, accountability, selflessness, and commitment. As a public speaker, he reminds audiences that sport does not build character—it reveals it.[4]

These coaches provide great examples of consistency between one's coaching philosophy and one's actions. They have been in the business a long time and figured out what works for their particular programs. As their experience illustrates, it is crucial to think systematically both about your philosophy and about how to implement it. When you face conflicts and tough decisions in coaching—whether related to playing time, facility use, or interactions with parents or officials—your credibility and continued success will depend on your ability to draw on a sound philosophy.

Establishing a Coaching Philosophy

You can develop your coaching philosophy by following these five steps:

1. Understand yourself and determine what is important to you.
2. Prioritize your values.
3. Identify your coaching objectives.
4. Express your coaching philosophy publicly.
5. Link your coaching philosophy to your coaching style.

Let's examine each of these steps in some detail.

Determining What's Important

The first step in developing a sound coaching philosophy involves self-reflection and understanding yourself. The key is to obtain self-knowledge. What is most important to you—family, caring, exercise, learning new things? What are your values? These questions are personal, and your answers should be as well. At the foundation, your philosophy is not about you as a coach but about your personal beliefs. What lies at your core? To help you determine your beliefs, work through exercise 3.1. First, brainstorm a list of the beliefs or values you feel are most important to you, then define them.

Exercise 3.1 Self-Knowledge of Personal Values

Value	Definition
(Example) Caring	Caring about the people around you (e.g., in your family or organization)

From International Council for Coaching Excellence, *Sport Coaches' Handbook*, eds. D. Gould and C. Mallett. (Champaign, IL: Human Kinetics, 2021).

Prioritizing Your Core Values

Once you have completed the chart in exercise 3.1, it is time to prioritize your values. To do so, turn to exercise 3.2 and rank order your five or six key core beliefs. For example, if *caring* is the core belief that you rate as most important, rank it as number 1. Alternatively, you can assign a percentage to each core value (make sure that the values add up to 100 percent).

Exercise 3.2   Prioritizing Your Core Values

Value	Definition	Rank (or percentage)
(Example) Caring	Caring about the people around you (e.g., in your family or organization)	1 (45 percent)
(Example) Effort	Giving strong, consistent, positive effort regardless of task	2 (30 percent)

From International Council for Coaching Excellence, *Sport Coaches' Handbook*, eds. D. Gould and C. Mallett. (Champaign, IL: Human Kinetics, 2021).

For some folks, boxes and rankings do not provide the best way to illustrate their values, and that is okay. We are free to be creative in this process and true to our own style and thought patterns. For instance, it may be easier for some of us to depict visually how our values fit together—perhaps in the form of puzzle pieces, where each piece represents a key core value. The pieces could be of similar size, suggesting similar levels of importance, or varied in size to indicate which are most impor- tant (see figure 3.1). If this approach appeals to you, con- sider also whether a certain piece might be located at the center to represent its impor- tance. In this way, you can think through your values and reflect on how they fit together to form a connected, unified picture.

FIGURE 3.1 Puzzle pieces as core beliefs.

Identifying Your Coaching Objectives

Exercises 3.1 and 3.2 help you lay a foundation for your coaching philoso- phy by understanding your core values. The next step is to begin translat- ing those values into effective coaching practice. More specifically, your values can help you identify coaching objectives, or goals for your athletes to reach. Coaching education experts identify objectives in various ways. For instance, Vealey suggests balancing a triad of objectives: optimal devel- opment, optimal experience, and optimal performance.[1] Martens refers to similar objectives in different terms: development, fun, and winning.[5]

A coach should reflect on how to define and prioritize these objectives based in part on the level of sport involved. For example, sport educa- tors can spend hours debating the importance of winning. At what age or level is it appropriate to focus on winning? No single answer exists, because winning is defined in a variety of ways. A U6 youth soccer coach might define winning not in terms of final score but based on whether her team consistently dribbles the ball in the right direction. Similarly, an age-group club swim coach might define winning in terms of whether the majority of his athletes achieve a personal best by season's end. In contrast, a coach in an NCAA Division I sport program might define winning solely on the basis of the scoreboard.

It is equally important to determine how one will put the objectives of development and fun into practice. Fun for a high school varsity softball team might involve allowing the athletes to choose their favorite drill, whereas fun in high-performance international sport likely depends primarily on winning in competition. The coach's beliefs and principles regarding these objectives exerts a strong influence on how they are defined and interpreted by athletes.

Objectives are often identified for coaches and participants by a sport organization. For example, Sport Australia (formerly the Australian Sports Commission) provides various guidelines ranging from starting at the grassroots level and creating an inclusive environment to the elite level of creating national pride and international success.[6] Another classic example of prioritizing beliefs and principles can be found in John Wooden's Pyramid of Success.[7] Based on his core philosophy of being a teacher first, Wooden provided the building blocks to help his athletes reach competitive greatness.

In all cases, developing good coaching objectives depends on prioritizing them according to the core values that underlie your philosophy.

Expressing the Philosophy Publicly

Articulating your core values and using them to inform your coaching objectives enables you to create a sound working coaching philosophy. Therefore, it is good practice to make a list of your principles and objectives, present them to your athletes and their parents (if appropriate for the level) at the start of the season, and remain true to them at the first sign of adversity. Table 3.1 provides examples of working philosophies in the words of great coaches. Exercise 3.3 provides space for you to write your own coaching philosophy statement.

Linking Your Philosophy to Your Coaching Style

Once you have engaged in self-reflection and thought about how your core values inform your coaching objectives, the next step is to consider the implications for your coaching style. Your style should be a direct reflection of both your philosophical beliefs and your personality. Our truest selves are revealed when we face tense or adverse conditions in coaching. For example, if you are usually laid back and communicate calmly with a high level of information and clear instruction, your athletes have grown accustomed to this behavior. If you suddenly become frantic when the game is on the line and communicate ineffectively, then you are doing your players a disservice.

In fact, consistency may be the most important component of one's coaching style. Athletes are more at ease, and thus perform better regardless of level, when they know what to expect from their coach. Consistency in style—expressed through both words and actions—helps build credible coaches.

TABLE 3.1 Exemplar Coaching Philosophies

Coach	Philosophy
Bob Ladouceur, award-winning high school football coach	Football is a vehicle for teaching life skills, such as respect, accountability, selflessness, and commitment. Sport does not build character—it reveals it.[4]
Jill Ellis, head coach, U.S. women's soccer	"I think part of my coaching philosophy is creating a connection. I think having an understanding of some of the players and knowing them on and off the field will definitely help me navigate being the full team coach. The players at this level are very professional and really know that whoever the coach is, they're going to need to perform. But I think knowing me will help build that bridge quicker."[3]
David Belisle, Little League World Series coach	"I learned coaching on my own that you have to make every player take pride in their role no matter how weak or strong they are. That's the beauty and biggest challenge of coaching: every kid is different. You have to recognize everyone's different abilities and push the right buttons to keep them enthusiastic. Everyone's involved, no one is slighted, we're all together."[8]
Kim Tortolani, former coach, U.S. U19 lacrosse and high school field hockey and lacrosse	"Balance my goal of developing players and creating successful teams with my underlying desire to win."[9]
Charlean Crowell, award-winning coach, Lower Russell County Youth Club, Alabama	"Crowell fills the emotional tanks of her players by satisfying their emotional needs for certainty, love, connection, and growth. Her willingness to teach the whole child and build relationships with students beyond their participation on sports teams shines through as she advocates for their success in academics, at home, and beyond."[10]
Muffet McGraw, former head coach, University of Notre Dame women's basketball	"That's why we're trying to teach our women to be strong, independent women and go into the job market and make the difference that they know they can."[11]

Exercise 3.3   Coaching Philosophy Statement

Based on your core values and priorities, write a coaching philosophy statement. Share the statement with colleagues and fellow coaches to help you identify any holes.

_____

_____

_____

_____

From International Council for Coaching Excellence, *Sport Coaches' Handbook*, eds. D. Gould and C. Mallett. (Champaign, IL: Human Kinetics, 2021).

COACHING SNAPSHOT

Nicknamed the "Iron Hammer" as an outstanding player and captain on China's 1984 gold-medal-winning team, **Lang Ping** went on to a very successful coaching career. Indeed, she was the first person to win an Olympic gold as both an athlete and a coach. Ping keeps it simple when explaining her remarkable achievements—*"Talent and hard work are equally important"*—while acknowledging a coach has many more things to consider and manage.

Coaching Philosophy and Context

A coaching philosophy makes a difference in any context. Generally, coaching contexts can be categorized as oriented toward participation (e.g., recreational youth sport), developing performance (e.g., school sport, sport club, youth sport academy), or high performance (e.g., elite, college, professional, and international levels). Each of these realms requires a distinct skill set, as well as targeted coaching beliefs and objectives.

Both your personal belief system and your coaching objectives must also mesh with the philosophy of the agency or organization with whom you work. For example, if a recreational youth sport coach espouses an ethic of development but behaves in a way that prioritizes winning (e.g., unequal playing time, focus on competitive outcomes), then problems will arise with key stakeholders. Sport leaders, parents, and athletes may question the coach's tactics, which are not congruent with stated beliefs. As this example illustrates, you must coach in a context that matches both your beliefs and your behaviors.

One great example of a coach who understands context can be found in the person of Charlean Crowell. As the 2019 winner of the Positive Coaching Alliance's Double-Goal Coach Award, Crowell has been recognized for helping young people develop into better athletes and better people. Crowell works in a system where many of her athletes come from a rural community in which many families live at or below the poverty line. As a result, resources are limited, but these athletes still want an opportunity to play. She helps meet that need by providing sport experiences focused on building self-esteem and confidence and making a difference for the local community.

In addition to the importance of an individual coaching philosophy, recent literature in recreational youth sport also highlights the importance of a community- or agency-based philosophy. For instance, one must be thoughtful about programmatic philosophy when working as a youth sport administrator and creating coaching development programs. In other words, in addition to formulating personal values and beliefs, it is also critical to articulate thoughtful programmatic values and beliefs. This process can be facilitated by the questions provided in the Programmatic Philosophy Toolbox sidebar.

Once you have answered these questions, you are ready to formulate a program philosophy statement. Essentially, your statement should answer the following questions from the toolbox: (a) What are the values of the agency? (b) Why do we run the programs we do? (c) What value do the programs provide to the community?

Programmatic Philosophy Toolbox

What are my personal values? Are they consistent with the community or agency values?

What are the values of the agency? Are these values consistent across programs?

Why do we run the programs we do?

What do we do?

How do we do it?

Whom do we do it for?

What value do the programs provide to the community?

Program philosophy has been described as the key factor in providing effective structure for community-based youth sport.[12, 13] In fact, articulating a clear, action-oriented philosophy constitutes the first step in implementing best practices in these settings, which tend to involve building multifaceted relationships with community sport leaders, parents, athletes, and sport administrators. The importance of philosophy in building best practices with sport constituents is represented in figure 3.2, which positions the philosophy as the central factor for working effectively with parents, implementing coach development practices, carrying out organizational and administrative duties, and creating programs that provide equity and access to youth sport participation.[12]

Despite the importance of program philosophy, research indicates that agency mission statements often go unarticulated or undelivered to coaches in both community-based youth sport and school sport.[14, 15] This disconnect needs to change. One way to initiate this change is to place mission statements at the forefront of all coaching education and coaching development programs.

One area that lacks sufficient treatment in the scientific literature is that of developing a coaching philosophy as an assistant coach. Consistency in the approach taken by members of a coaching staff plays a large role in determining success, whether the staff is coaching for participation, development, or performance.[16] Assistant coaches generally follow the lead and the beliefs of the head coach and therefore are rarely asked to develop their own philosophy. Yet all coaches should begin to formulate their own beliefs and objectives very early in their careers.

One study of preservice coaches found that coaches with little experience had difficulty writing belief statements. As a result, instead of addressing beliefs and core values, their statements of philosophy tended

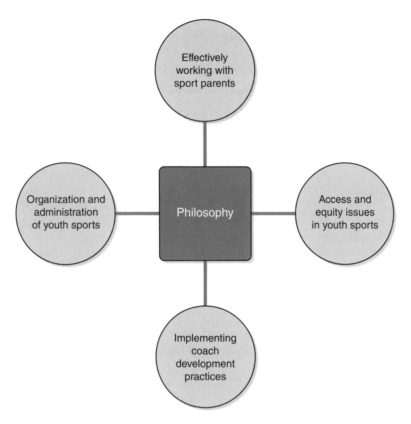

FIGURE 3.2 Model for working in sport communities.

Reprinted by permission from K. Collins and R. Barcelona, "Youth Sport Coaches' Perceptions of the Usefulness of a Statewide Coaching Education Program," *Applied Recreation Research and Programming Annual* 4 (2014): 1-30.

to focus on rules and regulations associated with how they would run their team and create a culture.[17] In response to this finding, the study's authors called for coaching education programs to increase their focus on early-career coaches and help them through the process of developing a philosophy. With a better understanding of their own beliefs, these coaches, who are often found in an assistant role, can better match their choice of sport context to what they believe is important in coaching.

Understanding Athletes

After gaining an understanding of your coaching context, as well as the duties you are undertaking, the next step is to develop a good sense of your athletes and their goals. To do this, you need to develop clear objectives. More often than not, coaches at all levels cite athlete development as an important outcome for their coaching practice. Development can include physical, psychological, and emotional components. For instance, some top coaches help athletes develop not only their physical and sport skills (e.g., technical, tactical, physiological) but also their life skills and a growth mindset.

Playing Time Versus Playing for Keeps

It was the travel league championship for girls' basketball in grades 7 and 8. All year long, Coach Belanger had made sure that her players got equal playing time in each game. She believed that at this level what matters most is for players to learn the game and that the best way to do so is to play in all situations, regardless of the outcome. She also stressed the importance of executing fundamentals, team play, and consistent effort, and that approach worked—her team, the Wildcats, entered the championship game undefeated. Although a few of her players were very talented, the rest of her team, like the other teams, exhibited a wide variety of skill levels. Fortunately for Coach Belanger, she had 10 players, so she was able to split her athletes into two balanced rotations—one led by Kelsey, the top player in the league, and the other led by Hannah.

With four minutes left in the fourth quarter, Kelsey's group had built an 11-point lead, and Hannah's group entered the game for its scheduled rotation. Though a hard worker, Hannah was not as strong at ballhandling as Kelsey was, and she struggled under the pressure of a full-court press and often lacked the confidence to take control of the game. At three minutes, the lead had dwindled to seven points, and the tension rose. Corinne, a forward in Kelsey's group who was sitting next to Coach Belanger on the bench, leaned over and said, "Coach, maybe Kelsey should go back in to make sure we win." Coach Belanger did not respond, but a knot was forming in her stomach. With two minutes to go, the lead was down to five. Coach Belanger was second-guessing her decision and feeling frustrated that she hadn't had the foresight to switch the order of the groups for the fourth quarter. The league allowed only one time-out per quarter, and she had already used hers.

She looked down the bench and made eye contact with Kelsey. What should she do? Should she put Kelsey in and preserve the win or let Hannah continue to struggle and potentially lose the game in the process? Coach Belanger caught herself in that moment and made a decision: "I'm not going to change what I've done all season. Fairness to the girls in the game now is more important than getting the W in this league. Hannah will stay in, and we will learn from this, whatever the result." Coach Belanger and the rest of the team sweated it out for the next two minutes, and the Wildcats won by two points. Coach felt a sigh of relief.

After the game, Hannah's mother approached Coach Belanger and said, "Thank you for leaving Hannah in the game at the end. I know she isn't the strongest guard you have, and I know everyone would have been more comfortable with Kelsey on the floor. You are the first coach in Hannah's five years of basketball who has given up a chance to win."

Life Skills Development

In recent years, the scientific literature has focused in part on the teaching and transferability of life skills through sport.[18-22] Scholars in this field argue that coaches are uniquely positioned to teach life skills and that doing so effectively hinges on articulating a sound philosophy and matching it with appropriate behavior. These factors enable coaches to make good use of their influence in creating a motivational climate, both for individual athletes and for the team. One report examined coaches who sought not merely to improve the technical and tactical skills of their student-athletes but also to put their players at the center of their coaching philosophy and use sport as a systematic tool for helping them develop life skills.[18]

Similarly, a set of studies looked at successful coaches who articulated clear philosophies stemming from their core beliefs and implemented a system of "tough love" in which actions that departed from the stated core values were not tolerated.[20-22] These findings indicated that a well-articulated philosophy serves as an important tool in a successful coach's toolbox. For example, in one study,[21] model high school football coaches exhibited well-established coaching philosophies that recognized the importance of helping athletes develop life skills (see figure 3.3).

The individuals observed in these studies were veteran coaches who had made good use of the opportunity to foster and adapt their philosophy over time. Novice coaches, on the other hand, likely model their approach on such experienced coaches. The potential pitfall here lies in the temptation for the novice to focus on behavior or outcome without developing core beliefs or understanding the reason for the behavior. For example, a young coach might hear of an experienced coach who suspends an athlete from all activities for two weeks. The young coach sees the outcome—the suspension—but not the other coach's three meetings with the athlete about values and behavior. The young coach might then interpret the situation based solely on the outcome and initiate the practice of suspending players for poor behavior on his own team. Thus the young coach is making a decision based on partial information, which is likely to produce problems down the road.

Growth Mindset in Coaching

Developing a climate for teaching transferable life skills requires a coach to develop a core-value system based in a growth mindset—that is, a mindset that views coaching strategies and behaviors as learned more than fixed (innate). In other words, a coach characterized by a growth mindset believes that she can improve her leadership abilities, whereas a coach with a fixed mindset believes that either you have leadership abilities or you don't—and therefore you cannot do much to develop

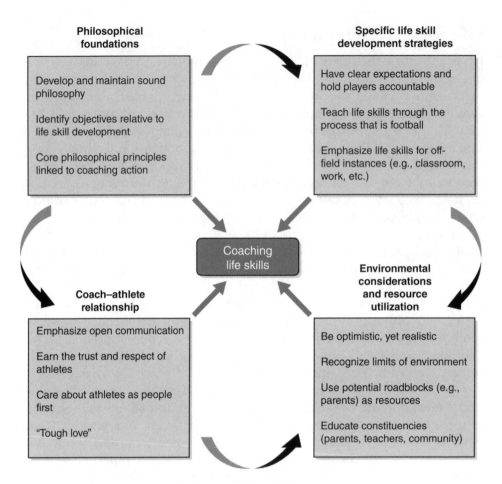

Philosophical foundations

Develop and maintain sound philosophy

Identify objectives relative to life skill development

Core philosophical principles linked to coaching action

Specific life skill development strategies

Have clear expectations and hold players accountable

Teach life skills through the process that is football

Emphasize life skills for off-field instances (e.g., classroom, work, etc.)

Coaching life skills

Coach–athlete relationship

Emphasize open communication

Earn the trust and respect of athletes

Care about athletes as people first

"Tough love"

Environmental considerations and resource utilization

Be optimistic, yet realistic

Recognize limits of environment

Use potential roadblocks (e.g., parents) as resources

Educate constituencies (parents, teachers, community)

FIGURE 3.3 Model for coaching life skills in football.

From D. Gould, K. Collins, L. Lauer, and Y. Chung, "Coaching Life Skills: A Working Model," *Sport and Exercise Psychology Review* 2, no. 1 (2006): 4-13. Reproduced with permission of British Psychological Society through PLSclear.

them. Research[23] has been done to extend original work on the growth mindset[24] to the leadership mindset of high school and college coaches. This research found that high school coaches generally viewed their overall coaching abilities as learned, whereas at the collegiate level, head coaches believed their abilities were more learned but assistant coaches viewed them as more innate. This divergence speaks to the potential differences between head and assistant coaches and validates the need for more systematic development of coaching philosophy by all coaches.

What does the choice between a growth mindset and a fixed mindset mean for one's coaching philosophy? A coach who leads a team with a fixed mindset models behaviors that encourage athletes to retain or adopt a fixed mindset, which often leads them to avoid risk, fear failure, and fail to reach their full potential. Thus a fixed mindset may lead to a lack of satisfaction. On the other hand, if coaches present their core beliefs and philosophical foundation as part of a growth mindset—one in which players and coaches alike can improve over time through small successes based on effort and challenge—then the team climate is characterized by positive development, which lies at the very core of what many coaches hold to be so important. Indeed, it is very difficult to believe in positive development as a core value yet approach sport and coaching with a fixed mindset.

A prime example of a growth mindset can be found in legendary basketball coach John Wooden. He preached about the importance of effort and consistently worked with players to help them get better every day. Each player varied in his level of improvement, but over time almost all of Wooden's athletes lived up to their potential. In fact, this consistent improvement constitutes his greatest legacy, and it was enabled by a growth mindset.

Athlete Development

Whether your coaching philosophy is based on developing life skills or on improving and developing a growth mindset, your athletes will approach sport in a myriad of ways. To help with this process, the Long-Term Athlete Development (LTAD) model provides coaches with guidelines for physical literacy, trainability, development, periodization, competition, and continuous improvement. According to this model, over the span of life, an athlete moves from early stages including an active start and FUNdamentals where motor development and enjoyment are the key focus, to later stages of training to win and being active for life. The ultimate goal of this model is to guide sport participation, training, competition, and recovery from infancy through adulthood.[25]

Seven-Stage Framework of LTAD

- Active start
- FUNdamentals
- Learning to train
- Training to train
- Training to compete
- Training to win
- Activity for life

As you might anticipate, the LTAD model carries implications for coaching philosophy. Specifically, this holistic approach to sport considers the physical, psychological, and social development of athletes and, as the name implies, calls on coaches to think not only about the here and now but also about each athlete's long-term development. In doing so, the model provides an important framework to aide coaches and organizations in systematically considering coaching and context, in which beliefs and behaviors fit over athletic development stages. In short, implementing the "sport for life" message associated with LTAD depends on a sound working philosophy, regardless of the stage at hand.

COACHING SNAPSHOT

Putting aside the 13 NBA championships (2 as player, 11 as coach), triangle offense, Native American spiritualism, and "Zen Master" label, the essence of **Phil Jackson's** success was his ability to establish a connection with each player as an individual while still being able to mold a team into a cohesive unit. As he said, *"Some coaches insist on having the last word, but I always tried to foster an environment in which everyone played a leadership role."*

Modifying and Adapting a Philosophy

Thus far we have examined the importance of developing a philosophy and putting it into action. The final step is to develop the ability to recognize when and how to adapt or modify your philosophy. Over time, your coaching philosophy will be tested, and standard practice would suggest reviewing your core values every season. To do so, ask yourself the questions provided in the Postseason Philosophy Reflection sidebar at the conclusion of each season. These questions, which can be found in a variety of coaching philosophy exercises, will help you address both the positive and the critical experiences of your season. It is best to conduct this review after some time has passed (e.g., a few weeks to a few months) since the conclusion of the season—when the season is still fresh in your mind but time has allowed any adverse situations or feelings to settle, thus enabling you to reflect with a clear head.

Beyond the postseason self-evaluation of philosophy and actions, there are three other key situations in which coaches should evaluate, and if necessary, modify their philosophy. The first type of situation involves a change in coaching context. For instance, will you now be coaching for performance rather than for participation? Or will you be joining a new organization and therefore needing to align with a different programmatic mission statement? In the second type, there is a change in your athletes. For example, perhaps you are now working with veteran athletes rather than novices. Have you coached such athletes before? Do they have varied motives for their own involvement?

Postseason Philosophy Reflection

Do my athletes know what is important to me?

Identify an incident that *reinforced* my philosophy and values.

Identify an incident that *challenged* my philosophy and values. What were the consequences? How did I respond?

Did I meet my goals and objectives for this season? How do I know?

If my athletes described me to someone unfamiliar with my team, what would they say?

- On my best day
- On my worst day

Was there an incident this season that I wish I could do over? Why? What would I do differently?

The third type of situation, and arguably the most valuable and effective, involves evaluating through the lens of sheer experience or structured opportunities for reflective practice.[26] Examples include coaching clinics and both formal and informal coach training, all of which provide valuable opportunities to talk with other coaches about your beliefs and behaviors. In these settings, experienced and novice coaches alike receive valuable input from their peers, and coaches of all levels should take advantage of such opportunities. Often, a casual conversation, occurring beyond the confines of the field or court, enables coaches to accurately reflect on and evaluate their beliefs and actions.

Developing a coaching philosophy is a hallmark of highly effective coaches, yet all coaches must *work* to stick to their philosophy. As the Playing Time Versus Playing for Keeps sidebar dramatizes, all coaches sometimes struggle to adhere to their philosophy and, at times, may stray from it. Strategies for adhering to your philosophy include writing it down and posting it ("ink it, don't think it"), regularly reviewing it and modifying it as needed, reflecting on it at the beginning and end of each season, and empowering a trusted friend or assistant to hold you accountable.

If you do get caught up in a situation and veer off course, what should you do? In part, it comes down to evaluation. As coaches, we spend considerable time evaluating our players, and in order to be most effective we also need to evaluate ourselves (for guiding questions, refer back to the Postseason Philosophy Reflection sidebar). But how do we evaluate our actions in the moment, especially when they may contradict our stated philosophy and values? To begin with, remember that modifying and evaluating your philosophy is a cyclical process;[5] that is, your response to a situation, along with the consequences of that response, directly affect the need to modify or confirm your beliefs.

For example, suppose that you coach hockey athletes of ages 8 to 10—an age group where players start to become more competitive but are still young and need to focus on fun, participation, and skill development. One day, in the heat of a particularly competitive match, your emotions get the best of you. As a result, you change your consistent strategy of equal playing time in order to keep the best players on the ice and go for the win. Then you argue with the referee over a call and find yourself telling your players in a loud, demanding voice, "Don't be soft! Go after them and go after them hard."

Later, as you head into the locker room with your players for a postgame talk, you know in your gut that you were out of control. What do you do now? One simple yet very effective strategy is to own your mistake. That is, tell your team what you did and why it was wrong. Apologize for your behavior and describe what would have been a better approach. Here is an example:

"Wow. That was a tough match. There were some battles out there. I want us to take a few important things from this game. First, I was not a good example of controlling my emotions. I should not have argued with the ref, and I shouldn't have lost my cool. I apologize for calling you 'soft.' I let myself get too competitive instead of focusing on what we wanted to do. Second, it's really important to me that we work really hard. Third, it's also important to me that we keep getting better at skills, and to do that, we need to have fun playing. I am going to do a better job of keeping those things in my mind while I coach."

It might also be a good idea, especially at this age level, to send a similar note to the parents and guardians of your players. That way, the message is consistently delivered. Such incidents provide a great opportunity for coaches to evaluate in the moment, acknowledge transgressions, and move forward in a better way.

Chapter 4

Key Coaching Functions

Dan Gould and Kristen Dieffenbach

Coaches fulfill many and varied functions. Some are fairly universal, such as instructing athletes, providing feedback, and executing administrative tasks. Others are specific to a certain coaching level or context; for example, some coaches must raise funds to support their programs, whereas others must engage in community service. Having acknowledged this variety, we focus in this chapter on the functions of leadership in coaching.

Leadership functions include setting the program's vision, implementing strategies to facilitate and deliver on that vision, and shaping the environment (or creating a suitable coaching climate) to facilitate the program's mission and goals. Coaching leadership also involves building relationships with a variety of program stakeholders (e.g., athletes, administrators, parents), particularly by learning to listen and asking good questions. In addition, coaches exercise leadership by planning and conducting practices and training sessions, as well as preparing for and coaching during competition; moreover, both practice and competition require coaches to exhibit leadership in reviewing and reacting to player and team behavior. Great coaches also review their own performance by engaging in purposeful self-reflection. Finally, an often-forgotten coaching leadership function involves maintaining one's own health and well-being.

Coaches as Leaders

In *Coaches Guide to Sport Psychology*, Rainer Martens drew an important distinction between coaches as leaders and coaches as managers.[1]

As managers, coaches perform essential tasks such as budgeting, staffing, scheduling competitions, and planning and organizing practices. As leaders, they set the program vision, develop goals and objectives linked to that vision, and help athletes achieve them. Unfortunately, as Martens observed, "too many teams are overmanaged and underled."[1] [(p. 33)] That is, too many coaches act merely as managers who keep the operation running smoothly rather than providing true leadership that helps athletes and teams identify and achieve major goals.

Of course, coaches must fulfill both management and leadership functions, and how they do so depends on their own attributes and the resources available to them. For example, a head coach who is very strong at creating a program vision (i.e., seeing the big picture) but weak on the management skills necessary for implementing that vision (i.e., following through on the details) might hire assistant coaches who possess strong management skills. In a much different example, youth sport coaches who work without pay—and whose work and family lives limit the time they can devote to coaching—often recruit parents to help with program management functions.

Thus delegation can be a critical tool for fulfilling coaching functions; however, coaches must understand that the ultimate responsibility still resides with them. For this reason, they must monitor their staff while taking care not to micromanage. They must also commit to improving in areas in which they are weak. For instance, a coach who is weak on certain aspects of management should not simply delegate but also work to improve in this area of responsibility—for instance, by taking a course in time management.

Setting the Program Vision

One of the most important functions of any leader is to set the organization's vision, and this is certainly the case for sport coaches. At a minimum, the head coach sets the vision for the team, if not for several teams (e.g., Swiss A, B, and C ski teams) or an entire program. Thus, it is essential to understand what goes into setting a program's vision. Fortunately, much has been written about creating corporate visions in the business world, and this literature can be applied to coaching. For instance, the process of building a company's vision was addressed in a classic *Harvard Business Review* article comparing successful corporations with unsuccessful ones.[2] The authors found that an effective vision included two key parts: core ideology and envisioned future.

Core ideology consists of the central value and core purpose of the organization or program. It endures over time and explains why the operation exists. For example, the Walt Disney Corporation embraces the core values of wholesomeness and imagination and exists to "make people happy" (its core purpose); in contrast, Merck, the pharmaceutical company, embraces the core values of science-based innovation, honesty and integrity, and corporate social responsibility in pursuit of its core purpose to "preserve and improve human life."[2] An organization's core ideology seldom changes, and it usually embraces only the relatively few core values that are truly central to it. Core values do not change when the going gets rough; to the contrary, they serve as enduring guides.

The envisioned future of a program or organization consists of an audacious long-term goal (e.g., 10-year or even 30-year) as well as vibrant descriptions of what it will look like to achieve that goal. For example, in 1961, U.S. President John F. Kennedy set the seemingly impossible goal of putting a human being on the moon within a decade, and he vividly described the significance of doing so. This hugely ambitious goal drove the NASA program that landed a human on the moon in 1969. Such goals are not sure bets, and they require tremendous effort to achieve, but they direct the organization's efforts and inspire those who work toward them.

Although coaches do not run major corporations, they are responsible for developing, operating, and sustaining successful athletic programs. Great coaches achieve these goals by intentionally and carefully setting a vision for their team or program. In many regards, this process parallels the process described in chapter 3 for deriving a personal coaching philosophy. In fact, it is crucial to align the two. After all, what coach would want to work in a program with a mission that differed greatly from his or her own core values? This need for alignment also makes it crucial for coaches who are interviewing for a job to identify and understand both their own core values and coaching philosophy and the values (written or otherwise) of the potential workplace. Coaches who find themselves in a system or situation where their personal values conflict with those of the organization face challenges that can undermine their job satisfaction, their ability to succeed, and even their well-being.

At the same time, setting a program's vision requires more than simply implementing one's own coaching philosophy. For instance, the program vision will certainly be affected by the philosophy of the sport organization, national federation, club, or academy for which one coaches. It will also be influenced by the local community and other program stakeholders, such as funders or, in the case of youth sport, parents.

For example, let us consider the Collegiate Leadership Academy established by the National Wrestling Coaches Association to serve U.S. collegiate coaches. This organization calls for collegiate head coaches to develop a vision and mission for their program. Specifically, coaches are directed to examine vision and mission statements from the NCAA, their own conference, their own institution, and, if available, their own athletic department and then align their program vision and mission accordingly (see table 4.1).

TABLE 4.1 Sample Vision and Mission Statements and Core Values

NCAA

Mission statement: "Our purpose is to govern competition in a fair, safe, equitable and sportsmanlike manner, and to integrate intercollegiate athletics into higher education so that the educational experience of the student-athlete is paramount."

Core values: "The Association—through its member institutions, conferences and national office staff—shares a belief in and commitment to:

- The collegiate model of athletics in which students participate as an avocation, balancing their academic, social and athletics experiences.
- The highest levels of integrity and sportsmanship.
- The pursuit of excellence in both academics and athletics.
- The supporting role that intercollegiate athletics plays in the higher education mission and in enhancing the sense of community and strengthening the identity of member institutions.
- An inclusive culture that fosters equitable participation for student-athletes and career opportunities for coaches and administrators from diverse backgrounds.
- Respect for institutional autonomy and philosophical differences.
- Presidential leadership of intercollegiate athletics at the campus, conference and national levels."

Big Ten Conference

"Since its inception in 1896, the pursuit and attainment of academic excellence has been a priority for every Big Ten member institution. But maintaining the conference's standard of competing at the highest level in athletics also endures as an important component of the Big Ten experience. Striking that balance between academics and athletics is integral to the Big Ten's identity. Recognized as one of intercollegiate sports' most successful undertakings, the Big Ten strives for success from its students not only on the field and in the classroom, but around the world as well."

Ohio State University

"The university is dedicated to:

- Creating and discovering knowledge to improve the well-being of our state, regional, national and global communities;
- Educating students through a comprehensive array of distinguished academic programs;
- Preparing a diverse student body to be leaders and engaged citizens;
- Fostering a culture of engagement and service.

We understand that diversity and inclusion are essential components of our excellence."

Ohio State University Athletics Department

Mission statement: "We foster a culture that provides the opportunity to develop our student-athletes through success in academics and competition to achieve excellence in life."

Core values:

- "Integrity: We will act with integrity and personal accountability.
- Education: We will educate each student-athlete with quality academic, competitive, leadership and social experiences to build a sense of responsibility and foster an appreciation for life-long learning.
- People: We will keep the well-being of our student-athletes, coaches and staff at the core of every decision.
- Excellence: We will excel in performance, achievement and service.
- Respect: We will celebrate a climate of mutual respect and diversity by recognizing each individual's contribution to the team.
- Innovation: We will encourage innovation, develop a curious mindset and embrace change.
- Community: We will enhance the lives of those in our university, city and state communities by helping and paying forward to others.
- Tradition: We will build upon our traditions which have been developed throughout our proud history."

Reprinted by permission from The Ohio State University. Retrieved from https://ohiostatebuckeyes.com/mission-statement [July 1, 2020].

Ohio State University Wrestling

Mission statement: "OUR vision for Ohio State Wrestling is in each one, help foster a relentless pursuit of personal growth through the pursuit of absolute permanent truths. Where love, gratitude and suffering bind us to our purpose and to a deep connection. Where each become uniquely them, yet the whole is always an integral piece of the equation. Where the elite lift those around them.

Damaging pride and fear is exterminated and truth and love are elevated. Me is overshadowed by we. We join together and pursue disciplines that lead to a life aimed at becoming elite!

Modeling the way IS the way. Together we build men who love each other, their sport, learning and pursue things that will lead to their development as the Best Version of themselves. Where we all transcend from those who believe to those who commit.

Goals For Team:

Educate, Graduate, Job placement for each one so that they may lead and inspire others.

Create the world's greatest training environment to inspire those whose purpose is to reach their full genetic potential.

Elevate and inspire those to cross the gap between believing and committing.

To create the world's best competition environment that moves the spirit of all in the organization to love each other.

Build a culture of truth and love. A culture of bold men who communicate genuinely with each other.

Build a culture whose foundation is deeply rooted in behaviors over rules.

Build men who value toughness and understand the power in chasing what is uncomfortable.

Over communicate and listen intently. Be vulnerable and real. Share truth. Always share truth.

Our word is our bond and we are measured by our actions and those things that are in our control."

Courtesy of Ohio State University Head Wrestling Coach Tom Ryan.

Unfortunately, it is not uncommon for stakeholders, including coaches, to be unaware of their organization's vision and thus miss out on the strengths and benefits to be gained from a clearly articulated common core of beliefs and values.[3] Vision and mission statements do little good if they merely rest on shelves or in computer files rather than being used. To be effective, a mission statement must be understood by all stakeholders, including athletes, coaches, administrators, and supporters. This awareness can be developed by posting values and vision statements both electronically and in prominent places at training and competition venues, reviewing them with team members on a regular basis, and engaging team members in discussions about what they mean and why they are important.

In addition, coaches, athletes, and other program stakeholders must be held accountable for implementing and adhering to the stated standards and values. Although successful programs and coaches are flexible and adapt to changing conditions that influence their programs, they do not stray from their program vision and key values. Less successful programs and coaches do.

Shaping the Environment

Once the program vision is set and the core values have been identified, a coach must work to shape the environment so that they can be implemented. Research reveals that through such efforts, coaches help create various types of climates that positively influence their athletes. For example, in one study, researchers interviewed 16 UK coaches who were considered experts in athletic talent development.[4] These coaches, who represented 13 sports, identified five general characteristics of effective talent development programs:

1. Long-term aims and methods for achieving them (e.g., long-term purpose and vision along with systematic planning)
2. Coherent philosophy and broad-ranging messages and support for them (e.g., role models, forums for open and honest communication)
3. Focus on appropriate long-term development rather than immediate or early success
4. Individualized and ongoing development (e.g., opportunities for many youngsters, flexible systems for variations in performance and physical development)
5. Integrated holistic and systematic development

Other researchers have taken a holistic case study approach in analyzing both a highly successful sailing program and a track-and-field program. In the sailing study, researchers found that the sport club's environment was characterized by a high level of cohesion that hinged on relationships between current elite athletes and prospective athletes.[5] They also observed a strong organizational culture, which valued open cooperation, individual responsibility, and a focus on performance. For example, the elite sailors felt a duty to help younger participants, and the norm called for always improving and openly sharing knowledge. The program also limited parental involvement while encouraging athlete autonomy. This strong organizational culture also helped club members overcome a lack of resources.

In the track-and-field study, researchers again found a culture of cohesion in which elite athletes voluntarily served as role models and mentors for younger club members.[6] They also observed that the club's board worked passionately to meet the club's needs and that families provided emotional, social, financial, and practical support for the athletes. The club's cultural paradigm was also characterized by common interrelated values, such as achieving excellence through cooperation and openness, maintaining a family orientation, treating each athlete as a whole person, and valuing successful development more than early results.

When the authors compared these two cases, they identified several common keys to success. In both clubs, elite athletes played important roles in the development of up-and-coming prospects, and prospects themselves worked with younger athletes. Each club also exhibited a strong organizational culture; norms that included open sharing of knowledge; an athlete performance process with a long-term development focus; a high degree of cohesion; and a focus on helping athletes develop related psychological competencies, such as responsibility, social skills, and a desire for excellence.

Finally, in a study of a highly successful Danish soccer club, researchers found that the club environment was characterized by a focus on player education and development.[7] That is, the club took a holistic approach to developing each young athlete as both a player and a person. For instance, training sessions emphasized informing and motivating athletes on the basis of individual player development plans. More specifically, the club attended to each player's development of desired characteristics, such as self-awareness, goal setting, management of performance and process outcomes, and social skills. In addition, key club values were featured prominently in the club's culture—for instance, strong family-like feelings; an attitude of working hard to compensate for any shortage of talent; a cooperative, open environment; and team achievement (using team skills, knowing team strengths and weaknesses, and using team resources and teamwork skills).

A talent development culture is a complex, almost living thing. It requires a collective effort of support and must provide value to those who supply the resources on which it is built. Although the coach plays a vital role in creating a team culture, a positive and supportive culture cannot be created or sustained by just one individual. Coaches can, however, facilitate and nurture the desired culture through their choices and actions. For example, one study examined best practices among coaches with long-term records of high performance and found that sustained success required them to enlist help from the right people—that is, people dedicated to a similar vision and work ethic.[8]

On a smaller scale, considerable research has been conducted on the motivational climates that coaches create within a team to help their athletes train and compete.[9] This research has shown that the social environment created by a coach exerts a strong influence on athletes' attitude, effort level, and learning. Specifically, when coaches establish a climate that is task oriented (i.e., focused on personal improvement and skill mastery) rather than ego oriented (i.e., focused on winning and comparing athletes with each other), athletes are more satisfied, give increased effort, persist longer in the face of adversity, and perform better and more consistently. This research has generated a number of practical guidelines for creating task-oriented climates:[10]

- Help athletes set self-referenced goals and emphasize individual challenges.
- Allow athletes to make meaningful decisions and give them responsibility for aspects of their own development.
- Meet with athletes to focus on individual improvements.
- Recognize and reward effort and individual progress.
- Allow athletes to work in small groups to help solve problems and make plans for progress.
- Provide individual player evaluations based on effort and individual improvement.
- Treat athletes as individuals and recognize that they improve at different rates.

Coaches also shape the environment in other important ways. For instance, one study found that Canadian intercollegiate sport coaches recruit athletes who exhibit certain characteristics or intangibles that they feel will mesh with the team environment they are trying to create.[11] Another study, focused on turnaround coaching leadership, examined collegiate coaches in the United States who led a formerly losing program to a national championship.[12] The study found that these coaches shaped team culture by instilling key program values, recruiting athletes who epitomize those core values, and holding athletes accountable to those values by means of rewards and penalties.

Both research and experience, then, show that one key function of a coach is to shape the environment in which athletes train and compete.

COACHING SNAPSHOT

Pat Summitt was known for her toughness, integrity, winning (eight national championships), and knowledge. She left no stone unturned in preparing her players for competition, and at game time she was an intense warrior. Still, Summitt never lost sight of the fact that her strategy and strength of will took back seat to a more important factor, subscribing to a slightly modified version of Theodore Roosevelt's famous quote: *"They don't care how much you know unless they know how much you care."*

Building Relationships

Ability and desire to relate to athletes are critical in coaching. The coach–athlete relationship provides a foundation for effective motivation, communication, mental preparation, and feedback. Coaches also need to build good relationships with assistant coaches, support staffers (e.g., sports medicine providers, strength coaches), program administrators, officials, and athletes' family members.

Early research in youth sport showed that coaches who are more encouraging and less punitive fostered athletes who were more motivated and more satisfied.[13] A synopsis of 25 years of this research produced the following relationship-building guidelines for coaches:[14]

- Encourage athletes often and sincerely.
- Minimize punitive and demeaning feedback, especially after mistakes.
- Reward effort as much as results.
- Provide technical instruction that is clear and concise.

Research reveals that when coaches create a caring climate—in which athletes know that their coaches care about them, support them, and respect them as individuals—athletes exhibit greater enjoyment, more positive attitudes, higher commitment, and more caring behavior.[15] Specific actions for creating a positive climate include asking players to introduce themselves to one another at the start of the season, greeting each player individually by name upon arrival at practice, setting clear public expectations about the importance of personal effort and improvement, and helping athletes build relationships with each other through strategies such as identifying teammates' strengths and working with a practice partner.[16]

Another study identified the following key components of the coach–athlete relationship:[17]

1. Closeness—mutual feelings of respect and trust
2. Commitment—mutual intention to maintain the relationship over the long term
3. Complementarity—cooperative actions

The study also emphasizes the fact that "coaches' and athletes' feelings, thoughts, and behaviors are interdependent" and that better coach–athlete relationships lead to desirable athlete outcomes, such as better leadership, motivation, and performance.[17 (p. 17)] To gain these benefits, both parties must clearly express their goals and their commitment to those goals; they must also find the most effective styles of working with one another. However, even as coaches facilitate a positive bond with their athletes, they must remain in command. Not only are they more knowledgeable than athletes, they are also legally and ethically liable for their players' health and safety.

Developing and maintaining an effective coach–athlete relationship also depends on the coach's ability to understand and recognize the athlete's feelings, thoughts, behaviors, and intentions.[18] To develop empathic accuracy, make a point to gather information regularly about your athletes. For instance, you might recognize that when a certain athlete snaps at others during practice, this behavior indicates anxiety or worry about the next game. Such insight can help you maintain empathy appropriately. For example, you might show support to an athlete who is late to practice due to losing a loved one but respond differently to one who regularly arrives late for no good reason. At the same time, reflect on your own actions to gain understanding of why you behave in the ways you do. You might, for instance, realize that you are displaying anxiety that makes your athletes feel anxious. Finally, seek to avoid any biases that might cloud your coaching judgment, such as assuming that African American athletes would not be interested in swimming because none have been on the team before.

An especially effective way for coaches to build relationships with athletes and other key stakeholders is to spend less time telling others what to do and more time asking questions. In *Coaching for Performance*,[19] sport coach and business consultant Sir John Whitmore argues that a coach's role is to "unlock people's potential to maximize their own performance"[(p. 10)] while "building awareness, responsibility, and self-belief."[(p. 19)] He encourages coaches to do so by asking questions. This approach shows athletes, fellow coaches, and support staffers that their opinions are respected. It also invites athletes (and others) to become more aware of what they are doing and gives them a chance to own their answer and commit to it of their own accord. Coaches can ask good questions by using the GROW model:[19]

> G or *goal* questions: What would you like to achieve? What are you hoping to accomplish?
>
> R or *reality* questions: What have you tried so far? What have you seen others do?
>
> O or *option* questions: What could you do? What would help you achieve your goal?
>
> W or *what will be done, when, and by whom:* As a result of our meeting, what can I expect to see you do differently?

Of course, asking good questions is not enough. Coaches must also listen attentively, both to ensure that they really hear what is being communicated and to show that they are listening.

Whitmore is not suggesting that coaches should never direct or tell others what to do; to the contrary, they must instruct.[19] He does contend, however, that the bedrock of good coaching involves a general shift away from telling others what to do and toward asking them questions that help them become more self-aware, take more responsibility, develop more self-belief, and become more self-efficacious. In our experience, this approach also greatly facilitates relationships and helps coaches become more effective.

Conducting Practices and Preparing for Competitions

Even in the most elite sport setting, far more time is spent in training and practice than in competition. As a result, daily practice sessions provide an excellent opportunity for coaches to help athletes develop physical, technical, tactical, and mental skills through drills, scrimmage play, and feedback. Unfortunately, coaches often overlook the need to align their practice plans with the team or program vision, and this misalignment can lead to problems including frustration and diminished outcomes.

Every good practice is founded on clear and well-prioritized objectives. To ensure alignment with program goals and vision, coaches must evaluate practice plans both before use (to support athletes) and after use (to assess progress). Even in the best circumstances, practice is constrained by the limitations of training resources, such as time, stamina, focus, enthusiasm, and facility access. Assessing and understanding these constraints will enable you to prioritize the daily practice objectives that are most likely to help your athletes make progress.

Coaching and training do not happen *to* athletes. Rather, effective training for talent development requires that athletes be engaged and working toward becoming "students of the sport."[20] To help athletes buy in, coaches can highlight and clarify training objectives in terms of both day-to-day activities and larger team goals. This approach reinforces the long-term vision and helps athletes develop a sense of competence. Coaches are teachers, and, as with academic curriculum design, the best practice plans are developed with an end goal in mind.[21] To ensure that a plan is effective, it is important to test progress along the way. Whereas an academic curriculum assesses progress through testing and achievement of cognitive developmental markers, training progress can be charted through sport models that provide athlete growth markers, such as the Long-Term Athlete Development (LTAD) model[22] and physical tests (e.g., 12-minute run, beep test).

In a competitive culture, an overemphasis on outcome often overshadows the unique opportunity that competition presents to evaluate training gains, test new approaches, and assess future training needs. The LTAD model suggests that a well-trained coach understands and uses the opportunities presented by competition as part of an overall plan to meet training goals and objectives rather than letting competition itself dominate the training focus.[23] This reverse emphasis, which places competition in the role of servant in the athlete development model, is especially important during the early part of the season when athletes resume training after the off-season. Downtime between training seasons provides an important physical and mental break that is essential for long-term growth in sport, and while athletes may continue to train at a lower level during this phase, a certain amount of detraining will still occur. Thus, the initial phase of training at the start of the season allows coaches to assess and address fitness needs as well as refresh safe training and playing techniques.

In most regards, training and competition are as different as two things can possibly be. For instance, most sports feature specific game-day uniforms, and some programs have game-only playing facilities. In addition, spectators charge the competitive environment, and the pace is often swift, with an emphasis on execution and little time for meaningful corrective feedback. In contrast, routine training allows for repetition and in-depth teaching practices. In fact, the marked differences between these two types of activity often constitute a difficult gap for athletes to negotiate as they strive to pull together their performance. Coaches can facilitate the transition from the learning environment to execution and fill in the performance gap by designing intentional practice plans that replicate or simulate competitive elements. Research on elite performance suggests that using a practice structure similar to that of competition or game play helps athletes improve their performance.[24] Examples include playing crowd noise over loudspeakers and running competition simulations complete with referees and a timer.

The most important element of both practice design and competition preparation may be the feedback loop or evaluation process. Without conducting routine evaluations, it is impossible to assess progress toward team objectives and goals or to make the necessary adjustments for continued improvement. Performing the necessary audits requires coaches to begin with their plan and a clear understanding of their objectives and how to measure or assess growth. Most coaches are comfortable and familiar with routinely assessing athlete progress—for instance, using timed runs to evaluate fitness gains. It is just as important to evaluate overall progress toward season goals and assess the effectiveness of the plan. Indeed, it has been suggested that reflection serves as a key to effective coaching as a leader and educator.[25] In order to design effective programs, then, coaches must develop the ability to collect appropriate information and feedback, understand the significance of the information collected, and use this knowledge to enhance future planning and coaching efforts.

Reading and Reacting to Developments

The cornerstones of sport performance include skill acquisition, motor learning, development of decision-making skills and core mental skills (e.g., focus, resilience), and, of course, physiological growth. None of these things can happen without guidance from individuals who possess the skills and resources to set up effective learning environments and provide appropriate guidance—namely, coaches.

Coaches need to be prepared to provide effective instruction across a wide variety of learning platforms and to understand and employ a range of teaching and motivational strategies. In order to align this process with the athlete-centered approach to coaching,[26] it is essential to consider individual athletes.[27] Though it can be challenging to do so, particularly for coaches of larger teams, conducting practices that engage various learning styles may improve athletes' learning and reduce negative outcomes such as burnout and dropout.

In addition to creating a solid platform for learning, with clear objectives and well-designed practice plans, you must also be able to conduct effective practices. High-quality practice design incorporates multiple teaching methods, including active teaching (e.g., providing instruction), shaping behavior (e.g., providing effective feedback), and providing learning opportunities (e.g., constructing an appropriate environment). It does *not* call for constant engagement with your athletes. To the contrary, in order to conduct effective practices, you must be able to step back, observe, reflect "in action," and respond and adjust as appropriate.[28] The ability to silently observe and assess the action while it is occurring and be able to provide meaningful and succinct feedback relevant to the current activity is important for maintaining practice momentum.

During any given practice, coaches are bombarded with cues related to athletes' behavior (e.g., on or off task), skill execution, and tactical performance, as well as their own administrative duties. Thus coaches must determine each cue's relevance and value in order to determine where to focus their efforts. To help make such judgments, coaches should determine core learning objectives for specific activities *before* practice takes place—specifically, during the plan development phase. These objectives can then help coaches determine which cues to focus on in their observation and feedback during each segment of practice.

When coaches provide athletes with meaningful, appropriately timed feedback about observed behaviors, they bring to bear both pedagogical and sport psychology skills that are essential for high-quality coaching. To enable positive learning, feedback should be specific, encouraging, and delivered in a manner that the athlete can understand.[29] Effective coaches intentionally provide both verbal (e.g., praise, instruction) and nonverbal feedback (e.g., silence, body language).[30]

COACHING SNAPSHOT

Sergio Scariolo's coaching career has been marked by adaptability, a tremendous rapport with his players, and his teams' success exceeding expectations. Working his way up from the youth level to an assistant coach at the senior level to head coach of the Italian Air Force team, Scariolo would go on to lead the Spanish national team to three EuroBasket titles and one World Cup title. He accepted an assistant coaching position in 2018 with the Toronto Raptors, a team that would claim an NBA championship the following year, proving that effective leadership and communication can overcome borders and the odds.

Learning and Reflecting

Both research and experience teach us that great coaches strive constantly to learn and improve their coaching. Through such activities as attending clinics and reading about other great coaches and leaders, they continue to learn about the science and art of coaching. These coaches also take an active approach by using the gym, pool, or track as a laboratory for testing both their own ideas and various possibilities from best coaching practices and developments in sport science.[31] They then reflect on these experiences and evaluate whether their coaching strategies are working as intended, why or why not, and for whom. As discussed in chapter 12, this reflective process is essential for growth in coaching.

There are many practical ways for coaches to reflect on their practice. First, they can set aside time each week to reflect on how their coaching is going. This debriefing session might involve asking questions such as the following:

- What went right with my coaching?
- What went wrong?
- Why did things go right or wrong?
- What should I stop doing?
- What should I keep doing?
- What should I start doing?
- Did my coaching actions align with my personal coaching philosophy and with the program's vision and core values?

We have also found that sport camps can provide a powerful setting for coaching reflection. For example, coaches might set aside one night a week to meet and discuss a topic of common interest, such as effective ways to reach parents or help players with mental preparation. They may also find it useful to discuss a particular athlete who is struggling or doing well. Through this exchange of ideas, they form a community of practice that allows them to learn from each other.

Similarly, an athletic director or head coach might schedule a monthly meeting for staff to discuss their coaching practices and what they are learning about coaching. Participating coaches might identify areas where they are struggling and ask the group to discuss ways of improving. Each coach might also present a useful coaching tip on a particular topic, such as motivation, nutrition, strength training, or conditioning.

Another technique we have found useful is for coaches to keep a simple log of lessons learned. As they go through the season, they can take time each week to reflect on what they have learned about coaching in general or about particular athletes or situations. For instance, one coach simply made a list of what worked and what did not work and then referred to it from time to time.

Finally, some coaches find it useful to develop a peer-mentoring buddy system in which two coaches meet periodically to discuss each other's coaching.

Health of a Coach

Leaders, teachers, and coaches cannot take care of their followers, students, and athletes unless they take care of themselves. Ironically, however, coaches often fail to heed this advice because they care so much about their athletes and their sport. They work long hours, don't necessarily eat well, and often fail to spend adequate time with loved ones. If unchecked, this pattern leads to diminished coaching performance and, in extreme cases, relationship issues and even divorce.

As noted by sport psychologist Jim Loehr, sustained high achievement in any field demands physical, emotional, and intellectual stamina.[32, 33] Therefore, sport leaders must learn to balance energy management and demands if they are to achieve and sustain peak performance. To this end, it is critical for coaches to manage their energy expenditure, both daily and over the course of a season. Effective energy management addresses multiple dimensions: physical (e.g., nutrition, exercise, sleep, and other healthy habits), emotional (e.g., management of emotions), intellectual (e.g., time management, avoidance of multitasking), and spiritual (e.g., understanding of one's purpose and deepest values). In contrast, being unable to manage one's energy can lead to coaching burnout, in which a once-enjoyable activity becomes a chore. An individual experiencing burnout feels both physically and emotionally exhausted and lacks the personal sense of accomplishment that coaching once provided. Motivation wanes, and the coach loses passion and often stops caring.

Research has shown that burnout usually results from chronic or prolonged stress. Specific causes of coaching burnout may include travel demands, the need to play multiple roles (e.g., coaching on top of a noncoaching full-time job), parental interference, pressure to win, and low social support.[29] Coaches may also be more susceptible to burnout when they are young or inexperienced and if they use a caring or people-oriented style.[34] In addition, female coaches may be more susceptible than men due to gender-based cultural expectations that can create role conflicts related to parenting, smaller support staffs, and differing leadership expectations and pressures.[35]

The bottom line is that if coaches want to be effective for the long haul, they need to take care of themselves physically, mentally, emotionally, and spiritually. To do so, they should engage in a healthy lifestyle, learn ways to manage their stress, and develop social systems for support in times of stress. These steps can help coaches avoid burnout while staying fully engaged.

Exercise: Meeting My Coaching Functions

Directions: If you are an established coach, consider these coaching functions and rate the level of engagement you need to have with each as well as your proficiency in meeting those functions. If you are a beginner coach, rate higher the functions in which you perceive that you should be most engaged and your anticipated proficiency at meeting them. Once you have created your personal ratings profile, identify the functions in which you most need to develop your proficiency. Ratings should be on a 1 to 5 scale, with a 1 meaning little engagement or little proficiency, and a 5 meaning high engagement or extensive proficiency required. Rate yourself on each primary action (not the bulleted items that follow some of them) involved in fulfilling the key coaching functions.

Coaching function	Engagement rating (1-5)*	Proficiency rating (1-5)**
LOGISTICAL MANAGEMENT FUNCTIONS		
Budgeting		
Planning		
Scheduling		
Time management		
Delegation		
LEADERSHIP—SETTING YOUR PROGRAM'S VISION		
Clearly write a core ideology. • Set the program's purpose. • Identify core values.		
Envision the future. • Identify an audacious long-term goal for the program.		
SHAPING THE ENVIRONMENT		
Create a talent development incubator. • Identify long-term aims and corresponding methods to reach them. • Provide a coherent philosophy and broad-ranging messages and support. • Focus on appropriate long-term development rather than immediate or early success. • Provide individualized and ongoing development. • Integrate holistic and systematic development.		

Coaching function	Engagement rating (1-5)*	Proficiency rating (1-5)**
SHAPING THE ENVIRONMENT *(continued)*		
Create a success-oriented club or program environment. • Involve senior athletes in the development of up-and-coming prospects. • Develop a strong organizational culture in which open sharing of knowledge is the norm. • Establish a long-term development focus. • Develop high degrees of cohesion within the club or team. • Focus on helping individual athletes develop psychological competencies.		
Create a success-oriented motivational climate. • Create a task-oriented (not ego-oriented) environment. • Emphasize self-referenced goals. • Allow athletes to make meaningful decisions. • Give athletes meaningful responsibilities. • Meet with athletes to focus on improvements. • Recruit athletes who epitomize core values. • Instill key values. • Hold athletes accountable.		
BUILDING RELATIONSHIPS		
Adopt a positive approach to coaching. • Provide encouragement liberally and sincerely. • Minimize punitive and demeaning feedback, especially after mistakes. • Reward effort as much as results. • Provide technical instruction clearly and concisely.		

(continued)

(continued)

Coaching function	Engagement rating (1-5)*	Proficiency rating (1-5)**
BUILDING RELATIONSHIPS *(continued)*		
Create a caring climate. • Ask athletes to introduce themselves to one another at the start of the season. • Greet each player individually by name upon arrival at practice. • Set clear public expectations for personal effort and improvement. • Help athletes build relationships with each other (e.g., identifying teammates' strengths, working with practice partners).		
Build an effective coach–athlete relationship. • Build closeness, trust, and respect with athletes. • Commit to long-term athlete relations. • Engage in complementarity. • Develop empathetic accuracy.		
Ask questions rather than merely telling or directing athletes as a coaching strategy. • Ask more questions. • Use the GROW model.		
CONDUCTING PRACTICE AND PREPARING FOR COMPETITION		
Write detailed daily practice plans with clearly identified objectives.		
Brief assistant coaches and athletes about daily practice priorities and objectives.		
Execute practices in accordance with practice plans.		
Develop an evaluation routine (e.g., weekly) to assess training progress and alignment with the larger program plan.		
Routinely evaluate practice.		
Debrief staff and athletes to discuss progress toward stated objectives.		

Coaching function	Engagement rating (1-5)*	Proficiency rating (1-5)**
REVIEWING AND REACTING		
Recognize and understand players' individual learning styles.		
Engage multiple learning styles in your teaching and coaching practice.		
Develop and practice effective feedback approaches.		
REFLECTING AND LEARNING		
Schedule regular appointments with yourself to reflect on your coaching.		
Schedule time to reflect on practice with other coaches.		
Maintain a log of lessons learned.		
Work with a peer-mentor buddy.		
MANAGING AND MAINTAINING YOUR OWN HEALTH		
Maintain physical energy (e.g., through nutrition, exercise, sleep, and other healthy habits).		
Maintain emotional energy (e.g., by managing emotions).		
Maintain intellectual energy (e.g., through time management, breaks, avoidance of multitasking).		
Maintain spiritual energy (e.g., through understanding of purpose and deepest values).		
Balance coaching with other life priorities.		

*1 = little engagement needed; 5 = high engagement needed

**1 = little proficiency; 5 = extensive proficiency

From International Council for Coaching Excellence, *Sport Coaches' Handbook*, eds. D. Gould and C. Mallett. (Champaign, IL: Human Kinetics, 2021).

Chapter 5

Core Coaching Skills

Sergio Lara-Bercial and John Bales

In the past, the job of coaching was thought of as mainly episodic and lasting from whistle to whistle. In this view, the work began when the coach first blew the whistle and athletes gathered round for instruction, and it ended when the whistle was blown for the last time and athletes were dismissed until the next practice or competition. This simple understanding addressed some of the realities of coaching, but what coaches do outside of practice and competition matters just as much—and sometimes even more. Today, coaches also set the direction for the team or program through vision and strategy, create effective training environments, engage in reflection in order to improve on past performances, build relationships, and cultivate a learning culture that enables success. This multifaceted work requires a broad set of core coaching skills, which together form the subject of this chapter.

These core skills are needed by all coaches, regardless of the context in which they work (e.g., youth sport versus professional sport). At the same time, a given skill may be more salient in certain situations—or applied in different ways or to varying degrees—and this chapter provides practical examples of how the skills can be deployed in real coaching situations. It also offers guidance for practicing the skills, making best use of them, and learning new ones. In addition, it can help you identify which skills you already possess, which ones you may be able to improve on, and perhaps some that you had not considered necessary until now.

Effective coaching has been defined as "the consistent application of integrated professional, interpersonal, and intrapersonal knowledge to improve athletes' competence, confidence, connection, and character in specific coaching contexts."[1 (p. 316)] In order to translate this knowledge into practice, coaches' efforts must be informed and guided by their philosophy, values, and beliefs.[2] And all four of these elements—knowledge, philosophy, values, and beliefs—are put into practice and brought to life by deploying core coaching skills.

Different aspects of the coaching job demand different combinations of skills. These skills, or competences, are acquired rather than inherent, which means that they can be learned—either formally (through acquisition of formal qualifications), nonformally (e.g., by attending coaching clinics), or informally (e.g., via self-reflection or discussion with other coaches). Core coaching skills can be classified into four main groups that overlap and complement each other:

- *Teaching skills.* This category includes all skills that directly affect a coach's ability to help athletes learn and improve their performance—which of course is a key part of coaching.
- *Management skills.* Skills in this group relate to overall planning and organization—that is, putting in place the necessary elements to maximize effectiveness and efficiency and thereby increase the chances of positive athlete outcomes as defined by the program.
- *Leadership skills.* The skills included in this category help accomplish program goals by facilitating the contributions of all members and influencers and calibrating personal and common goals.
- *Analytical skills.* This set of skills enables the coach to evaluate and monitor the needs and performances of all program members (i.e., self, athletes, staff) as part of a cycle of planning, reviewing, and adjusting.

The core coaching skills covered in this chapter are listed in table 5.1.

TABLE 5.1   Core Coaching Skills

Teaching skills	Management skills
• Setting up and standing back • Explaining • Demonstrating • Questioning and listening • Providing feedback • Differentiating • Designing activities	• Strategizing • Setting goals • Planning • Organizing
Leadership skills	**Analytical skills**
• Modeling • Communicating • Applying emotional intelligence • Motivating • Safeguarding	• Observing • Recording • Analyzing • Evaluating • Self-monitoring

Teaching Skills

While coaches should always strive to develop their athletes holistically, it is central to the mission of coaching to help athletes improve their technical and tactical abilities. Therefore, effective coaching requires teaching skills. Effective teaching, however, goes beyond merely passing on information to students or athletes.

Moreover, coaches need to be aware of the difference between improvement and learning. Improvement is temporary and can be achieved quickly—within a given session or activity. Learning, on the other hand, is permanent; that is, the skill is retained and retrievable even if not practiced for a period of time. Learning also takes time (please see chapters 10 and 12). With this distinction in mind, let us now examine the essential actions that coaches must perform effectively in order to foster both short-term improvement and long-term learning.

Setting Up and Standing Back

This skill is particularly useful when we are unfamiliar with a group or wish to introduce a new skill. When teaching a new skill, it is tempting to immediately provide technical instruction such as an explanation or demonstration, and this may be the right choice if we know our athletes' baseline level for the skill. Often, however, it is advisable to start by assessing which elements of the skill most need to be taught and for which athletes. In this way, we avoid explaining or demonstrating elements that they have already mastered and can focus instead on what is most needed.

To implement the approach of setting up and standing back, we can design or develop an activity or drill that encourages athletes to execute the specific skill (whether technical or tactical) that we wish to assess. The activity can be as simple or as complex as needed and can be shaped as either a closed skill (with no contextual interference) or an open skill. The key is to be very clear about the skill that we are encouraging the athletes to perform.

Explaining

The word *explain* literally means to make plain. Thus, explaining is the art of clearly telling athletes what they need to do, as well as how and why. Here are some recommendations for delivering effective explanations:

- Run through the explanation in your head before giving it to your athlete.
- Focus on a few specific points and be succinct.

- Use language that is clear and free from ambiguity.
- Concentrate on what *to* do rather than what *not* to do.
- Explain not only what to do but also how and why.
- Create mental pictures and use vivid language that athletes can remember easily.
- Attend to your body language during the explanation; an aggressive demeanor can arouse fear and reduce the athlete's ability to process information.
- After explaining, question the athlete to check for understanding.

Demonstrating

The purpose of demonstrating is to increase athletes' understanding of what is being taught by providing a model.[3] Demonstrations are typically combined with explanations but can exist on their own. In other cases, a coach may be intimidated by the prospect of demonstrating a complex technical skill. If so, the coach can ask for demonstrations by players who already grasp the technique, either within the same age group or from an older group; alternatively, the coach might use pictures or videos of famous athletes demonstrating the skill.

Here are some keys to giving effective demonstrations:

- Can all athletes see the demonstrator?
- What is the best angle or position for seeing the required elements of the model?
- Do the athletes need to see the full skill or only a segment of it?
- Can the observation be aided by using certain cues, anchor words, or imagery?
- Is the demonstration pitched at the right level of difficulty, or will it look unattainable to your athletes?

Questioning and Listening

The coach–athlete relationship should be a two-way interaction, both in general terms and with regard to teaching in particular. More specifically, the process of questioning and listening provides coaches with a powerful way to promote and guide athletes' learning. Despite sounding simple, effective questioning and listening require practice and preparation. Here is a five-stage framework for coaches:[3]

1. Prepare the question.
2. Present the question.
3. Encourage athletes' responses.

4. Process athletes' responses.
5. Reflect on the questioning process.

Given the fluidity of coaching and sport, it may not always be possible to prepare the question in advance. Over time, however, following this type of protocol will make even ad hoc questions more effective.

Question format also matters. Different types of questions promote different levels of thinking. For instance, questions such as "Did you?" and "Can you?" tend to generate simple yes-or-no answers. In contrast, questions such as "What?" and "When?" (or "How many?") tend to promote lower-order thinking and elicit factual information. And questions such as "How?" and "Why?" tend to elicit complex or higher-order thinking and deeper analysis.

Providing Feedback

In sport, feedback consists of information about an athlete's performance. It allows athletes to recognize good current performances and create reference points for improving future ones.

Effective feedback considers multiple factors, including time constraints and the athlete's mental readiness. When time allows, it is beneficial to engage the athlete through the positive questioning process described in the preceding section. And in all cases, the coach must gauge how much information the athlete can process at a particular time and adapt the feedback to that limit.

Of course, the quality of the content also matters. Effective feedback addresses only the aspects of performance you are focusing on in the current session. Where possible, it should also be objective—that is, supported by evidence. In addition, it must go beyond merely identifying elements to change or improve and point the way to a solution; that is, it should enable the athlete to see a way forward and know what to do next.

Much has been written about balancing positive and negative feedback and the effect on how people receive the information. In a popular tool, known as the "sandwich technique," negative feedback is inserted between two pieces of positive feedback. While this technique may be effective in specific circumstances (e.g., when building rapport or when working with children), it can also undermine the value of your feedback if the athlete figures out what you are trying to do and shuts down.[4] Therefore, it is now generally recommended for coaches to provide feedback transparently and objectively in the context of a healthy coach–athlete relationship and a learning culture in which feedback is perceived not as a reprimand but as an opportunity to improve.

Effective feedback fosters athletes' awareness of their own performance, and athletes who can self-evaluate and self-correct enjoy a great advantage. For instance, this ability provides them with many opportunities to improve their skills via self-coaching (after all, the coach will not always be there). It also enables them to be more self-reliant in competition, where opportunities for feedback from a coach may be limited.

Differentiating

A coach's athletes may be operating at different stages of development and therefore require different kinds of guidance and coaching intervention. For this reason, catering to everyone's needs in the program is a fundamental coaching duty. One way to do so is by using the inclusion spectrum framework (ISF; see figure 5.1).[5] Originally developed to support coaches whose participants have special needs, this approach also offers a useful way to conceptualize differentiation and adapt sessions and programs for athletes of differing ability levels.

The ISF shows various ways in which an activity can be presented and modified within the same group to ensure that every athlete is able to join in, learn, and experience a certain level of achievement and success:

- *Open activity.* Everyone can play without the need to modify the activity.

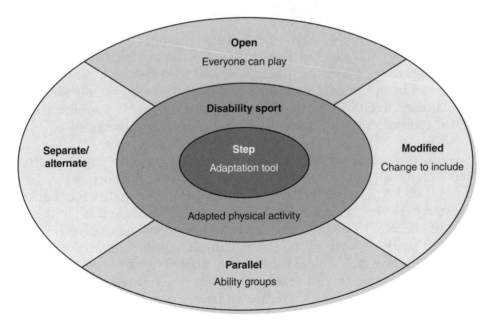

FIGURE 5.1 The inclusion spectrum framework.

© Pam Stevenson and Ken Black. Used with permission.

- *Parallel activity (ability groups).* Athletes are grouped according to ability and engage in the same activity or a modified version as appropriate for their needs.

- *Separate or alternate activity.* The coach sets up different activities for different ability groups. This differentiation may continue throughout the session, or the coach may set up the separate activity for the lower-ability group as a step toward rejoining the main group later in the session.

- *Adapted physical activity or disability sport.* The coach uses activities, games, or sports based on existing modalities such as boccia, wheelchair basketball, or sitting volleyball.

- *Modified activity (change to include).* Everyone does the same activity, but the coach incorporates a number of changes to support all athletes taking part. In one method of modification, known as the STEP model, coaches make activities, games, and drills either easier or harder on demand.[5] This approach also helps coaches emphasize different areas of the activity by changing the constraints. Each letter of STEP stands for a different category of factors that can be altered:[5]

  Space—changes in the size of the playing area, the distance to be covered, or the target area

  Task—changes in the task itself, such as running versus skipping, passing a ball with the hands versus the feet, and varying the scoring system or time constraints to adjust the level of opposition or realism (e.g., drill versus game)

  Equipment—changes in the implements used (e.g., size or weight of ball, size of racket or bat head, height of hurdle)

  People—changes in group composition, number of people involved, allocation of roles, or constraints placed on certain athletes

Designing Activities

Activity design involves developing drills and games that help athletes improve and learn. In order to be effective, it must be informed by a clear understanding of the skills or concepts we want to teach. With this understanding in hand, we can either look for appropriate activities from our own repertoire or that of another coach or develop new ones. A good starting point can be found in the STEP model described in the preceding section. Then, in order to keep the activity on track, we can ask questions such as the following: Does this activity accomplish what I want it to? What could I change to emphasize the skill I want participants to practice?

COACHING SNAPSHOT

Once the director of recreation and athletic program coordinator at a small college, **Ron Lykins** went on to apply his knowledge and experience in adapted sports with great success in various contexts. For a decade he directed training of coaches and taught youth adapted sports, and he would become the winningest international wheelchair basketball coach ever, coaching both men's and women's teams and revolutionizing how the game is played.

Management Skills

Successful coaches spend at least as much time shaping the environment to make it performance ready as they do acting in it.[2] Doing so requires them to engage in the following activities: strategizing, setting goals, planning, and organizing.

Strategizing

Strategizing involves plotting a course of action that maximizes the chance of success. For our purpose here, strategy addresses the long term rather than the narrower approach of preparing for a particular game or competition. When developing a long-term strategy for a program or squad, the following key elements need to be considered.

- *Vision.* The fundamental starting point for strategizing is to develop a vision that clearly states the ultimate goal that will drive the strategy. For instance, a coach might want her program to be recognized as the go-to place for the best athletes in the state or region because of the quality of coaching. Alternatively, a coach's vision might focus on competitive achievements (i.e., championships) or the number of college scholarships earned by athletes in the program.
- *Philosophy and values.* A coach's actions should be informed by his philosophy and values, which must be aligned with his vision and be positioned at the heart of everything he does (see chapter 4).[2]
- *Gap analysis.* An effective strategy is informed by a clear understanding of where the program or its athletes currently stand. One popular way to paint this picture and identify options is to conduct a SWOT analysis, which have been used in business and military settings since the 1960s. As the acronym reflects, a SWOT analysis identifies strengths, weaknesses, opportunities, and threats in order to shape strategy and inform decision making.

Once the vision is developed and the gap analysis has been completed, the results can be used to set or adjust program and athlete goals.

Setting Goals

Setting clear goals helps coaches and athletes achieve success. Goals offer direction and purpose for our day-to-day activities; in addition, by providing tangible objectives, they enhance our motivation. Clear goals also help us determine whether we are going in the right direction at a given point in time.

Goals can be classified according to either their content or their time frame. In terms of content, they can be categorized as follows:

- *Dreams.* Dreams, and ambitions, get us out of bed in the morning, bring smiles to our faces, and light up our eyes. They may also help us pull through difficult times by reminding us of our ultimate objective—for example, a college baseball player who dreams of playing in The Show. By themselves, however, dreams and ambitions rarely get the job done.

- *Outcome.* Outcome goals focus on the end result of a particular performance—prevailing in a game, race, or fight; winning a medal or championship; or simply finishing in a particular position. As with dreams, outcome goals do not achieve much by themselves. Nonetheless, they are sometimes necessary because they focus our efforts on a particular target. For instance, they help coaches and athletes analyze the components of performance that eventually lead to success. These elements give rise to the next category—performance goals.

- *Performance.* Performance goals set the standard that must be met in order to achieve outcome goals. Thus they allow coaches and athletes to translate outcome goals into specific, tangible objectives and measuring sticks. For instance, in order to have a chance of winning the 100-meter Olympic final, you need a time of about 9.7 seconds. Thus setting performance goals is a fundamental step for coaches in planning how to help their athletes reach desired standards. It also informs the development of process goals.

- *Process.* Process goals help coaches break desired performance into its key components. This analysis enables them to plan training cycles and sessions around specific, measurable objectives that provide clear direction and reference points. For instance, in order to achieve the performance goal of holding opponents to no more than 60 points, a basketball coach might create per-game process goals of limiting the opposition to fewer than 7 offensive rebounds, 10 trips to the foul line, and 12 fast-break points. In turn, each process goal leads to a set of actions (and training tasks) that contribute to its achievement.

With regard to time frame, goals have traditionally been classified as either short-term (1 to 4 weeks), mid-term (4 weeks to 12 months), or long-term (12 months or more). Your own timing, of course, will depend on the duration for which you anticipate working with a particular group or athlete. In any case, athletes need both a long-term view of development and a sense of the milestones they need to hit at key times. At the same time, goal setting also requires review and adjustment due to the fact that progress tends to occur nonlinearly.

Effective goal setting requires the application of certain principles. Specifically, effective goals are specific, moderately difficult but realistic, applicable to both practice and competition, recorded, linked to achievement strategies or action plans, tailored to the athlete's personality and motivations, agreed with and owned by the athlete, and frequently evaluated.[6] Goal setting failures often happen either because the athlete does not understand the process or because of insufficient planning and support for strategies that could enable success.

Planning

As mentioned in chapter 1, the word *coach* originates from the Hungarian *kocsi* and reflects the process of taking someone from where they are now to where they want to be in the future. Thus coaching is defined less by episodic delivery of coaching sessions and more by long-term development, which may take months or even years. This long-term focus is also echoed in the definition of coaching offered by the *International Sport Coaching Framework:*

> A process of guided improvement and development of athletes and participants in a single sport and at specific stages of development.[2 (p. 14)]

Therefore, in order to facilitate development, coaches must look beyond session planning and embark on mid- to long-term goal setting. In this process of nested planning, coaches work backward from mid- or long-term goals to develop a comprehensive plan of coaching cycles and associated sessions that enable an athlete or team to achieve desired objectives over time.[7] This type of planning ensures that when developing a session plan, coaches can see how each drill or activity links not only to the session's learning objectives but also to the mid- and long-term goals. In this way, coaches protect themselves from the potential loss of concentration caused by the day-to-day issues that arise in athletic programs and retain their focus on the big picture.

Organizing

Sport coaching takes place in a dynamic environment. Therefore, effective and efficient coaches use highly developed organizational skills to ensure that all the pieces of the puzzle are in the right place at the right time. Organizational skills can be divided into three main groups: organizing the practice environment, organizing for competition, and organizing the team.

Organizing the Practice Environment

Coaches must think carefully about what is required for each training session to achieve its objectives. One good way to make sure that nothing slips through the cracks is to allot space in your session planner to detail these elements. Essentials to consider include the following:

- *Risk assessment.* Coaches have a duty of care for their athletes. In this role, they must carry out a comprehensive risk assessment for the activity to ensure the health and safety of athletes, staffers, self, and, where appropriate, parents. More specifically, an overall risk assessment should be conducted for the whole season before the first practice commences; thereafter, a risk assessment should be completed for each session.

- *Equipment.* Once the session plan has been developed, the coach should review it and note the equipment needed for each activity. In turn, the equipment should be checked for faults and prepared prior to the session. If possible, this preparation should involve the athletes to help them understand what is needed for a successful session, appreciate the value of the coaching role, build their self-reliance, and develop their technical knowledge of the sport. If anyone else is using the same practice area, the coach also bears responsibility for ensuring that equipment is put away expediently to allow the next group to start on time.

- *Attendance.* Every coach should set up a system for recording attendance at practice. Athletes need to receive a consistent message that training is important. The system should also allow the coach to know in advance how many athletes or players will be at a given session so that it can be planned accordingly. To this end, athletes (or, if necessary, their parents or guardians) should be encouraged to alert the coach if they are going to miss a session.

- *Practice flow.* Delivering a good coaching session requires much more than putting together a collection of drills, activities, or games. Beyond making pedagogical choices, coaches need to account for other factors that affect the quality of the experience and the resultant learning.

  - *Transition management.* Adequate transitions between drills and activities help maintain the flow of a session and minimize time wasting and concentration loss. One way to manage transitions—when feasible for the facility and the number of athletes—is to create distinct zones with appropriate equipment beforehand so that athletes can move seamlessly from one to another.

  - *Assistant coaches.* In most contexts, assistant coaches constitute a luxury, and we want to maximize their contribution to the session and to the athletes. At the same time, we want to ensure that their time with athletes is satisfying and that they themselves continue to develop. In order to create a sense of value and belonging among assistant coaches, include them in the development of the season and session plans.

  - *Punctuality.* Practice should always begin on time. The best way to develop an urge in your players (and their parents!) to be on time is to make sure that you start on time. Athletes generally dislike coming into a training venue to find that activity has already begun. This regularity sends a powerful message to all involved that arriving late is not acceptable. Practice should also end on time. Athletes (and their parents) lead busy lives, and their schedules should be respected. A coach who consistently runs out of time should consider covering less content per session or explore ways to manage time more effectively.

Organizing for Competition and Organizing the Team

Competition can be a tense time for athletes and coaches regardless of the level or standard involved. Coaches' preparation for and management of competition can exert a major influence on both the quality of the experience and the outcome. Meanwhile, running a team (or squad) of athletes demands that coaches closely manage a myriad of processes to ensure that everything is in place for things to run smoothly. Head coaches can fulfill this function themselves or delegate it to assistant coaches, team managers, back-room staff, or supportive parents. Both of these topics—organizing for competition and organizing the team—are covered in detail in chapter 6.

Leadership Skills

Leadership skills have been defined as those that facilitate accomplishment of program goals by enabling effective contributions from all group members and meshing personal goals with goals held in common.[8] Without effective leadership, even the most elite group may not reach its potential. Indeed, the annals of sport are full of teams and athletes who seemed to be destined for greatness but failed to fully succeed. They had all the ingredients—funding, facilities, and talent—yet somehow things never came together for them. In many cases, the reasons for this disappointment can be traced back to inadequate leadership.

To help you provide your athletes with effective leadership, this section reviews some of the fundamental skills required of successful leaders. These skills include modeling, communicating, applying emotional intelligence, motivating, and safeguarding.

Modeling

According to social learning theory, we learn behaviors from our environments through observational learning.[9] Specifically, we pick up cues about the rules of engagement and the functional processes that operate in a particular context by observing and interacting with others in our environment.[10] Therefore, although modeling is rarely described as a coaching skill, it plays a leading role in the coaching process. Indeed, whether knowingly or unwittingly—and often without saying a word— coaches set the tone and expectations for their athletes and program supporters through their own behavior and demeanor.[11, 12] The power of modeling also means that athletes' behavior is affected by the behavior of various other people in their lives, such as parents, teammates, and assistant coaches.

Given this often-unspoken reality, coaches are well advised to carefully review the environmental cues to which their athletes are exposed on a day-to-day basis. In this vein, a study of serial winning coaches found that this exclusive group made a conscious effort to create what they termed a "visible culture"—one in which actions speak louder than words.[12] This culture becomes especially powerful when it is lived and enacted by all staff and especially by charismatic and experienced players, thereby catalyzing the rest of the group. Selected behaviors that help develop a visible culture are presented in the following list:[12]

- Always being on time
- Always being prepared
- Wearing appropriate clothing
- Maintaining high standards of personal hygiene
- Practicing correct manners
- Respecting and appreciating all
- Taking a genuine interest in the people with whom you coach and work
- Being proactive
- Being willing to go the extra mile and leave no stone unturned
- Keeping emotions under control
- Being accountable for one's own mistakes

Communicating

Effective leaders not only develop a compelling vision but also communicate it clearly to the people who will be working to realize it. Coaches, then, must be able to communicate effectively in order to guide athletes, staff, and other stakeholders through the day-to-day activities that serve their vision for the sport program. To put it the other way around, miscommunication often causes problems that could otherwise be easily avoided. Thus communication is an essential element in a coach's toolbox. Effective communication can be considered in terms of two distinct domains: creating the environment and exchanging information.

Creating the Environment

- *Building rapport.* Taking time to develop rapport with the people we communicate with is as important as the content of what we are communicating. A good rapport builds trust and predisposes the other person to listen to what we have to say in a much more open and receptive way. Rapport is built by taking an interest in the other person as a human being and not just as an athlete, colleague, or parent.

- *Opening a two-way channel.* It is important that the communication avenues we create in our coaching environment are two-way. The degree to which the two channels are open at a particular time or whether one prevails over the other will depend on context and situation. One-way channels are easier to manage, but in the long run they can lead to those around us feeling disempowered and belittled, which will likely affect their level of engagement and performance.

- *Communication media.* In today's world, coaches have a multitude of ways in which they can communicate: face-to-face, phone and videoconference, email, text message, social media. The decision as to which means to use will depend on factors such as content, timing, who the receiver is, etc.

- *Timing and frequency.* Timing and frequency are fundamental parameters in the creation of a good communication environment. Depending on what needs to be communicated, coaches have to find the right time to do so. In the same vein, the frequency of communication has an impact on how it is received. There is a fine line between being iterative and consistent, and becoming white noise that those around us take no notice of.

Exchanging Information

The purpose of communication is to exchange information with others, and information flows between people through various channels. No agreement has been reached as to which channels matter most, but consensus holds that all channels influence the final outcome of any instance of communication. Drawing from this research, the Coaching Communication Wheel has been developed to raise coaches' awareness of the various means by which information is shared, even if unwittingly.[13] This model is summarized in table 5.2.

Applying Emotional Intelligence

Emotional intelligence (EI) has been defined as the ability to recognize one's "own and other people's emotions, to discriminate between different feelings and label them appropriately, and to use emotional information to guide thinking and behavior."[14] EI has been posited as a fundamental ability for high-performance coaches who operate in the dynamic and pressurized environment of competitive sport.[15] More broadly, the

TABLE 5.2 The Coaching Communication Wheel

The lyrics (the actual words)	The music (how things are said)
• Use simple language that can be easily understood. • Use specific and unambiguous language (leave little to interpretation). • Chunk information to aid retention. • Use positive language that tells people what they need to do, not what they don't. • Avoid rambling on.	• Tone and pitch impact people's attention. • Tone can influence the interpretation of the lyrics. • "Painting a picture": Use memorable and consistent language. • Storytelling can get a point across better than factual speaking.
The dance (our body language)	**The silence (what is not said and why)**
• Face and hand gestures: Feelings are first communicated and received through these two channels (i.e., aggression, excitement, disappointment). • Body stance: An open stance is welcoming and will put people at ease. • Body level: The height of your body in comparison to the people you are addressing has a significant impact on how the information is received. • Body proximity: Respecting people's personal space is a key element for successful communication.	• Provide athletes with time to try and work out a solution to a problem or challenge. • Convey a sense of trust and promote self-reliance. • Encourage others to speak up. • Take a step back and pick up cues from the athletes and the environment.

© Sergio Lara-Bercial

International Sport Coaching Framework,[2] drawing on earlier work,[1, 16] proposed that coaches must possess not only professional knowledge but also interpersonal and intrapersonal knowledge and skills (see chapter 1). Thus EI is a fundamental skill for sport coaches who work in any coaching context or domain. Here we focus on two key aspects of emotional intelligence: self-awareness and empathy.

Cultivating Self-Awareness

A study of consistently successful international coaches identified emotional intelligence—and especially self-awareness—as a strong contributing factor to continued success.[17] These coaches demonstrated very high levels of self-awareness related to their emotions, personality, behaviors, coaching practice, and overall performance. This self-awareness allowed them to anticipate problems; tailor their behavior to a given situation, person, or group; and exercise optimal control over their emotions. The researchers concluded that this heightened self-awareness fed into an emotional intelligence that was critical to the coaches' capacity to lead successfully and cope with the stresses of the environment. It was also thought to contribute to the coaches' own learning ability.

COACHING SNAPSHOT

Gordie Gillespie demonstrated the transferability of core coaching skills during the course of his nearly 60-year career, coaching both males and females, at the high school and college levels, and three different sports. And his teams won more than twice as often as they lost, collecting four national college baseball titles and five high school football championships along the way. Yet Coach Gillespie never lost sight of what was most important, advising his peers to *"Love your players for who they are, not what they can do for you. Kids will see through the coach whose only concern is himself."*

Practicing Empathy

The coaching process has been increasingly recognized as a complex social and cognitive system.[18, 19] In this context, the quality of the coach–athlete relationship has been proposed as a critical success factor for effective coaching,[20, 21] and that relationship can be understood in terms of the 3+1Cs model:[21]

- Closeness—affective ties between athlete and coach, such as mutual trust, respect, appreciation, and liking
- Commitment—explicit dedication to the common goal
- Complementarity—collaboration and mutual responses, such as ready support and overall friendliness
- Co-orientation—interdependence, or the degree to which coaches and athletes seem to have a shared understanding

As these elements suggest, the quality of the coach–athlete relationship is determined in considerable part by the coach's ability to recognize and empathize with the emotions, feelings, needs, and desires of others (typically athletes, but also other stakeholders). This empathy enables the coach to understand and cater to athletes by providing athlete-centered coaching.[22] It is not, however, enough by itself. The quality of the coach–athlete relationship also depends on the ability of the coach and athlete to coordinate objectives and efforts.[23] Thus empathy provides only the starting point for the coach and the athlete to create a shared understanding as the basis for their work together.

Based on this perspective of optimal empathy as shared understanding, coaches should engage in the following practices:[24]

- Seek formal and informal opportunities to speak with athletes individually, both about sport and about other topics.
- Develop a culture in which everyone's opinions are shared through consistent opportunities for athletes' voices to be heard and valued nonjudgmentally.
- Review and evaluate communication strategies to ensure that coaching messages are received in the manner intended.
- Promote opportunities for social interaction between athletes and coaches.
- Attend to both verbal and nonverbal cues.

Motivating

Legendary coaches are thought of as great motivators, and the web is full of motivational quotes and stories attributed to the likes of Vince Lombardi, Pat Summitt, John Wooden, and Sir Alex Ferguson. Motivation can be simply defined as a force that compels someone to do something, and it is typically discussed in terms of a dichotomy between high and low levels. For instance, a certain player is said to be either highly motivated or lacking motivation. Psychologists, however, prefer to describe motivation in terms of quality—that is, where it comes from and how sustainable it is. In this view, motivation can be either internal or external, and internal motivation (i.e., personal desire, such as desire to learn) is more adaptive and sustainable than external motivation (i.e., external factors, such as rewards or punishment).

Researchers in sport psychology and sport coaching have dedicated considerable time and effort to motivation because of its contribution to how we think, feel, and behave. Three key theories that examine motivation in sport are achievement goal theory (AGT),[25, 28] self-determination theory (SDT),[26, 29, 30] and mindset theory (MT).[27] Full treatment of these theories lies beyond the scope of this chapter, but all three conclude that coaches and significant others play a large role in creating a motivational climate that is either adaptive, maladaptive, or something in between. Table 5.3 summarizes key features of these models that may contribute to an adaptive motivational climate.

TABLE 5.3 Adaptive Motivational Features of Sporting Climate and Athlete Responses

Climate features (coaches and significant others)	Athlete responses
• Define success in terms of personal and group improvement (self-referenced success). • Praise effort and hard work over ability. • Support athletes in setting personal goals. • Promote internal competition not as a ranking mechanism but as a chance to stretch each other and improve. • Provide informational feedback. • Value and care about all athletes as people. • Build a sense of community (belonging). • Give athletes choices. • Promote and value initiative and decision making by athletes.	• Enjoy practice and games. • Understand success in terms of improvement and progression (self-referenced success). • Aim for success based on hard work. • Enjoy being challenged to improve and prefer tasks that stretch them. • See mistakes as opportunities to learn. • Exhibit resilience. • Feel a sense of belonging. • Support and help each other. • Gain inspiration from other people's success. • Enjoy competition and put results in a healthy perspective. • Self-evaluate and focus on what they can do to improve. • Show initiative and independence.

Of course, athletes may be driven not only by internal motivation but also by external factors, such as scholarships, fame, and financial rewards. However, focusing primarily on external motives—which lie mostly out of one's control—is more likely to lead to negative athlete outcomes, especially when things do not turn out as expected. In contrast, a positive motivational climate that fosters internal motivation can buffer and mitigate the inherent challenges and stresses associated with sport.

Safeguarding

A fundamental skill for coaches is being able to keep themselves, athletes, and others associated with the program safe from harm. Safeguarding has two key components:

- Prevention: putting the measures in place to minimize the chances of anyone coming to harm
- Action: the step we take once an incident has occurred or when we have suspicions that someone may be harmed in the future

Analytical Skills

So far, we have described coaching largely as a goal-led decision-making process.[7] Of course, we base our decisions on the information available to us, and information that is accurate and reliable enables us to make sound decisions. For this reason, we also need to develop analytical skills, which allow us to observe, record, analyze, and evaluate the performance factors that we wish to affect. In short, analysis helps us determine how to achieve desired effects in our athletes. It also helps us monitor our own performance.

As part of this process, we can monitor aspects of performance such as the following:

- Technical skills, such as biomechanical movement analysis
- Tactical strategies, such as execution of set plays in basketball or the offside trap in soccer
- Key performance indicators, such as stroke rate in rowing, passes completed in field hockey, and first-serve rate in tennis
- Trends, such as the most-used elements in gymnastics floor routines or the proportion of athletes using positive versus negative splits in the 800-meter race
- Personal factors, such as mood, exertion, and intrinsic motivation

In fact, in today's technology-driven world, we can virtually measure anything. With so much power at our disposal, we must think carefully about what is worth measuring, whether a given factor can be measured accurately and reliably, how we can make sense of the resulting data, and how to use that information to help athletes (see chapters 6 and 10).

Observing

Coaches should observe athletes constantly, both in training and during competition. High-quality observation requires high-quality preparation. Detailed discussion of this topic is provided in chapter 10.

Recording

Research indicates that coaches have only a limited capacity to recall what happened during a training session or game.[31] This limitation derives from the human brain's inability to maintain both broad and narrow focus simultaneously, which makes it difficult if not impossible to keep track of everything occurring in the coaching environment. That difficulty is heightened by the speed at which sporting actions take place. Given these challenges, we must find ways to ensure that the data informing our decisions are recorded accurately and consistently.

This demand applies regardless of whether we gather and analyze data through traditional means (e.g., checklists, spreadsheets) or with the aid of advanced software. That choice depends on factors such as our own skill level, budget, and time constraints, as well as the availability of support staff (assistant coaches and eager parents can be very helpful in this endeavor). Regardless of what approach is used, we must clearly identify what to record, how, and by whom.

Analyzing

The coach's ability to analyze data is a critical step in the monitoring process. The purpose of the analysis is to extract discrete information from the data that will support performance evaluation and subsequent decision making. For more on this topic, see chapter 10.

Evaluating

After the data have been analyzed, it is time to evaluate or interpret the data to understand what it means for the athletes or team. This process is delicate because it requires the data to be put into context. To do so, the coach must have a mental model of the desired performance level and the athlete's or team's stage of development. The coach then faces the difficult task of deciding a number of things, such as the following: What are the central cause–effect relationships? Will intervention work? If so, how might it be scaffolded to address key issues? For more discussion of this process, see chapter 10.

Self-Monitoring

Coaches are typically aware of the importance of monitoring athlete and team performance. In recent times, however, they increasingly realize that success also requires them to engage in self-monitoring.[2, 32, 33] For discussion of this topic, see chapter 12.

Exercise: Core Coaching Skills Self-Assessment

Please complete the following self-assessment form. If you are already coaching, think about your last season. If you have yet to coach, consider your experiences at school, work, or in the community.

Core coaching skills	On a scale of 1 (not competent at all) to 5 (very competent), note down how competent you feel in each of the skills listed on the left	Write down how much of a priority this skill is for you and your team/program over the next 12 months 1 – High priority 2 – Medium 3 – Low	Pick the 3 skills with the lowest combined score and write what you need to do to improve on them (i.e., ensure I have the checklist with me; make more time to talk to parents)	In this column jot down any support you need to be able to perform the skill better (i.e., go on a training course; an assistant coach; certain equipment)
TEACHING SKILLS				
Setting up and standing back				
Explaining				
Demonstrating				
Questioning and listening				
Providing feedback				
Differentiating				
Designing activities				

Core coaching skills	On a scale of 1 (not competent at all) to 5 (very competent), note down how competent you feel in each of the skills listed on the left	Write down how much of a priority this skill is for you and your team/program over the next 12 months 1 – High priority 2 – Medium 3 – Low	Pick the 3 skills with the lowest combined score and write what you need to do to improve on them (i.e., ensure I have the checklist with me; make more time to talk to parents)	In this column jot down any support you need to be able to perform the skill better (i.e., go on a training course; an assistant coach; certain equipment)
MANAGEMENT SKILLS				
Strategizing				
Setting goals				
Planning				
Organizing				
LEADERSHIP SKILLS				
Modeling				
Communicating				
Applying emotional intelligence				
Motivating				

(continued)

(continued)

Core coaching skills	On a scale of 1 (not competent at all) to 5 (very competent), note down how competent you feel in each of the skills listed on the left	Write down how much of a priority this skill is for you and your team/program over the next 12 months 1 – High priority 2 – Medium 3 – Low	Pick the 3 skills with the lowest combined score and write what you need to do to improve on them (i.e., ensure I have the checklist with me; make more time to talk to parents)	In this column jot down any support you need to be able to perform the skill better (i.e., go on a training course; an assistant coach; certain equipment)
LEADERSHIP SKILLS *(continued)*				
Safeguarding				
ANALYTICAL SKILLS				
Observing				
Recording				
Analyzing				
Evaluating				
Self-monitoring				

From International Council for Coaching Excellence, *Sport Coaches' Handbook*, eds. D. Gould and C. Mallett. (Champaign, IL: Human Kinetics, 2021).

Chapter 6

Program Management

Bob Crudgington

Coaches are commonly wished "Good luck!" before a competition. And, undoubtedly, a bit of good fortune—a friendly call by an official, a slip by an opposing defender—can give a team and its coach an unexpected situational advantage. Moreover, coaching (and, in particular, high-performance coaching) can be a dynamic, complex, and nonlinear endeavor that requires flexibility and fluidity in shaping the sporting environment.[1] However, attributing a great coach's perennial championships to luck would defy all statistical probability. Legendary coaches such as Harry Hopman, Pat Summitt, and Sir Alex Ferguson did not win by chance. Rather, like every coach of consistently great athletes and teams, they applied strong organizational skills and effectively managed the training and competition environments.

Managing a sport program involves skills and knowledge that extend beyond the teaching, tactical, and technical skills typically associated with a sport coach. These traditional skills are usually applied in the form of activities intended to engage athletes and enhance individual or team performance.[2] Effective coaches also apply other types of professional expertise, such as organizational and planning skills relevant to the specific context of their program. For instance, they must provide the program with clear direction and elicit the support and best efforts of stakeholders—including players, coaches, parents, and administrators—to ensure that agreed-on objectives can be met. This work requires coaches to apply a broad set of skills that include both the interpersonal (e.g., negotiation) and the intrapersonal (e.g., reflection) as appropriate for specific contexts.[3] To learn more about these contexts and the appropriate and effective application of coaching skills in them, please refer to chapters 1 and 5.

Establishing a Program

Every coach who achieves long-term success understands the need to develop not just an athlete or team but a program. A sport program can be defined as an amalgamation of "complex organizational processes involving athletic directors, program administrators, sports leaders (e.g., athletic boards), coaches and parents, and athletes."[4 (p. 310)] As the program manager, and as an influential leader, the coach needs to take a structured approach to planning and preparing for training and competition in specific contexts.[5, 6]

As discussed elsewhere in this book, sport programs generally operate in one of two broad contexts—performance sport and participation sport. In either of these environments, program objectives are typically aligned with certain kinds of outcomes—for instance, participation by children, adolescents, and adults in a recreational context or strong competitive performance by athletes who are emerging, performance oriented, or elite.[7] This chapter refers occasionally to participation sport but emphasizes performance sport and the challenges and opportunities presented to coaches who develop and manage programs in that context.

The International Council for Coaching Excellence has identified a number of core coaching functions related to program development and management.[7] These functions include setting a vision, creating a strategy, and shaping the environment—each of which is guided by the philosophy and core values that underpin the program (see chapters 2 and 3). Let's examine these functions in some detail.

Setting a Vision

Many sport organizations have developed a strategic plan that outlines goals and objectives and identifies key strategies for achieving them. In this way, developing the vision often serves as the first stage in the process of strategic planning. In building such a plan, an organization develops a shared vision that reflects its purpose or reason for existing and what it wants to become in the future. The plan reinforces this vision by documenting the organization's core values.

The organization can then use its vision statement and core values to inform a mission statement articulating its overall direction and scope. An effective mission statement reflects the aspirations of its stakeholders and the organization's culture by aligning practice with core values, and thus provides the foundation for goal setting.

Mission statements vary in terms of level and intent. In terms of level, they might address a team, program, or entire organization. In terms of intent, they might focus narrowly on performance or address broader concerns. For example, several years ago, the New York Yankees organization stated its mission as follows: "The New York Yankees' ultimate goal every year is to win the World Series; anything less is a failure."[8] Clearly, this mission focuses solely on a certain outcome—winning—and says nothing else about values. In contrast, the National Basketball Association articulated a succinct mission statement based on values: "Our calling: Compete with intensity, lead with integrity and inspire play."[9] In yet another approach, organizations that focus on participation tend to emphasize inclusion and development. For instance, here is the mission statement for the Capalaba Warriors, a local rugby league club in Australia: "Provide a fun, safe, enjoyable environment that encourages all participants to reach their full potential no matter what their aspirations may be."[10]

In some cases, setting a vision constitutes a core coaching function on the team or program level within the context of a larger organization. For example, in 2008, New Zealand Rugby collaborated with its stakeholders and provisional unions and developed the vision for its organization: "Inspiring and Unifying New Zealanders."[11] Within the performance sphere, the coaches and players developed a separate vision or motto for the successful All Blacks: "Better people make better All Blacks." In 2004, the players organized a session including binge drinking and participated in subsequent displays of antisocial behavior after losing an international match. This event acted as a trigger for the coaches to call for a change in culture, behavior, and team leadership in order to improve the team's performance both on and off the field. The new All Blacks vision was geared toward empowering players and coaches and encouraging them to take the initiative.[12] This approach enabled program stakeholders to feel a strong connection to their own performance context while also aligning with the vision and aspirations of New Zealand Rugby.

A mission statement also carries implications in relation to the coach's own philosophy and values, and chapter 5 provides good insight into how to align these elements through effective goal setting. This alignment helps coaches give consistent messages to key participants.

COACHING SNAPSHOT

New Zealand All Blacks coaches **Graham Henry** (left) and **Steve Hansen** managed the world's most dominant rugby program superbly during their cumulative 16 years as head coaches, winning more than 86 percent of their team's matches. The All Blacks became a standard of excellence in the sporting world, and their coaches have been expected to maintain and build on the program's principles, strategies, practices, and rituals to keep it at that level.

Creating a Strategy

A strategic plan generally lays out a long-term direction including major objectives, priorities, and strategies to enable the organization to achieve its vision. The plan is often endorsed by the organization's management committee or board. In sport settings, the plan may address facilities, member recruitment, marketing, finances, funding, use of volunteers (e.g., officials, grounds staff, statisticians), and, of course, participation- or performance-related topics. As a result, the organization's strategic plan often provides a framework for the coach's planning process. That process may also need to consider other coaching factors, such as age-group or discipline-specific factors, sharing of facilities and equipment, staff employment, scheduling, and transitional elements of the program such as the recruitment of new players and staff and the retirement of others.

In many cases, a strategic plan also serves as the working document for operating at a strategic level and evaluating progress against stated performance objectives. In these cases, planning should reflect the strategic goals of the organization, and any reporting of results should be aligned with the relevant strategic objectives. To assist with this review process, strategic plans include measures of success, or key performance indicators, for each strategic area. For instance, the United States Tennis Association has established an objective of growing the game, and it measures progress toward this goal in terms of yearly participation statistics. Examples in high-performance settings include win–loss ratios, premierships, and world championship medals. In contrast, a junior league or sport club might choose indicators related to member satisfaction, participation numbers, player retention, or graduation to high-performance programs (e.g., college scholarships).

In many cases, strategic considerations also include commercial factors, such as game attendance, media exposure, and funding or sponsorship levels. Although these measures may not be linked directly to the activities of the program coach, the quality of coaching—and of the training and competition experience—exerts an influence on participation and involvement by family members and volunteers (e.g., officials, administrators).

Shaping the Environment

In both setting a vision and creating a strategic plan, coaches must be keenly aware of the external environment in which their programs operate. They must also be highly attuned to the internal environment created by the program itself.

External Environment

For a representation of external environmental factors, see figure 6.1.[13] This external layer includes everything outside the program that can affect it. In the context of sport, these factors may include political issues (e.g., related to owners, board of directors, paid staff, or parents), economics (i.e., resources), sociocultural values and customs, and any legal issues (e.g., constraints, laws, other conditions associated with competition or training).

Internal Environment (Setting)

This layer relates to the program's organizational structure, staffing, and culture. In high-performance programs, staff may include assistant coaches, consultants (e.g., strength and conditioning, medical, and performance psychology staff), and, of course, athletes—whose contribution, ironically, is often marginalized or forgotten. In participation programs,

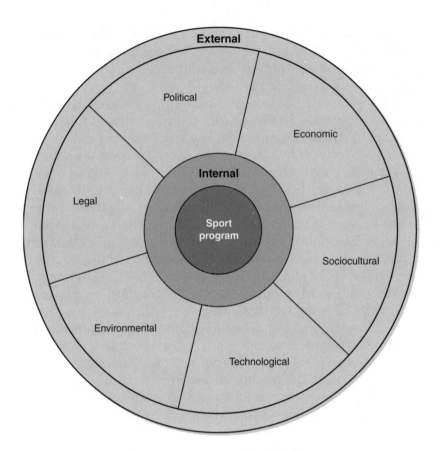

FIGURE 6.1 Sport programs are affected in part by external environmental factors (in contrast, internal factors, not specified here, relate to the structure of the organization or program itself).

Reprinted by permission from P. Davidson and R.W. Griffin, "The Environmental Context of Management," in *Management: An Australian Perspective*, 3rd ed., edited by P. Davidson and R.W. Griffin (Brisbane: Wiley, 2006), 67-97.

on the other hand, direct stakeholders may include players, their family members, and volunteers (e.g., coaching assistants, team managers, officials). Regardless of program context, coaches must cater to the needs of various stakeholders and, where appropriate, seek their input.

In large associations, a program's internal environment may also be influenced strongly by the overall organizational structure and its relationship to the learning culture of the program.[14] In other words, the organizational structure can directly affect the coach–athlete relationship.

Managing a Program

As discussed in the preceding section, the sport setting is shaped by multiple layers of influence. Coaches must understand these layers, as well as a range of psycho-socio-cultural influences, in order to lead and manage the program effectively. This shaping of the environment requires the coach to demonstrate organizational and leadership skills. Specifically, all coaches must be competent in four key categories of functional program management: planning, directing, managing, and monitoring.[15]

Program Planning

Planning is a core competency of coaching (see chapter 5). The process of planning is beneficial because it does the following:

- requires coaches to think through what to do and how to do it;
- enables coaches to clarify goals, tasks, and processes;
- greatly reduces the misdirection of energy or resources; and
- provides direction and purpose for the coach and team, thus enabling commitment to the task at hand.

Planning is necessary at all organizational levels and in all coaching contexts. For instance, as discussed earlier, large sport organizations generally develop a strategic plan that outlines organizational goals and strategies for their various sections or departments. In contrast, this section focuses on the planning in which a coach must actively engage.

Coaches need to develop specific plans both for their squads or athletes and for themselves. Individual plans should focus on the athlete's holistic development regardless of the setting (e.g., participation or performance). That is, they should include actions for personal development, participation, and performance. Although most planning focuses on the program itself, or its internal environment, coaches also need to consider factors in the external environment—for instance, available resources, rule changes, and even the activities of opposing teams or organizations.

Let us now consider how the process of planning applies to a sport program. As shown in figure 6.2, the environment may initially appear complex, perhaps even chaotic, but the planning process is generally structured and often hierarchical.

Operational Planning

Whereas strategic planning addresses the long term, operational planning addresses the middle term and is often subject to review on an annual or seasonal basis. In many sport programs, operational planning falls to the coach on a yearly basis and focuses on managing the day-to-day activities associated with training and competition. The resulting plans usually reflect the organization's overarching strategic plan and contain the same elements: objectives, strategies, and actions to achieve desired organizational and program outcomes.

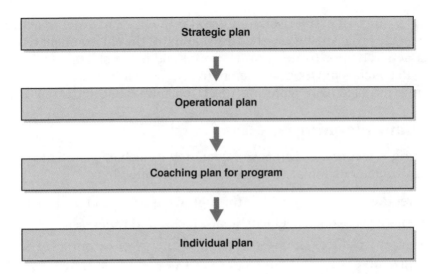

FIGURE 6.2 Potential planning instruments used by a sporting organization.

At the same time, they differ from strategic plans in being more specific and providing more detail about elements such as budgets, staff responsibilities, time frames, and measures of success. This type of planning is particularly prevalent in high-performance organizations but may still apply in programs focused on participation and development. For example, even though a recreational sport club does not focus on elite performance, it still needs training and playing facilities, organized rosters and schedules, and coaches and volunteer staff.

Coaching Planning

This level of planning addresses the coaching that goes into the program's day-to-day activities. It is often driven by an experienced coach, and it relates directly to the athletes' training sessions and competitions. It typically includes a variety of plans—for assistant coaches, other support staff, individual athletes, and squads. These plans may address scheduling, such as periodization and peaking for competition in performance sports, as well as training and competition calendars for recreational programs.

High-performance organizations often take a multidisciplinary approach to planning, and coaches may therefore be required to coordinate interventions related to sport science programs (e.g., physiology, psychology, nutrition, recovery) and athlete welfare programs (e.g., personal development activities). In fact, in many elite sport programs around the world, the head coach serves informally as a chief executive officer by coordinating the efforts of various specialists. In contrast, participation and development programs tend to have limited resources, which means that coaches carry out many tasks themselves. Examples include conducting warm-up and cool-down processes, supervising conditioning activities, and inviting consultants to address topics such as nutrition and recovery.

Planning for the day-to-day is a key component of coaching.[16] However, it can be problematic due to any of various reasons, such as the context of the program including the level of performance (e.g., meeting expectations in competition) or competing agendas among players and other coaches. Planning can also be complicated by changes in weather or access to facilities and equipment, competition programming, unavailability of players due to injury or other commitments, and changes in staffing. As a result, coaches need to develop contingency plans—for instance, alternative training venues (e.g., indoor training facilities), modified training activities, and altered competition strategies if key players or staff are missing.

Individual Planning

Individual plans are flexible and should respond to the athlete's needs; in fact, they may well include input from the athlete.[12, 17] This level of planning is viewed as a core competency for high-performance coaches, regardless of whether it is focused on performance, ongoing development, or monitoring and evaluating progress toward stated goals and objectives. Of course, in programs focused on participation and development, individual planning caters to the developmental needs of each individual. Regardless of the coaching context, effective coaching ensures that every participant is catered to in terms of developing their confidence, connection, competence, and character.[3] Coaches can create inclusive practices by keeping notes about individual players and their progression and providing appropriate levels of feedback and communication to every member of the program. Thus, coaching plans should be designed both for the context in which the program operates and for each individual athlete.

Structure–Freedom Continuum

As a manager, a coach is required to systematically plan, implement, monitor, and review progress toward goals and objectives in the short, middle, and long term. In doing so, the coach makes deliberate, organized attempts to control as many as possible of the variables that influence performance outcomes. However, this effort also requires balance between structure (e.g., detailed planning, management, goal setting, and analysis) and fluidity in responding to a dynamic landscape (e.g., delivery, negotiation, decision making, evaluation, and working with others) in order to optimize athlete and team outcomes.[6, 18, 19] This lesson was learned the hard way by U.S. soccer coaches, who for years tried unsuccessfully to apply coaching methods from American football—characterized by highly structured technical instruction and strategies—to a sport that requires a great deal of reactive spontaneity.

Program Directing

When one applies for a coaching position, the underlying values and culture of the hiring organization are not always apparent. As a result, it can be difficult in the beginning for coaches to ensure that their own values and philosophy align with the organization's vision and mission (assuming they exist). To avoid this pitfall, it is worth devoting the time to studying the organization's vision, strategic plan, and any supporting documentation. To put it another way, the coach's behaviors must align with the organization's rhetoric; otherwise, the lack of alignment can cause tension between key actors in the organization.

In cases where the organization lacks a formal vision or mission statement, coaching applicants should consider trying to determine why. They might also consider exploring whether the organization is open to developing such a document. The absence of a vision or mission statement also requires the coach to ask key organizational stakeholders to identify the organization's mission and goals.

When reporting on professional and high-profile sports, the media often produce stories about clubs or franchises bringing in a new coach to address perceived cultural issues in order to improve on-field performance. Indeed, organizations often stress the need for a cultural change when they recruit a new head coach or high-performance manager. Yet the notion of culture is somewhat amorphous, and there is no consensual definition of it. Some broad conceptions of culture have been offered—for instance, values that hold the organization together, meanings shared by people in the organization, or simply "how we do things around here." In any case, whether a coach is hired to improve a program's culture and performance or to maintain its existing excellence, he or she must understand the concept of culture and how to create an effective one.

Many sport organizations have created a mission statement, reinforced it over time, and embedded it into organizational life in the form of culture and traditions. In such cases, a new coach should look for signs of this culture and its connection to the organizational mission. Doing so can help the coach understand what should be continued and what needs to change.

The most popular framework for examining culture in business, and especially in sporting organizations,[20-22] posits three levels of organizational culture: artifacts, values, and underlying assumptions. Artifacts are usually observable and are often used to reinforce the culture. More specifically, material artifacts include documentation, posters, trophies, or clothing. Artifacts can also be intangible—for instance, routines, rituals, traditional stories, mottos, and sayings (which may take the form of public statements, including mission statements).

Values, on the other hand, can be detected through the behavior of individuals; examples include work ethic, integrity, punctuality, and respectfulness. As an observer, the coach can look at how people respond to the environment—for instance, the conditions of the training area, equipment, and facilities—and how they interact with each other. In addition, shared values are reflected in the behavior of the group and in patterns related to which behaviors are rewarded and which are punished.

The third level of organizational culture—underlying assumptions—is often more difficult to evaluate. In fact, it may require considerable observation and questioning of participants about the values espoused by the organization. Suppose that an organizational value of hard work assumes that only hard work will lead to success. This belief might affect how players respond to injury or fatigue. For instance, rather than asking a coach or medical consultant about adjusting the training load to improve recovery or seeking treatment, group members might simply continue with a high-intensity approach to training and competition in order to model the coach's ethos of hard work. Over time, this decision could lead to a decrement in performance due to untreated injuries or fatigue through overtraining. Thus the common saying: "The standard you walk past is the standard you accept."

Culture can also be a pervasive force in programs focused on participation. For example, some junior developmental programs espouse personal development but emphasize winning in their actions, and this disparity can influence coaches and players and affect the expectations of parents and other stakeholders (e.g., volunteers, organizational staff). An inappropriate emphasis on performance and winning reduces player retention, increases the risk of overtraining and burnout, and deprives late developers and new participants of playing time and coaching attention. In addition, in many programs, the principles of age-appropriate practice are lacking, despite considerable research on long-term player development and participation.[23-25] This lack can present a challenge to the coach, who may feel called to be a change agent in the program.

Organizational culture can be not only challenging to understand but also difficult to link to performance. This is true in part because performance is also affected by other variables, including members' levels of involvement and positive interactions with each other, the consistency of values and behaviors across the organization, and the capacity to adapt to environmental changes (refer to the previous section on planning). In sport contexts, attempts to understand or change organizational culture are often complicated by the political and almost chaotic nature of sport coaching.[26] Nevertheless, researchers have examined the role of sport leaders in changing organizational culture and improving the consistency of performance.[27, 28] This research indicates that coaches affect the performance of sporting organizations, both on and off the field, through their capacity to influence and direct program participants toward common goals and standards.

COACHING SNAPSHOT

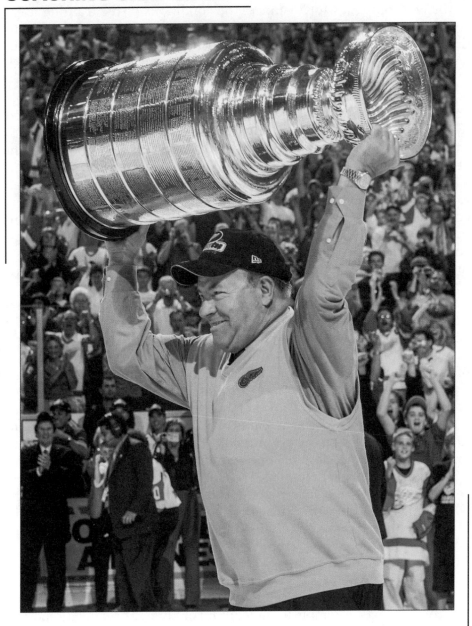

Very early in his career, as coach of the Peterborough Petes in the Ontario Hockey League, **Scotty Bowman** adopted an approach that would serve him well throughout his coaching career: *"Know what you've got. Get your players to do what they can do. Find a way."* Bowman applied his program evaluation, player development and motivation, and innovative strategies to win a record 14 Stanley Cups (9 as head coach, 5 as an executive) with four different organizations.

Program Managing

As outlined earlier, managing a program effectively requires a coach to plan and direct both culture and practice in a specific setting. In high-performance contexts, coaches must not only manage the coaching process but also handle various administrative tasks.[6, 18] Examples include compliance reporting to various stakeholders, as well as working and interacting with athletes and a wide range of other people (e.g., sport science consultants, administrators, officials, members of the media, and other coaches). Coaches may also be required to manage other resources needed to carry out their plans, including funds, equipment, and facilities.

Managing these resources requires coaches to oversee a number of day-to-day activities within the internal or coaching environment. These activities include implementing anti-harassment and antidiscrimination policies (including policies for accommodating pregnancy in sport), attending to risk management, selecting and recruiting athletes, and addressing issues such as performance enhancement and social drug use. Many organizations designate certain staff members to manage finances and resources, but it still falls to the program leader to ensure that resources are prioritized and maximized to meet the specific needs of their athletes and coaching staff, thereby enabling them to achieve intended outcomes.

Because of recent scandals associated with such issues as doping, date rape, and sexual abuse in sport, more and more organizations make it mandatory for employees (including coaches) to report any instances or potential instances. As a result, the days of coaches handling or even investigating such issues "internally" are over; in fact, coaches who do not report issues in these areas are highly likely to be fired. Therefore, it is absolutely essential that coaches understand the sponsoring organization's policies and procedures pertaining to mandatory reporting obligations.

At the amateur, college, and professional levels, many programs are limited in their finances, access to facilities and equipment, logistical capacity, and, of course, time. In many cases, coaches are provided with a financial budget for accessing services and supporting the technical and tactical development of their athletes. Resources are also needed for an athlete welfare system, including injury prevention and management, mental health services, and sport science services from specialized consultants (e.g., biomechanist, strength and conditioning coach, performance psychologist, nutritionist).

In the performance context, coaches may also be required to report on the progress of on-field performance by squads and athletes, appraise the work carried out by coaching staff and consultants, and track expenditures against financial accounts and budgets. These review practices can work well if the planning process includes a costed operational plan with clear time frames and measurable markers of success.

In addition to managing resources and staffing, coaches in all contexts also manage relationships, which requires them to develop interpersonal knowledge and skills as a core component of their coaching practice.[3, 7] Many performance-oriented programs have established a governance and administration framework to support the coach in the role of program manager. Programs in participation contexts also engage stakeholders, and in some cases these relationships can become problematic if not managed effectively. For instance, some coaches take on the challenge of working with athletes of differing ages, abilities, and aspirations.

In children's sport, this challenge can be heightened by the actions of participants' parents, who exert considerable influence on their children's experience of sport[29, 30]—an effect that can be either positive or negative.[30-32] For instance, inappropriate parental behavior—such as conditional regard, overcontrol, unrealistic expectations, and overemphasis on winning or punishment—can increase the pressure to perform and affect a child's personal development. These effects run counter to the aims of a coach who seeks to enhance a player's competence, confidence, character, and connection through sport participation.[3, 7] Therefore, it is well worth a coach's time to educate parents about their influence on their child's experience in order to create a supportive environment for all participants in the program.

To foster positive coach–parent relationships,[31] coaches should clearly communicate the program philosophy and outline behavioral expectations for both participants and parents. In this vein, it is fully appropriate for coaches to provide clear guidelines for parental behavior during training and especially during competition. Many sporting organizations develop a code of conduct for parents and spectators in order to prevent inappropriate behavior, and coaches should establish a clear expectation for all stakeholders to abide by this code. Nevertheless, it is unclear how effective these strategies are in promoting adaptive adult behaviors.

Program Monitoring

As the saying goes, "Not everything that can be counted counts, and not everything that counts can be counted." The wisdom of this phrase is appreciated by veteran coaches who have extensive experience in managing teams and programs. At the same time, modern sport is characterized by sport science interventions such as load monitoring, fitness tests, and sophisticated software, all of which has brought about a proliferation of performance analysis in professional and Olympic sports.

In order to measure the progress of individual athletes and programs, we must identify key performance indicators (KPIs) that can be measured and ensure that they provide valid assessments of what they are intended to measure. In regard to measuring success, one pair of researchers stated that "it's not always possible, but to be able to confirm, or question/reject [our] methods, it's necessary to come up with performance indicators."[33] (p. 67)

KPIs can be divided into lag indicators and lead indicators.[34] Lag indicators relate to output or competitive results. For example, a high-performance program goal might target finishing in the top four in a major competition or helping players obtain scholarships or professional contracts. In the participation context, a lag indicator might be linked to the number of participants who return in the following season. Lead indicators, on the other hand, relate to activities that, if carried out, will lead to desired results—for instance, incorporating a targeted fitness program to improve endurance in a player or team or providing fun and engaging activities to spur motivation and effort. Thus lag indicators are associated with outcome goals, whereas lead indicators are usually linked to the process goal-setting activities covered in chapter 5.

Coaches in performance programs should identify lead indicators or measures derived from athletic training and performance that provide feedback about athlete or team progress. Here are some examples:

- Physiological indicators (e.g., endurance testing via multistage shuttle run or $\dot{V}O_2$max test)
- Application to training (e.g., completion of training logs, attendance at training sessions)
- Competition performance

In a participation program, the coach might devise other methods of measuring progress, such as the following:

- Attendance at training and games
- Level of engagement or activity in competition
- Progression in skill development or competence

The information collected from this process (lead indicators) can often form the basis of feedback in the form of dialogue between the coach and the athlete. This process may also lead to changes in coaching and training or in other aspects of program operation.

Lag indicators, on the other hand, often help the coach formulate and monitor strategic management activities, such as establishing long-term objectives and reviewing overall performance. For example, a college basketball coach who reviews the season might discover that team performance tended to fade in the last 10 minutes of important games. Thus, by looking at game statistics, the coach has identified a lag indicator that points out a need to improve performance in crunch time. In response, the coach could set up a new conditioning plan to improve players' aerobic capacity. To measure progress, she could monitor two lead indicators—proportion of training dedicated to aerobic endurance across the season and improvement in whole-squad results for the multistage shuttle run (with a target of 10 percent improvement by the start of the competition season).

Physical Measures

Physical measures include physiological (e.g., endurance and strength) and anthropometric (e.g., body type including skinfolds and height) testing of athletes that can be used for various purposes, including the following:[35]

- Identifying strengths and weaknesses
- Monitoring progress
- Providing feedback
- Educating coaches and athletes
- Predicting performance potential

Testing protocols should address characteristics appropriate for the sport in question and should be specific, practical, valid, and accurate.[35] Many sport organizations use physiological testing to assess athletes against certain criteria for selection into representative or professional programs. In other words, they use sport-specific protocols to assess whether athletes meet certain performance benchmarks and possess certain physical attributes (e.g., what is required to finish in the top eight at the Olympic Games). For example, in some team sports, aerobic endurance has been identified as a key to maintaining performance over the duration of a match or tournament. Thus, an organization might require athletes to meet a benchmark for a relevant test, such as the multistage fitness test, in order to be eligible for a squad.

This type of testing should be standardized to minimize variance in conditions; that is, quality control needs to be applied. For instance, skinfold measurements of athletes are often undertaken to monitor their general condition. To ensure that the results provide valid feedback, the testing needs to be conducted by an accredited practitioner, and if possible by the same person over an extended period. Testing should also be conducted in such a way that the results are precise, reliable, and interpretable. These standards can be difficult to maintain, particularly in the field, where results can be affected by factors such as performance surface and weather conditions. In addition, coaches need to ensure that athletes understand the reason for testing and that the athletes sign an informed consent form to confirm their acceptance of the process.[35]

Various types of tests are available to coaches:

1. *Laboratory tests.* This type of testing measures an athlete's physical responses to training and is particularly relevant in cyclical, repetitive sports with heavy physiological demands, such as cycling, rowing, athletics, and swimming. Examples include blood lactate tests, anaerobic tests (cycle, treadmill), and $\dot{V}O_2$max tests (using various ergometers). These tests should be conducted by qualified staff through certified laboratories, but coaches should still manage the process by providing participating athletes with adequate feedback.

2. *General field testing.* This approach is also used to obtain general markers about an athlete's condition and response to training. Examples include the multistage fitness test, the sit-and-reach test, and various strength and power tests. Many sport programs also use anthropometric testing. General field tests offer the advantage of enabling us to compare general results across various sports for benchmarking. As with laboratory tests, these tests should be conducted by appropriately qualified staff, especially in the case of gymnasium exercises where maximum loads can increase the chance of injury to athletes through poor technique or improper safety practices and equipment.

3. *Sport-specific field tests.* These tests are often most useful to coaches when bringing various skill factors into general field testing—for example, agility tests in which athletes dribble a ball, carry a glove and field a ball, or hit a target. This type of testing can be motivational for athletes and provide sport-specific feedback.

All forms of testing, including physiological testing, affect program resources. For instance, tests can involve significant monetary cost, and this is particularly true of laboratory tests. The testing process also takes time, which is of course a valuable commodity for both athletes and coaches. In other words, even as physiological testing enables coaches to monitor program progress, it can be disruptive to training. Therefore, coaches need to weigh scheduling concerns against the value of testing when deciding which tests to use.

Training Measures

Training records provide great value and can be maintained through training diaries or training logs. Many types of training logs are used in sport, particularly in programs that are decentralized and therefore need to gather information into a central database, or athlete management system. Coaches can also turn to any number of training apps that make it easy for athletes to upload their training data to an online database using a mobile device such as a smartphone or tablet.

In some sports, global positioning system (GPS) devices offer another way to measure some aspects of an athlete's workload. These devices can measure speed and distance covered in real time, thus providing coaches with accurate workload data for each athlete during training sessions; in team sports, they also facilitate appreciation of positional differences. In addition to providing useful training feedback, GPS devices and other technology—such as movement sensors, heart rate monitors, high-speed cameras, and video editing software—can also serve as useful tools for skill acquisition and tactical development in competitive events (see chapter 10). These types of technology also allow coaches to compare the performances of athletes in geographically separated programs where they don't have access to them on a day-to-day basis. For example, coaches can monitor performances and training loads of individual athletes, assess key factors in their coaching plans, and adapt them to achieve program objectives (e.g., periodization, training volume, intensity).

In addition, while recognizing that athletes respond to training in idiosyncratic ways, coaches must ensure that the training load for each athlete is properly managed to ensure athlete well-being and reduce the risk of injury. For instance, for athletes who engage in high-risk activities such as hard throwing (e.g., pitching in baseball and softball; fast bowling in cricket), coaches may set a limit for the maximum number of throws per week. Such limits should take account of the athlete's stage of development.

In addition to these external approaches, training load can also be measured through internal methods, such as rating of perceived exertion.[36] In this method, the athlete provides a rating of intensity (perceived effort) for each session on a scale of 1 to 10, where 1 indicates lowest intensity and 10 denotes extreme intensity. Coaches then simply multiply the rating for a given session by the duration of the session to produce an indicator of effort for each athlete. This method is used quite commonly in a number of football codes including soccer, American football, and rugby union. Because such measurements require the individual to interpret the rating scale consistently, athletes may need a degree of experience to develop their expertise in making reasonably accurate assessments. When the testing is done properly, the resulting data provide coaches with insight into how athletes are coping with training and competition.

Finally, although coaches who work in recreational or participatory sport for youth typically lack the time and capacity to use advanced training measures, it may still be possible and useful for them to assess their athletes. For instance, given the growth of physical inactivity, many children enter sport programs without basic physical literacy or fundamental motor skills (e.g., jumping, hopping, throwing, catching). In such cases, it is useful to assess athletes for these skills, which form the basis for acquiring most fundamental sport skills.

Athlete Well-Being Measures

Researchers have become increasingly interested in developing ways to document the effect of a sport program in order to adapt training loads, improve performance, and reduce the chance of injury.[37-39] For example, a stress recovery questionnaire has been used extensively to monitor overtraining in athletes in a variety of sports.[40] Recent years have also seen a growing interest in athletes' psychological well-being, and research has revealed an increase in mental health problems among athletes.[41] Researchers have posited that this increase may result from overtraining, concussion, or identity crisis (often relating to a transition out of sport due to a career-ending injury or diminished ability to perform). Addressing these issues requires us to go beyond monitoring and adapting training loads. Instead, these challenges should be considered one part of understanding the person in context—that is, the individual athlete within the wider scope of study or vocational obligations, social pressures (including from friends and family), and potential commitment to other sport programs or sponsors.

A Significant Finding

One study investigated how the organizational culture and structure of the Australian Institute of Sport (AIS) affected the learning culture of athletes participating in an elite sport program—specifically, their sport-specific learning and development of a second, nonsport career.[14] The AIS was created by the Australian government to provide world-class facilities and coaches for Australia's developing elite athletes. As is the case at many U.S. colleges, selected athletes are provided with a scholarship to move to the institution in order to develop their elite skills in a chosen sport. The AIS also encourages athletes to develop vocational skills through education and workplace learning, but, unlike the colleges, it does not serve as an educational provider itself.

Through a series of interviews and surveys, the study identified major factors that the athletes contended with when moving to the institute—for instance, leaving home, living and breathing their sport, and facing intense pressure to deliver elite performance in order to maintain their scholarships. The researchers found that athletes recognized the importance of developing a "fallback career" and therefore greatly valued education and developmental experience in the workplace. In order to handle this dual load—high-pressure athlete training and performance and crucial career preparation and development—the athletes were required to be highly organized. Striking this balance proved difficult in the environment provided by the institute, which focused on athletic performance. In many cases, experienced athletes learned to cope with the environment by developing time management skills and negotiating with their coaches about training schedules.

Using Technology in Program Management and Monitoring

In the past decade, as easy access to networked digital devices has exploded, technology use in sport has proliferated, especially for the purposes of sensing, communicating, and analyzing data.[42-44] Advanced design and miniaturization have led to the development of microsensors, communication methods, and processors that give coaches powerful new ways to collect training and competition data, analyze it, and provide feedback. Some emerging technology even uses algorithms that can identify training and technical strategies to enhance performance. This type of technology is relatively inexpensive, generally noninvasive for the athlete or team, and useful in providing immediate feedback to the athlete or coach.

Recent years have also brought the development of numerous apps designed to help coaches and players plan and manage training and performance. These programs, which are inexpensive and can be easily downloaded to computers and mobile devices, address many areas of coaching. Examples include TeamSnap and Teamstuff for administration, planning, and communication; Hudl, Coach's Eye, Sports Clip Maker, and Excelade for video performance analysis; TrainingLoad and AthleteMonitoring for fitness and nutrition; and Headspace, Lucid, and SportPsych Performance Coach for psychological aspects.

Advances in digital technology—including both software (apps) and hardware (e.g., sensors, GPS units, high-definition cameras) are available to coaches and players in both performance and participation settings. With options ranging from inexpensive apps to high-cost performance-oriented technology, coaches can select from a range of tools to suit their budget and their program. In all cases, technology should be used judiciously. Although technological advancement has enabled more evidence-based coaching and training, it has its own limitations and comes with the potential to overburden a coach or coaching staff.[42] Therefore, like any other resource, technology should be incorporated into the planning process, not only to ensure that its use provides a clear benefit but also to account for the costs in terms of financial and human resources.

Of course, this process carried implications for coaching in terms of planning training sessions, taking a flexible approach to scheduling, and providing athletes with ongoing support. The researchers concluded that although the AIS structure affected the learning environment through its own organizational objectives, this influence operated differently according to the experience of each athlete. When athletes were given appropriate flexibility by coaches, they were able to develop not only their sport performance but also their life skills. Indeed, these two skill sets—on and off the field—complemented each other.

Exercise

Suppose that you are coaching at an educational institution where athletes are required to meet academic requirements in order to remain eligible.

- Describe coaching strategies to help athletes develop skills in their chosen sport as well as ensure they are able to successfully complete their study commitments.

_____

_____

_____

_____

_____

_____

_____

- Design a monitoring program to track athletes' well-being and their progress in both their studies and their sport.

_____

_____

_____

_____

_____

_____

_____

- Identify the variables you would measure, how you would gather the information, and what benchmarks or indicators you would put in place to alert you immediately when an athlete struggles with schoolwork or sport participation.

_____

_____

_____

_____

_____

_____

_____

From International Council for Coaching Excellence, _Sport Coaches' Handbook_, eds. D. Gould and C. Mallett. (Champaign, IL: Human Kinetics, 2021).

Chapter 7

Athlete Development Models

Joe Baker and Nick Wattie

Despite increasing interest in the process of identifying and developing talent—as well as a growing body of research on expertise in sport—successful athlete development remains elusive. The uncertainty of this process, and its inherent difficulty, are easy to observe in professional sport drafts, which repeatedly expose teams' inability to reliably predict athletes' future level of performance.[1] Furthermore, the complexities involved in optimal athlete development are reinforced by research showing that performance at one stage of development does not necessarily predict performance in later stages (as reflected, for instance, in the low rates of "conversion" from junior international to senior international levels).[2] The process of athlete development is also constrained by the finite number of positions available for athletes in high-performance sport—positions that become increasingly scarce as athletes progress to higher levels.[3]

Beyond the limitations of forecasting and selection, the process of athlete development is also affected by a number of other factors. For example, both overall athlete development and rate of skill progression are influenced by biases in developmental environments (e.g., socioeconomic status) that affect access to resources and quality of training.[4, 5] Development and progression are also influenced by personal characteristics, such as the timing of growth and maturation,[6] as well as genetic factors[5] and "innate giftedness."[7] They may also be affected by unique constraints imposed by a given activity itself. For instance, relatively immature sports typically require fewer hours of accumulated practice to reach elite levels of performance (e.g., compare the relatively new sport of "ultimate" to much older sports like boxing or baseball).[3] In another example, the age of peak performance for a given sport may influence the timing and feasibility of various stage-based participation behaviors.[8]

These constraints—environmental, individual, and task related—and their interaction complicate our understanding of athlete development.[3] Fortunately, models and theories can help us create a blueprint and guiding principles that will help us navigate this uncertain process. This work is not merely an academic preoccupation; to the contrary, numerous popular books advocate for one or another model of athlete development (e.g., deliberate practice, discussed later in this chapter). These lay models are often considerably distilled or modified from the original research, and as a result they vary in quality. Rarely, however, has anyone compared different models or types of models. This chapter helps to fill that gap by reviewing two major categories of athlete development models: researcher driven and practitioner driven. Rather than providing an exhaustive summary of the numerous athlete development models, our goal is to highlight different classifications and explore what they can contribute to our understanding of optimal coaching.

Models of Athlete Development

As coaches and trainers are well aware, athletes at different phases of development have different training needs. A comprehensive model of athlete development could allow us to allocate appropriate resources for different phases of growth and maturation and make evidence-based decisions about talent selection. However, athlete development models are only as good as the evidence on which they are based; for example, if a model lacks validity, then a large number of athletes might go unselected despite their potential for success.

This section considers some of the most widely used (or at least widely talked about) models in sport research and practice today (see table 7.1 for a list). A comprehensive discussion of these models lies beyond the scope of this chapter; instead, the following subsections elaborate on four models, provide general insight into how they were developed and can be applied, and discuss their strengths and weaknesses. These four models are presented briefly in figure 7.1.

Researcher-Driven Models

As the term suggests, researcher-driven models typically result from extensive hypothesis testing as part of an organized research program. Here we consider two models that are widely used in sport research: deliberate practice and the Developmental Model of Sport Participation (DMSP).

TABLE 7.1 Prominent Athlete Development Models and Approaches

Model or approach	Description
RESEARCHER DRIVEN	
Developmental Model of Sport Participation (DMSP)[9]	Proposes that athletes move through three qualitatively different stages (sampling, specializing, investment) on their way to expertise.
Deliberate practice[10]	Proposes that expertise is determined by intense focus on accumulating deliberate practice (i.e., highly effortful, highly relevant training).
Nonlinear pedagogy[11]	Focuses on manipulating critical task constraints, emphasizing practice variability and representative (i.e., game-like) learning tasks, and linking perceptual information with movement outcomes.
Athletic Talent Development Environment (ATDE) model[12]	Models the athletic environment, the roles of each component, and their interrelations in the talent development process.
Differentiated Model of Giftedness and Talent (DMGT)[13]	Distinguishes between giftedness (possession of natural abilities in the top 10% of age peers) and talent (skill development in the top 10% of peers active in the same field).
PRACTITIONER DRIVEN	
Foundations, Talent, Elite, and Mastery (FTEM) model (Australia)	Uses research and practitioner experiences to propose that athletes move from fundamental stages to mastery.
Long-Term Athlete Development (LTAD) model, or Canadian Sport for Life (CS4L)	Posits stages of development in which developing elite athletes move from an active start to training to win.
Performance or Talent Pathway (UK)	Proposes a pyramid-based system in which athletes move from community sport through podium stages of development.

Deliberate Practice

Over the past 25 years (see Gagné[13] for a review), considerable attention has been given to the concept of deliberate practice developed by Anders Ericsson.[10, 14] This approach posits that expertise is attained not simply through training of any type but through prolonged engagement in a specific type of training. These deliberate practice activities require cognitive or physical effort that does not lead to immediate personal, social, or financial rewards; in other words, they are performed solely for the specific purpose of improving performance. While the concept of deliberate practice was initially developed using data drawn from the field of music, Ericsson argues it applies to the acquisition of expertise in all areas of human endeavor, including sport.[15] The concept has been widely treated

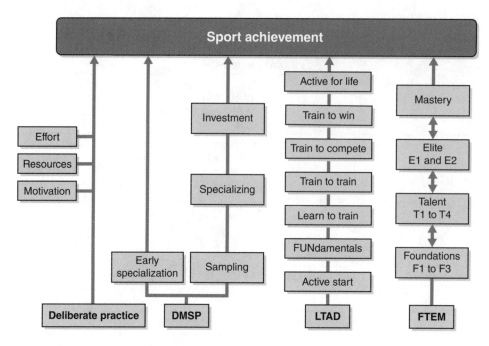

FIGURE 7.1 Comparison of athlete development models.

in popular science books, including the international bestsellers *Outliers*,[16] *Talent Is Overrated*,[17] *The Talent Code*,[18] *Bounce*,[19] and *The Sports Gene*.[20]

Deliberate practice studies in sport have consistently revealed that experts spend more time in training than their lesser-skilled peers. More important as it relates to deliberate practice, experts also spend more time participating in the specific activities that are most relevant to acquiring the essential component skills for expertise.[21, 22] Since deliberate practice focuses on accumulating a large amount of training, it involves a solitary focus on sport-specific training. Therefore, unlike models of athlete development (e.g., DMSP) that focus on participating in a range of sports and physical activities during early development, the deliberate practice approach emphasizes engagement in training as early as possible.

Evidence for this approach comes from nearly a century of research supporting a strong, positive relationship between time spent in practice or training and level of skill development.[23] Essentially, this approach suggests that the "developmental clock" is ticking and therefore that any time spent outside of deliberate practice could have been better spent elsewhere. In this view, athletes who spend all of their time in deliberate practice gain a developmental advantage over their peers who spend time in nondeliberate practice activities. This advantage becomes difficult to make up later in development.

How "Deliberate" Is Your Practice?

Although some elements of the concept of deliberate practice have been challenged, the notion that training should be effortful and should address areas of weakness is supported by good evidence. Therefore, it is advisable to evaluate your practice designs periodically in order to determine how well they fit into your long-term athlete development plan and whether they could be redesigned to be more deliberate. This type of evaluation requires a bit of planning, as well as some understanding of your athletes' areas of weakness and what is developmentally appropriate for your athletes. However, even though it can be a complicated process, it begins with some basic questions:

1. What factors affect performance in your sport?
2. How does each of your athletes score on these factors?
3. What key factors does each athlete need to improve in order to continue developing?
4. How can you better design practice to promote this improvement?
5. How do you plan to continually adapt practice to challenge athletes and keep them progressing toward desired outcomes?

Although it is relatively uncontroversial to assert that elite performance requires highly specialized training, the supposed need for early specialization has been challenged. Understanding the evidence for and against early specialization matters because early specialization can be associated with several serious developmental consequences such as dropout and injury.[24, 25] Fortunately, other models of development, some explored in the following sections, argue that early specialization is not a requirement for exceptional athletic performance.

Applied Implications: Deliberate Practice

- Pros: Emphasizes the role of the coach and the training environment in facilitating high-quality training for athletes. Highlights the role of personal agency in determining attainment.
- Cons: Undoubtedly oversimplifies the influence of biological factors and predispositions on ultimate levels of performance. Has been interpreted as requiring early specialization, which is associated with negative consequences (e.g., dropout, injury).

Developmental Model of Sport Participation (DMSP)

Contrary to the deliberate practice approach, the DMSP, developed by Jean Côté and colleagues,[8, 26] emphasizes a broad range of sport participation during early development. Based on research involving elite athletes from Canada and Australia, the DMSP proposes that athletes move through a number of developmental trajectories during their sport experience. Although the model discusses the development of recreational athletes, we focus here on the elements of the model that focus on elite athlete development.

Research on the DMSP suggests that most athletes move through three qualitatively different stages on their way to expertise—sampling, specializing, and investment. The sampling stage involves participating in a broad range of sports with an emphasis on enjoyment and the development of general physical movement skills (i.e., physical literacy).[27] Then, in the specializing phase, this broad range of sport participation is reduced as athletes begin to focus on one or two sports and train with increasing intensity. In the final stage, investment, athletes exhibit a nearly singular focus on intense training resembling deliberate practice with an emphasis on training for performance (rather than for enjoyment).

Despite the DMSP's differences from deliberate practice, it does allow a potential role for early specialization. Specifically, it acknowledges that some athletes achieve exceptional performance through a highly specialized training program that starts early; consider, for instance, Tiger Woods. Even so, research on the DMSP suggests early specialization is a less-than-ideal pathway to elite athlete status due to potentially negative consequences of this type of engagement during early development.

Applied Implications: DMSP

- Pros: This model's multidimensionality likely does a better job than the deliberate practice model at representing the nuances of athlete development. The early role of play-like activities provides a good foundation for fundamental motor skills, physical literacy, and intrinsic motivation.

- Cons: Although the model is widely discussed in research, its validity requires further verification using larger samples from more countries. The model also likely oversimplifies patterns of youth sport participation (early diversification versus early specialization).

Practitioner-Driven Models

As indicated by the label, practitioner-driven models are either developed or widely used by practitioners. In other words, these models have generally emerged from experiences "in the trenches" as practitioners determine what works and what doesn't through an ongoing process of trial and error.

COACHING SNAPSHOT

Informed by science and guided by practice, the American Development Model employed by USA Hockey established a framework that associations both in ice hockey and other sports use to develop their athletes most successfully. ADM Technical Director **Ken Martel** was a key figure in designing, testing, refining, and then communicating the model to the benefit of many coaches and athletes.

Long-Term Athlete Development (LTAD) Model

One of the most widely known models of athlete development in the world is the Long-Term Athlete Development (LTAD) model (known in Canada as Canadian Sport for Life, or CS4L), which was developed by Richard Way, Istvan Balyi, and their colleagues.[28] The current version of this model has seven stages.

1. *Active start.* Consists of the period from 0 to 6 years of age and involves introducing the developing athlete to a broad range of movement opportunities in order to develop the ABCs of movement (agility, balance, coordination, and speed).
2. *FUNdamentals.* Covers ages 6 through 8 in females and 6 through 9 in males and focuses on further development of fundamental movement skills through a challenging and fun multisport environment.

3. *Learn to train.* Focuses on ages 8 through 11 in females and 9 through 12 in males and encompasses the developing athlete's initial forays into more formalized types of training. Here, the emphasis is on general sport training rather than specialized training or competition.

4. *Train to train.* Includes the period from ages 11 through 15 (females) and 12 through 16 (males), which is roughly reflective of the adolescent growth spurt. During this time, athletes focus on consolidating the basic skills and capacities specific to their chosen sport (e.g., aerobic versus anaerobic energy systems; specific forms of strength, speed, and agility). In this critical stage of elite athlete development, training and competition are driven by highly nuanced sport-specific requirements.

5. *Train to compete.* Focuses on the period starting at 15 years in females and 16 years in males and lasting up to 21 years in females and 23 years in males. This is the first stage in which training focuses on competition and athletes specialize in a single sport. Athletes in this stage are highly committed and display high-performance potential.

6. *Train to win.* Occurring in early adulthood (18+ and 19+ for females and males, respectively), this stage of the high-performance athlete development model focuses on podium performance and achievement at the highest levels of competition. Emphasis is placed on providing the highest quality of support, coaching, and other developmental resources.

7. *Active for life.* Encourages athletes to continue with lifelong participation in sport.

Applied Implications: LTAD

- Pros: This model is widely used internationally to structure athlete development and provides an easy-to-understand structure for framing the phases of athlete development.
- Cons: The model lacks empirical validation, and the stages are likely too generic to capture sport-specific nuances (they require considerable modification to be sport specific).

Foundations, Talent, Elite, and Mastery (FTEM) Model

The FTEM model, developed by researchers and practitioners at the Australia Institute of Sport, is among the newer athlete development models.[29] Similar to other models, this approach posits that athletes move through a series of stages on the way to expert-level performance. In this case, there are four macrostages and 10 nested microstages. The foundations macrostage emphasizes development of the fundamental movement skills and physical literacy necessary for more advanced involvement in sport.[27] This stage includes three microstages—F1, F2, and F3—which mark progression through the stage with subtle differences in focus but the same general emphasis.

More specifically, the F1 microstage focuses on the "participant's early exposure to a variety of movement experiences that afford . . . a broad range of essential movement foundations."[29 (p. 1324)] F2 then emphasizes refinement of the movement experiences gained in F1 through continued exposure to a range of sports and physical activities. Finally, F3 involves increased commitment to training and stronger emphasis on the development of sport-specific skills or formal engagement in competition. Typically, this phase relates to initial involvement in traditional club or school sport.

Next comes the talent macrostage, which focuses on developing the qualities and attributes associated with a high-performance athlete. During this stage, coaches and trainers work to identify and develop the "raw materials" of future elite performers. Athletes entering this phase rank among the top 10 percent of performers for their age and competition level. The stage has four microstages. In T1, athletes demonstrate their potential through either formal or informal talent identification processes. T2 then focuses on verifying talent before moving on to the more advanced training environments emphasized in T3. To round out this macrostage, T4 involves transitioning from junior national or international levels of performance to the senior or open level. Here, athletes focus on obtaining the highest levels of support for continued development, such as a university or college scholarship or being drafted to play for a professional team.

The final two macrostages represent the highest levels of skill development. The elite stage includes two microstages—E1, which involves athletes who represent their country at international competitions, and E2, which relates to athletes who are podium hopefuls in these competitions. The final stage, mastery, is restricted to those few who achieve repeated international or professional distinction.

One characteristic that makes the FTEM model unique is the notion that athletes can leapfrog over stages. That is, although the model's stages are presented in a linear fashion, the creators propose that the trajectories of athlete development are in fact dynamic and that many athletes make rapid changes in their capacities. For example, an athlete who switches from one sport to another (e.g., through a talent transfer approach[30]), may move from the elite (E1 or E2) stage back to the talent (e.g., T1) stage while acquiring and demonstrating key capabilities in the new sport. Similarly, a truly exceptional performer may skip stages on the way to the elite level of competition. As a result, this model can account for athletes who are "rapid experts" rather than "slow experts."[3]

Applied Implications: FTEM

- Pros: Developed based on current research *and* practitioner experience. Recognizes the need for models to reflect current knowledge while being presented in a manner that is useful for practitioners.
- Cons: Assumes that athletes can be easily placed into stages of development. Stage nuances are sometimes difficult to discern (e.g., F1 versus F2).

Key Issues for Athlete Development Models

The models we have discussed so far reflect the large body of research conducted on athlete development over the past few decades. However, while we know a considerable amount about the value of specific types of practice—as well as the importance of designing training environments that are developmentally appropriate—many nuances of athlete development remain unknown. Several of these issues are discussed in the following sections: disabilities, stages versus continuous adaptation, the nature of talent, integration of theory and practice, and generic versus sport-specific models.

Athletes With Disabilities

The past two decades have brought considerable growth in disability or parasport; however, nearly all models of athlete development are based on data from samples of nondisabled individuals. The domain of parasport is incredibly complex and encompasses various forms of ability and injury classifications. Moreover, the time course of development—including factors such as starting age, participation in other sports, and other developmental milestones—may differ appreciably from those of nondisability sports. In particular, athletes' developmental trajectories can be influenced by whether their disability was congenital or acquired. As a result, while the theory of deliberate practice is a general theory of expertise, which theoretically should apply to parasport, the diversity of athlete histories may influence the profile of accumulated practice in this population. Similarly, athletes' unique histories, as well as the availability level of parasport activities, may affect an individual's ability to sample diverse sports during the early stages of athlete development, as prescribed by the DMSP.[8, 26]

Notably, two stages have recently been added to the LTAD model for athletes with disabilities: awareness and first contact. These stages reflect the need to increase awareness of available activities for individuals with disabilities and to ensure that their first contact with sport results in a positive experience. However, these new components, which are particularly geared to individuals with acquired disabilities, may not be sufficient; indeed, they highlight the fact that generic models can be problematic. Thus, it has been suggested that we may need disability-specific or sport-specific models (e.g., addressing wheelchair sports or sports designed for athletes who are blind).[31] Clearly, we could use greater focus on the development of models based on data from a range of parasports and athlete populations.

COACHING SNAPSHOT

Darren Cahill is keenly interested and involved in player development, contributing to the maturation and improvement of such players as Lleyton Hewitt, Andre Agassi, and Simona Halep. Son of an Australian rules football coach and once a highly ranked professional tennis player himself, Cahill entered into coaching with an appreciation of the coach–athlete dynamic in the development process.

Stages of Development Versus Continuous Adaptation

Most models of athlete development assume that athletes move through clear stages of development, but this position has been criticized. For example, one group of researchers propose that a better way to conceptualize athlete development is through a period of continuous adaptations to specific training constraints.[32, 33] In this view, development is seen not as a progression through various predetermined stages of development but as a process of moving along a continuum from no skill (or very low skill) to elite or exceptional skill.

A Place for Talent?

Many models of athlete development are implicitly grounded in one or another notion of athletic talent—that is, the idea that there is something to be developed and that it requires an optimal learning environment for maximal skill acquisition. However, research emphasizes that our understanding of talent identification (e.g., what it is, how it could be measured) is surprisingly limited.[34] In fact, a review found insufficient evidence to conclude that the notion of talent carries any relevance for coaching practice.[35] The implications of this finding are amplified by evidence indicating that coaches' selection decisions have low predictive accuracy[1] and are often biased (e.g., open to relative age effects[3]). Indeed, our limited understanding of talent raises important implications for models of athlete development that emphasize early entry and suggests significant difficulties for athletes trying to enter later (e.g., after athletes have already been placed in competitive and/or high-performance "streams").

Better Integration of Theory

Researchers in sport science and a range of related disciplines (e.g., education, psychology) have developed highly sophisticated models of exceptional development. However, these models have not been adequately evaluated for their relevance to athlete development. This lack derives in part from the fact that it is not easy for coaches and trainers to translate the models' complex theoretical concepts to applied sport settings. This type of work needs to be done either by those who create the models in the first place or by applied sport scientists who can bridge the gap between theory and application. Unfortunately, these scientist-practitioners are less common than they need to be, especially at younger and lower levels of competition.

Generic Versus Sport-Specific Models

Coaches and practitioners commonly report struggling with the fact that athlete development models often take a "one-size-fits-all" approach.

Clearly, general models such as the ones explored in this chapter have gaps when applied across different sports. Consider, for example, the time frames for development denoted by the LTAD model and how they would apply differently in artistic gymnastics versus marathon running. Similarly, in the context of competitive gymnastics, which currently requires early specialization and deliberate practice, it may not be feasible for participants to sample multiple sports in the manner recommended by the DMSP.

In addition, although general guidelines may be valid for the development of certain qualities (e.g., strength, flexibility, speed), coaches who need to make decisions about athlete development are often constrained by the coaching traditions and the structure of their chosen sport. Similarly, while general guidelines can be useful, they do not leave room for important differences in pedagogy or coaches' ability to design practices that improve skills while also being developmentally appropriate, safe, and enjoyable (regardless of the level of competition or the number of other sports in which an athlete participates).

Finally, athlete development models often do not sufficiently address the challenge of individual variation. Athletes differ based on individual characteristics (e.g., anthropometrics, physiology, psychology, maturity) and developmental circumstances (e.g., geography, socioeconomic status), to name but a few factors. In summary, in many ways, general athlete development models see only the forest and not the trees.

Exercise: Designing an Athlete Development Model for Your Sport

While keeping in mind the reasonable concerns about using stage-based models to describe the trajectory of athlete development, use the information provided in this chapter to create an outline of athlete development in your sport. Make sure that your plan accounts for the various age divisions and levels of competition related to your sport. Pay specific attention to the following questions:

1. What descriptors or skills distinguish one stage of development from another? Can these factors be measured objectively? Are they general (e.g., related to age) or sport specific (e.g., related to movement quality or competition outcomes)?

2. How linear or dynamic are the processes of development in your sport? In your experience, do athletes regularly move up and down the stages of development? Does your model adequately capture all developmental nuances among athletes in your sport?

3. Could your model be applied in real-world settings? For instance, does it offer value to a coach who must decide which athletes get to move forward in the system? Or is it too complicated to be understood or, for that matter, too simple to be meaningful?

4. What is missing? No model is perfect, and improvement requires knowledge of where the gaps are. What elements of your model are incomplete? What is required to fill these gaps?

_____

_____

_____

_____

_____

_____

_____

_____

_____

_____

_____

_____

From International Council for Coaching Excellence, _Sport Coaches' Handbook_, eds. D. Gould and C. Mallett. (Champaign, IL: Human Kinetics, 2021).

Chapter 8

Psychological and Social Development of Athletes

Karl Erickson, Martin Camiré, and Jenelle N. Gilbert

When asked about the benefits of sport participation, people involved at all levels of play often note that athletes learn about themselves and develop desirable personal qualities and skills. To cite just two examples, the Women's Sports Foundation lists leadership, confidence, and teamwork as benefits of sport participation for girls, and high school football coach (and former NFL player) Joe Ehrmann believes that his primary role as a coach is to develop young men of integrity.[1] As these views suggest, coaches not only help athletes develop sport skills but also influence their psychological and social development. Indeed, many notable coaches, including football coach Urban Meyer, view psychological and social development—commonly known as mental skills and life skills, respectively—as primary aims of their coaching.[2, 3]

Because athletes are not stuck or fixed at their current capacity levels, effective coaching entails "thinking developmentally" about how athletes change over time and working to promote positive growth. In order to contribute to positive development, we must first recognize the capacity for growth in each athlete and adopt a growth mindset.[4] In other words, a growth mindset is critical not only for our athletes themselves but also for our own thinking about them. From this perspective, we can also acknowledge that some athletes develop sooner or at a faster pace than others. We must also recognize that growth does not happen immediately; to the contrary, long-term change requires long-term effort that continuously links short-term coaching actions to long-term developmental goals. In essence, then, thinking developmentally means continually asking ourselves where we want our athletes to end up and how we can help them get there.

Promoting Positive Athlete Development

All athletes have real and potential strengths or assets—for instance, ability to work hard, ability to think on one's feet, charismatic personality—that can be promoted progressively.[5] Effective coaches contribute to this youth and athlete development not simply by preventing or fixing problems and negative outcomes but also by proactively encouraging positive outcomes, such as improved mental and life skills. Putting this perspective into practice requires us to recognize that all athletes are more than simply sport performers; they are also people with multiple interests and capabilities. It also requires us to apply meaningful understanding of psychological and social development.

Research shows that a human being is a complex, integrated system of multiple elements and that human development is a holistic process. For example, an age-group athlete's performance might be influenced by (among other things) genetics, family finances, educational expectations, religious beliefs, peers, coach relationship, and the coach's knowledge. As a result, optimal athlete development requires coherence and convergence between performance enhancement and psychosocial development. Each of these factors influences—and therefore carries the potential to enhance—the other. For example, as athletes learn mental skills, they can use them to increase sport performance. In turn, success in sport performance may encourage them to use the same skills in other areas of life (e.g., school). Moreover, seeing their efforts produce positive change in multiple settings may circle back and increase their confidence and sense of control during sport performance.

To summarize, effective coaching facilitates both performance and psychosocial development.[6] Furthermore, since human development is multifaceted, effective coaching for positive development also requires us to create a fit between an athlete's internal assets as a whole person and external supports such as coaching strategies.[7] In determining this fit, we must consider the athlete's stage of athletic development as defined by competitive level and age with respect to psychosocial growth. Athletes at different stages have different developmental needs in the physical, psychological, and social realms;[8] therefore, creating an optimal fit for positive development may require us to adapt coaching approaches to an athlete's stage-based needs. By making such adaptations and thinking developmentally, we can help athletes progress through the stages of athletic development.

Sport science research offers a number of athlete development models—for example, the Developmental Model of Sport Participation[9] and the Long-Term Athlete Development model.[10] Fortunately, the major stage-based tenets of various models have been integrated into a concise, coaching-focused form in the *International Sport Coaching Framework* produced by the International Council for Coaching Excellence (ICCE).[11] This framework (figure 8.1) addresses competitive level and age by differentiating recreation- or participation-focused levels of competition from performance-oriented levels and then subdividing athletes by age (child, adolescent, or adult) or performance level (emerging, performance, or high performance). The resulting six coaching domains can help us think clearly about our athletes' developmental needs and how we might adapt our coaching strategies, including those intended to promote the development of mental and life skills. In other words, it can help us create a better fit.[8]

For example, many of the psychological and social factors relevant to sport are just emerging in children, including how they perceive themselves and how they interact with and compare themselves to teammates and other children. As a result, coaches can exert substantial influence at this stage—for instance, by emphasizing and rewarding effort to lay the foundation for a productive work ethic, recognizing personal improvement and learning, and deemphasizing social comparisons between children. Furthermore, children are particularly sensitive to competitive pressures, and coaches can set the foundation for a healthy relationship to competition through the ways in which they structure competitive experiences and interact with their young athletes, specifically to prioritize and reward effort and improvement over competitive outcomes. Coaches must also account for the influence of parents, who exert the most influence on their children's sport participation during these early years and may be either reinforcing or undermining such a growth-oriented approach to competition.

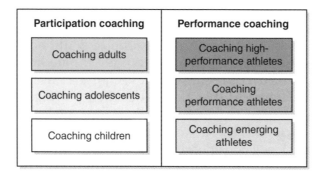

FIGURE 8.1   The six coaching domains.

Reprinted by permission from ICCE et al., *International Sport Coaching Framework, Version 1.2* (Champaign, IL: Human Kinetics, 2013), 23.

Similarly, the unique psychosocial characteristics of adolescents offer both opportunities and challenges.[12] Adolescence is often marked by personal exploration and change as young people try to figure out who they are and who they will be as adults; among other things, this effort involves exploring personal interests, educational and career aspirations, social preferences, and ways of interacting with others. During this stage, peers exert major social influence, and young people shift their focus away from their parents and toward their friends while also making comparisons with peers and facing the associated pressures. Thus, as a period of great change and openness to new ideas and behaviors, adolescence provides coaches with an opportunity to promote psychological and social development by teaching mental and life skills in sport.

The specifics of this opportunity may be shaped by the competitive level at which we coach. For example, in the performance domain of adolescent sport, the increasing experience of competition may provide especially fruitful material for athletes to practice mental and life skills, such as handling tough losses, working hard and persisting in training, and working effectively with teammates who do not easily get along. In contrast, the participation domain may free coaches from performance pressures and thus allow them to prioritize discussion and practice of mental and life skills without fretting about immediate effects on wins and losses. Regardless of competitive level, however, the increasing prominence of peer groups in adolescent athletes' lives can exert unpredictable effects. In addition, most adolescents now live in a daily environment pervaded by social media (e.g., Snapchat, Instagram, Facebook), which can influence their developmental experiences for either good or bad and may be particularly influential in this age group.

Developing Athletes' Mental and Life Skills

As noted earlier, effective coaching now involves facilitating athletes' development both on and off the field[6]—in other words, helping athletes enhance not only their physical, technical, and tactical skills but also their mental and life skills. Both children and adolescents need to develop mental and life skills in order to transition to adulthood and thrive in endeavors beyond sport. These assets are not innate but are trainable, and coaches can help ensure that athletes acquire a variety of mental and life skills that will benefit them long after their playing days are over.[13]

To this end, researchers have long called for purposely designed training programs to develop these skills, particularly in children and adolescents, who experience considerable psychological changes during these critical life periods.[14] In response, several programs have been implemented for mental skills training (MST) and life skills training (LST).[15,16] Of particular importance for this chapter, many of these programs have been found to facilitate psychological and social development (for reviews, see Dweck[5] and Camiré[17]). This research shows us that coaches can strongly influence athletes' learning of mental and life skills and thus their psychological and social development—if these efforts are given deliberate attention and take into account athletes' stages of development. In summary, it appears that well-conceived programs play an important role in helping athletes experience positive developmental outcomes.

COACHING SNAPSHOT

While systematic mental training programs are important, so too is a coach's ability to respond appropriately and spontaneously to an athlete's psychological and emotional needs at critical moments. Consistent, supportive feedback from a coach can help an athlete conquer the many challenges presented in sport.

Mental Skills Development

Mental skills, also referred to as cognitive skills or psychological skills, are trainable mental abilities that underpin successful performance, a positive approach to competition, and overall personal well-being. Examples of mental skills include imagery, relaxation, and self-talk, which can be used to manage competitive stress and focus one's attention.[14] In terms of MST programs for athletes, several research-focused interventions have been conducted in various countries (e.g., United Kingdom, France, Australia, United States) with children, adolescents, and emerging adults in a wide range of sports (e.g., swimming, gymnastics, football).[18-24] Overall, these interventions have shown that athletes of all ages can develop the mental skills of attentional control, imagery, focus, relaxation, self-talk, mental toughness, resilience, and self-regulation.

No matter how well conceived an MST program may be, it can succeed only if it is delivered effectively; in other words, coaches play a crucial role in the developmental process. Specifically, coaches are responsible for creating the caring climate in which positive development can occur.[13] Doing so is no easy task, but research has shown that coaches can develop the ability to teach both mental and life skills as part of their everyday coaching.[13, 25, 26] That is, the ability to facilitate mental skills development is not an innate coaching style or personality characteristic but a competence that all coaches can develop and improve with effort.

Once coaches recognize that mental skills are important to their athletes' success, they can teach these skills in many ways.[27] Some coaches focus on developing sport-specific outcomes and take what is known as an *implicit* approach, which is based on the belief that athletes learn how to use mental skills by seeing their coaches use them.[28] For instance, imagine a basketball coach whose team is losing by three points with only a few seconds left in the game and no timeouts remaining. With no way to stop the clock and get the team organized for a last-ditch scoring effort, the coach can at least make purposeful use of relaxation and stress control strategies, such as deep breathing and calm, purposeful communication, and hope that the players will do the same. Observing a good model, however, is only the first step in the learning process,[29] and athletes may not be able to complete the rest of the steps without guidance. This challenge may be especially evident among younger athletes at earlier stages of athletic development who are not as cognitively mature as those in adolescence or early adulthood.

Given this complexity, many sport psychology professionals assert that coaches need to teach such skills not only by example but also directly—that is, *explicitly*—rather than assuming that they will be learned by chance or mere observation.[30, 31] This explicit teaching generally involves helping athletes develop conscious awareness of key skills, plan for and reflect on them, and consider where and how they might be used in real-life situations. Given the wide variety of mental skills that may be relevant to different athletes and specific strategies, this section provides an overview of several general strategies that can be tailored to your particular objectives, athletes, and contexts to help you teach mental skills intentionally and explicitly. These general suggestions constitute teaching strategies that can be adapted and applied to any targeted mental skill (e.g., attentional control, imagery, focus, relaxation, self-talk, mental toughness, resilience, self-regulation).

Use Handouts

When teaching mental skills through an explicit approach, coaches can use an MST workbook or handouts to support training activities. For example, when teaching about goal setting, coaches can provide athletes with handouts featuring the key principles of the goal-setting process (e.g., recording goals and revisiting them regularly), the different types of goals (e.g., daily, short-term, long-term), and characteristics of effective or SMART goals (i.e., specific, measurable, adjustable, realistic yet challenging, and time-based). Though the SMART principle was originally developed for business,[32] sport psychology professionals have modified it for sport and advocate it for teaching athletes about goals. Summary information for use in handouts can be found in applied sport psychology textbooks[33] and other coach-focused resources,[27] including freely available online resources. Thus, handouts can serve as a formal resource when coaches introduce mental skills; figure 8.2 shows an example of a brief handout developed for goal setting.

Develop Worksheets

Worksheets (i.e., paper-and-pencil activities) can also be used to help athletes apply newly learned information about using mental skills. With goal setting, for instance, a worksheet might ask athletes to develop their own daily, short-term, and long-term goals based on information shared in the handout. When designing a worksheet for younger athletes, coaches should include starter sentences to help them stay focused on the task at hand. Here is an example: "Complete the following sentence. 'My goal for today's practice is to . . .' (Remember to make your goals SMART.)" Adolescent athletes, on the other hand, may benefit from a more open-ended approach, such as thought prompts (e.g., "How can you get the most from today's practice?") or scenarios to which they can respond (e.g., "Playoffs are in three weeks—what do we need to do to make sure we're at our best when it counts?"). Regardless of the format, asking athletes to share their goals allows you to check their comprehension of the goal-setting process; it can also give you insight into their sport objectives.

A goal is a statement about something you want to achieve. When developing goals, it can be helpful to think about when you would like to achieve them. As a result, athletes often set long-term, short-term, and daily goals.

- A long-term goal might identify something you want to accomplish in the next year or by the end of the season.
- A short-term goal serves as a stepping-stone to the long-term goal and might specify something you want to accomplish within the next three to six months.
- Daily goals indicate the tasks that you work on each day to help achieve your short-term and long-term goals.

For example, a basketball player might set the following goals:

- By the end of the season, I want to increase my free throw shooting percentage to 75.
- By midseason, I want to increase my free throw shooting percentage to 70.
- Each day after practice, I will shoot 50 free throws.

In this example, you can see how the daily goal will help the basketball player achieve the short-term goal, which in turn will help achieve the long-term goal.

Now let's practice identifying effective goals. In the following table, the left column includes three goals that a swimmer might set at the beginning of the preseason. Identify whether each goal is long-term, short-term, or daily.

Sample goal	Which type is it?
Before each practice, I will warm up on my own and work on my flip turns for 10 minutes.	Long-term Short-term Daily
I want to decrease my personal best time for the 100-meter fly by 0.25 second by the end of the season.	Long-term Short-term Daily
By the time league meets begin, I want to be making smooth transitions in my flip turns and to have decreased my 100-meter time by 0.1 second.	Long-term Short-term Daily

To get the most from your goals, write them down and post them in a visible spot, such as your locker or your smartphone's home screen. Seeing them often will help you stay focused on them.

Now it's your turn. Develop three goals for your sport. Remember to be specific.

Long-term goal: _____

Short-term goal: _____

Daily goal: _____

From International Council for Coaching Excellence, *Sport Coaches' Handbook*, eds. D. Gould and C. Mallett. (Champaign, IL: Human Kinetics, 2021).

FIGURE 8.2 Goal-setting handout and worksheet (combined).

Figure 8.2 presents a worksheet (bottom portion) combined with handout-type information (top portion). For more ideas and examples, consider the *USTA Mental Skills and Drills Handbook*,[34] which provides numerous worksheets and activities that can be easily adapted to sports other than tennis.

Use Social Media and Other Technology

Some athletes may feel reluctant to learn mental skills because the process seems daunting to them, especially if they do not experience immediate success. In this case, you may be able to pique their interest through the use of technology, such as a post on social media or a sport-related website about a favorite athlete who regularly uses mental skills. For instance, you might use video clips that show obvious use of mental skills, such as a baseball player taking a deep breath as part of his routine at the plate. You might also choose some clips that require your athletes to infer the use of mental skills, such as a soccer forward getting back on her feet quickly after a tackle and likely using strategies to refocus and control stress in the heat of the moment.

Such tools may serve as a catalyst for adolescent athletes to apply mental skills in their own sport. They also allow you to engage your athletes in spirited discussion about their use of mental skills. These activities are critical in helping your athletes complete the rest of the steps in the observational learning process.[29] These approaches can be used with athletes of all ages. However, they may work better with adolescents than with younger children due to their keen interest in social media and their greater freedom to use it.

Use the Natural Training Environment to Teach Mental Skills

Mental skills can also be taught effectively in the natural training environment, either through a classroom approach or in a stand-alone format. In one example, mental skills were taught to 17- and 19-year-old elite male soccer players on the soccer pitch, where they participated in drill-based sessions that focused on physical and mental skills simultaneously.[35] The athletes were introduced first to a specific mental skill and then to a series of manipulations that modified the traditional drill format to more directly emphasize competitive situations requiring that skill.

For instance, in a drill that typically requires small groups with an equal number of players, the format was manipulated to make the teams unequal in either number or ability, thus creating challenges that required the players to use mental skills in order to respond effectively.[35] Another example involved a drill that typically emphasizes using only one touch when receiving and moving with the ball and then shooting on goal. In this case, the format was manipulated so that athletes were expected to achieve perfect target passing. If the coach decided that a pass was not accurate, the athletes were instructed to restart the drill. In both examples, a modified sport task created challenges that gave athletes the opportunity to work intentionally on using mental skills—arousal control and self-talk, respectively.

To enhance learning, the drills were performed in rounds.[35] Before each round, the athletes were directed to focus on a particular aspect of the chosen mental skill and use it during the next round. In addition, throughout the drill and at its completion, the coach facilitated brief guided-reflection discussions with the athletes about their use of the skill (i.e., asking athletes what worked, what did not work, and why). This practical approach helped athletes learn authentically as they gained immediate experience in using the mental skills and applying new insights along the way.

To put these lessons into practice, coaches should employ similar tactics.[36] For instance, when updating physical drills to include a mental skill focus, coaches should use explicit and intentional teaching points to emphasize key messages about learning mental skills, debrief immediately after drills, and encourage and guide athletes to engage in shared reflection about their experience of attempting to use a given mental skill.[28, 35] Reflection is crucial to learning because it provides time for athletes to evaluate their use of mental skills, make connections about what helped (or did not), and identify how they can use the skills in the future.[37]

Such opportunities will arise not only in sport but also in other life domains. When mental skills developed in sport are used outside of sport, they become life skills.[31] Many researchers believe that teaching life skills and promoting athletes' positive development constitute a coach's most important task when working with young and adolescent athletes.[38]

Life Skills Development

Life skills, which are broader in scope than mental skills, can be developed in sport but enable individuals to succeed in the various environments in which they live—for instance, school, work, home, and community.[39] These skills can be behavioral (e.g., effective communication), cognitive (e.g., decision making), interpersonal (e.g., teamwork), or intrapersonal (e.g., goal setting). In order for a skill learned in sport to be considered a true life skill, it must be used by athletes in settings beyond sport. If transfer does not occur, then the skill can only be considered a sport skill. This distinction underlines the fact that coaches must work deliberately to help their athletes develop the confidence to use the skills they have learned through sport in everyday life situations.[31]

Several research-based programs for life skills training have been conducted with young people ranging from six years old to adolescence.[40-42]

Generally, such programs demonstrate the feasibility of helping partici-pants learn both physical skills within sport and life skills (e.g., team-work) that were reported to be used beyond sport. However, research evidence indicated that life skills transfer beyond sport was not always optimal, because the children often lacked concrete opportunities to practice using their skills in the classroom. Such findings reinforce the notion that coaches must work deliberately and systematically to help athletes not only develop life skills but also find opportunities to use them outside of sport.

COACHING SNAPSHOT

Coach **Lisa Alexander**, whose Australian national netball teams won 81 per-cent of their matches, knows the value of developing leadership and being an effective leader. Her holistic approach to coaching emphasized producing not just great athletes but great people who benefitted from their sport ex-periences for a lifetime.

As with mental skills, researchers have called for the creation of programs to help coaches learn to teach life skills. A few such programs were recently developed for youth sport coaches and physical education teachers in Australia and Spain.[43, 44] These programs proved useful on a number of levels. Specifically, coaches exhibited more life skills teaching behaviors in their everyday coaching, which led to positive outcomes for athletes in the form of enhanced cognitive and goal-setting skills.

The following sections describe concrete strategies that you can integrate into your coaching plan in order to teach life skills in a deliberate manner.

Connect Mental Skills to Nonsport Settings

Because mental skills can be transferred and used successfully outside of sport, the strategies outlined in the Mental Skills Development section of this chapter can also be used by coaches who want to teach life skills. However, in order for transfer to occur, coaches must consistently emphasize the link from sport to other life domains. One way to do so is by continually highlighting the similarities between sport and life. For example, setting sport goals and working toward them in daily training can help athletes achieve success, and coaches can teach athletes to use the same process to set life-related goals (e.g., developing effective study habits and achieving good grades). Thus, the teaching of life skills can build on the teaching of mental skills by simply deliberately helping athletes extend the content or target of the mental skill beyond sport to other important areas of life.

Deliberately Teach Life Skills

In addition to making connections between sport and real life, coaches should be deliberate when teaching life skills. For help in this regard, coaches can turn to several life skills programs for youth that include lessons and planned developmental activities to aid learning. For example, SUPER (Sports United to Promote Education and Recreation)[45, 46] and First Tee[47] use planned lessons to teach life skills alongside sport skills. Participants are encouraged to use their newly learned life skills (e.g., goal setting, conflict resolution, emotion management) in both sport and nonsport settings and are given assistance in developing a plan to do so.

For example, participants are taught and reminded about the STAR principle. According to this principle, when faced with a difficult situation, they should "Stop and take a deep breath; Think of all the alternatives to the problem; Anticipate the consequences for each alternative; and Respond with the best choice."[48 (pp. 108-109)] Upon returning to the sport site, they report and discuss their experiences in using the life skills on their own outside of sport. Sharing their positive experiences, as well as discussing initial challenges, helped the athletes better understand and continue transferring life skills to various areas of their lives.[40] Furthermore, although the support of caring adults is important in this process, hearing from peers was deemed at least as valuable as receiving feedback from coaches.[40] This deliberate process can be adapted and applied to any desired life skill, and coaches are encouraged to think creatively about how to incorporate it appropriately for their athletes' stage of development and particular context.

Provide Opportunities for Athlete Leadership

In addition to planned lessons and activities, life skills can be taught in more traditional sport contexts by allowing students to lead practice drills and by using various practice combinations. Allowing students to lead selected drills gives them opportunities to develop leadership, teamwork, and decision-making skills.[17, 28] Younger athletes can lead the team or small groups through familiar drills, either with a partner or individually, and adolescent athletes may be given the option of creating and teaching new drills to their teammates. Doing so requires athletes to take on the responsibility of teaching a learning objective, make a plan to address it, and implement the plan. In order for this process to work, the coach must allow athletes to take the lead (with appropriate guidance for their stage of development) even though things may not always go as intended. Indeed, learning from mistakes and experiencing the process fully are crucial to life skill development, particularly when learning and practicing leadership.

Practice combinations, on the other hand, can take various forms. For example, including girls and boys of similar abilities in a coed practice provides an opportunity for the athletes to develop mutual respect and better understand equity issues.[49] In another beneficial combination, university athletes can volunteer to assume the coaching role in a training session with a high school or community team.[50] When these role models promote the importance of education, they can inspire younger athletes to begin setting goals and imagining the possibility of attending university themselves. Similarly, coaches who work with mixed-age teams (or in clubs with teams in multiple age groups) can create athlete mentoring programs in which older athletes are paired with younger ones and given explicit responsibility to provide support for both sport and life challenges.

Teach Life Skills in Classroom Settings

Planned developmental activities to teach life skills can also take place in a classroom setting. One example can be found in the Psychological UNIFORM curriculum, in which adolescent athletes learn life skills (e.g., goal setting, confident mindset, and coping with adversity) through multimodal instruction.[19, 50, 51] Specifically, athletes participate in interactive lectures and in-class activities, complete homework assignments, engage in physical drills (the only activity performed in a gym or open field space), complete reflective journal entries, and watch film clips of skills in action and respond to guiding questions.[19]

All of these instructional activities are informative, but the use of movie clips is one of the most popular due to its entertainment value.[28] Coaches highlight the educational aspect of each clip by providing guiding questions that seek information about the character's use of the featured skill. Athletes are also asked to reflect on how they can use the same skill in their sport and in their daily lives outside of sport. Thus, the discussion encourages and helps athletes to develop both their mental skills (for use in sport) and their life skills (for use outside of sport).

Develop Life Skills Courses for Training Schools

Sport-focused schools (variants of which are rapidly developing around the world) provide another unique opportunity to teach various life skills. For example, one sport-focused school staged 60-minute developmental classes twice a week in which adolescent athletes were taught life skills and values alongside their regular curriculum.[52] In one activity, athletes classified values (e.g., fairness, honesty) and then identified the behaviors required to live in accordance with those values.[52] Through this activity and subsequent discussion, students learned to become self-aware, apply their values, and develop holistically as athletes and people. Coaches can use similar activities with younger athletes by providing more guidance throughout the process.

Use Off-the-Field Settings for Life Skills Training

Life skills can also be taught and practiced in a context away from the classroom or natural training environment. For example, athletes can develop organizational and decision-making skills by planning a healthy meal and then purchasing the needed food items.[49] During the meal, athletes should be praised for making healthy food choices and encouraged to discover alternative options for any unhealthy choices they may have made. This strategy has been used successfully with players from 10 to 17 years of age, and coaches noted that it also promoted good team communication and cohesion. In this approach, athletes could be given responsibility for specific meal components either occasionally or on a regular basis (e.g., weekly), depending on the length of the season.[3] This type of activity emphasizes the importance of roles (i.e., through different team members taking on and completing the different tasks required to make the full meal) and being dependable both for oneself and others. As with leadership experiences, athletes engaged in these activities should be allowed to take on as much responsibility as is appropriate for their developmental level.

Invite Athletes to Engage as Volunteers

Life skills can be developed through volunteerism both in sport-related settings and in nonsport experiences.[17] For example, athletes might help run a sport clinic at a community center for underprivileged youth, serve meals at a local homeless shelter, or spend time with abandoned animals at a rescue site. Coaches can prepare athletes for such experiences by talking with them about compassion, empathy, and our responsibility to help others; athletes can also be asked what types of services they would like to perform. When volunteerism is conducted as a team, it also provides athletes with opportunities for team building.

Because the process of planning and organizing volunteer experiences can be a challenging endeavor,[53] coaches may want to engage the assistance of a parent manager. In fact, additional adult involvement may be necessary in some instances, particularly when working with younger athletes. In any case, athletes should be allowed to lead the volunteer experience as much as possible in order to maximize their development of life skills. In addition, as with other off-field activities, it is crucial for athletes to be given opportunities to put their new life skills to use in real-world situations. Much like sport skills, life skills need to be trained for and practiced in order to be learned most effectively.

Use Unplanned Teachable Moments

Planned developmental activities provide an organized, deliberate format for teaching life skills; however, valuable learning experiences can also result from unplanned opportunities. For example, when athletes engage in behavior that contradicts the life skills they have been taught, coaches should capitalize on these opportunities by reviewing relevant life skills and reminding athletes to use them. These teachable moments give coaches the opportunity to demonstrate consistency in their expectations. Depending on the situation and the age of the athletes, possible approaches include reteaching certain life skills, leading a discussion about their importance,[52] and helping athletes brainstorm alternatives to inappropriate behavior.[54] In order to make full use of teachable moments, coaches need to remain mindful of the life skills they wish to emphasize, watch for examples of athletes using them (or not using them), and use those examples to highlight important points and explore possibilities.

Table 8.1 summarizes the coaching strategies discussed in this section for helping athletes develop mental and life skills.

TABLE 8.1   Coaching Strategies for Teaching Mental and Life Skills

Strategies	Examples
Create handouts that explain specific mental and life skills.	Provide information about effective goals and goal setting.
Provide worksheets that help athletes use newly learned skills.	Include matching exercises, vignettes, or other paper-and-pencil activities.
Highlight elite athletes' use of skills by incorporating content from social media, video-sharing websites, and sport-related sites.	Discuss the examples with athletes and ask them to reflect on how they can use the featured skills.
Conduct drill-based sessions in the natural training environment.	Emphasize mental and life skills and prompt athletes to reflect about them.
Develop lessons that teach life skills alongside sport skills.	Select training tasks/drills that require the use of life skills (e.g., problem solving) in order to successfully complete the sport activity.
Encourage and help athletes to use life skills in both sport and nonsport settings.	Highlight instances when athletes tried to use life skills (successfully or unsuccessfully) and lead a discussion about what worked or didn't work.
Allow athletes to lead practice drills as developmentally appropriate.	Have a different athlete lead the team warm-up each practice.
Use various practice combinations.	Boys and girls can train together; university athletes can help run a practice for younger athletes.
Create planned developmental activities.	Use film clips with lessons and guiding questions to promote athletes' awareness of key values.
Plan a team meal and give athletes responsibility for specific components.	Have the athletes plan the different steps involved and help assign tasks as appropriate.
Organize volunteer experiences for athletes to serve others in need.	Contact local community centers or charitable organizations to see how athletes might help meet community needs.
Capitalize on teachable moments to consistently promote expectations about the use of skills.	When something goes wrong or doesn't work during practice, pause to highlight and lead a brief discussion about the potential use of life skills to make improvements next time.

Supporting Psychological and Social Development Efforts

The preceding sections have provided general approaches and tangible strategies for teaching mental and life skills—that is, some "things to do." However, in order for such initiatives to fully succeed, coaches must also ensure that their programs include two underlying components: a well-crafted coaching philosophy and a positive connection with athletes.

Coaches who have successfully taught mental skills and life skills to their athletes rely on a well-formed coaching philosophy that emphasizes the development of these skills (see also chapter 3 of this book).[31, 52] Because their philosophy helps them to be consistent, these coaches are well positioned to create and implement planned developmental activities while also taking advantage of unplanned teachable moments. More specifically, a coherent and deliberately considered philosophy can help coaches define acceptable behavior, continually communicate clear messages about that behavior, reinforce or reprimand athlete behaviors as needed, discuss the process of behavioral learning, and align it with their overall coaching rationale.[3] Thus it is well worth the required time for coaches to think about how mental and life skills fit into their overall coaching philosophy.

COACHING SNAPSHOT

Known for his enthusiasm and optimism, Liverpool manager **Jürgen Klopp** has very successfully spurred his athletes on to exceed their perceived individual and collective team abilities. He also admits that while helping his athletes develop as individuals and players, he has had to mature and grow as a coach and person to better meet the responsibilities of his role.

The second underlying component involves a positive connection between coaches and athletes. When coaches value their athletes as people and establish supportive, respectful relationships with them, athletes are more likely to learn and use mental and life skills.[17, 31] One way in which coaches can show respect to players is to reprimand them without belittling them; in other words, support players who make mistakes "instead of having them incur the coach's wrath."[3 (p. 25)] Coaches can also nurture positive connections by talking *with* athletes, rather than "at them," and by engaging them in conversation about their lives outside of sport.[55] This approach treats athletes as people first and reminds coaches to interact with them holistically. A related strategy involves maintaining contact with athletes during the off-season,[3] which extends the coach–athlete connection beyond sport and encourages athletes to continue using life skills. A wealth of research evidence demonstrates that these simple efforts are critical for athletes' psychological and social development.[56, 57]

Though coaches can and should teach mental and life skills to their players, conflict can sometimes ensue when coaches attempt to fulfill both roles.[58, 59] For example, athletes may be unwilling to discuss competitive anxiety with a coach if they perceive that doing so could affect their playing time. On the other hand, a coach who knows that an athlete is facing challenges outside of sport may find it difficult to excuse the athlete from practice or competition due to the coach's desire for a positive performance outcome. In such situations, coaches may support their efforts in other ways, such as engaging the services of a sport psychology consultant.

Tips for Promoting Athletes' Psychological and Social Development

1. "Thinking developmentally" means working to promote positive change in our athletes over time.

2. Mental skills and life skills are real-world indicators of positive psychological and social development for athletes.

3. Successful teaching of mental and life skills requires a sound coaching philosophy focused on athlete development and high-quality relationships with athletes.

4. To optimize the teaching of mental and life skills through sport, coaches must make use of deliberate strategies both on and off the field.

5. Coaches who do not feel comfortable teaching mental and life skills can employ the services of a sport psychology consultant to teach these skills.

Working With Sport Psychology Consultants

Research shows that with directed effort, coaches can learn the importance of teaching mental and life skills and change their behavior to positively influence their athletes' development of these skills. At the same time, some coaches who value these skills shy away from addressing them due to a perceived lack of time, resources, or competence. In these situations, coaches can benefit from support, and one possible solution is to bring in a sport psychology consultant (SPC).

While the task of finding an SPC may seem daunting, it is actually quite easy once a coach knows where to look. The most direct approach is to search the online directories of professional organizations dedicated to sport and exercise psychology—for example, the Association for Applied Sport Psychology, the Canadian Sport Psychology Association, and the British Association of Sport and Exercise Sciences. These websites can be used to make contact with SPCs who are either located in your area or are able to work with you and your team remotely or online (such arrangements are common for many SPCs). Coaches whose financial resources are limited (which is the case in many youth sport programs) may prefer to contact a local university to seek the assistance of a sport psychology graduate student. Because of their novice status, student consultants charge much lower fees (or perhaps none at all, in the case of master's-level students), and they often welcome inquiries from coaches and sport organizations at every level in order to develop their consulting skills.

Other important considerations include the nature of the coach–SPC relationship and the SPC's ethical boundaries. Some SPCs assume a staff position and work alongside coaches, whereas others play a less prominent but still important role for the team. In either case, and before beginning to work with the team, the SPC should clearly communicate expectations about confidentiality to all involved parties (e.g., athletes, coaches, parents). For example, a coach or parent might expect the SPC to share information provided by an athlete, but doing so could damage the SPC's relationship with the athlete, thereby minimizing the SPC's value in future work together. At the same time, the SPC may need to communicate about an athlete with other counseling professionals if the athlete presents with clinical issues that the SPC is unqualified to address. Therefore, it is crucial to establish clear expectations with all parties ahead of time.[60]

When beginning their work together, the coach and SPC should identify certain skills for the athletes to learn. This determination can be made either through focused discussion in which the coach describes specific scenarios in which the athletes struggle (e.g., competitive anxiety, hesitant performance) or through the use of formalized assessment tools that indicate strengths and weaknesses in athletes' mental skills (see Burton and Raedeke[27] for examples). From there, the coach and SPC can determine how much time will be dedicated to teaching and learning the identified skills, as well as when and how.

For instance, a coach might prefer that athletes learn these skills through focused activities in the classroom or before the start of training sessions. If so, the SPC could create handouts and worksheets to help athletes learn about the skills and the importance of using them. The SPC could also teach skills (e.g., relaxation via diaphragmatic breathing) and then provide supervised practice opportunities. Alternatively, the coach might want athletes to learn mental skills as part of physical drills performed in the natural learning environment (e.g., on the softball field or soccer pitch). The coach might need to help create these teaching activities, depending on the SPC's sport-specific knowledge. A third option would be to combine these two approaches; for instance, the SPC might work as a consultant who helps the coach incorporate the teaching of mental and life skills into daily coaching practice.

Exercise

Skill synergy

Identify a favorite sport drill that is frequently used in practice. Given the suggestions provided in this chapter about manipulating drills, how might this drill be changed so that athletes can learn and practice their mental skills alongside their physical ones?

_____

_____

_____

_____

_____

How the pros do it

Identify a successful professional athlete and find some information about this person—for instance, social media posts or content from sport-themed magazines or websites. Present information about this professional's use of a particular mental skill, either through a discussion or in the form of a brief handout (as suggested in the chapter). Help participants reflect on the professional's use of the skill and identify areas in their sport where they could benefit from using the same skill.

_____

_____

_____

_____

Let's help out!

Lead a discussion about participants' interests outside of sport as well as opportunities to engage those interests in the community by volunteering to serve others. What might such opportunities look like, and what life skills might they emphasize?

_____

_____

_____

_____

_____

From International Council for Coaching Excellence, _Sport Coaches' Handbook_, eds. D. Gould and C. Mallett. (Champaign, IL: Human Kinetics, 2021).

Chapter 9

Physical Development of Athletes

Vern Gambetta

Developing athletes from their initial engagement with a sport to their first step onto the winner's podium is a long-term, multifactorial process. Moreover, in order for athletes to achieve their ultimate potential, athlete development demands professional guidance from coaches. This process has become even more challenging due to societal changes that have resulted in declining fitness among young people even as the expectations and demands placed on athletes have increased. This complexity means that coaches must be able to balance the art and science of coaching in order to optimize athlete development.

More specifically, physical training must incorporate a multifaceted approach that integrates various training modalities (e.g., medicine ball, stretch cord, dumbbells, body weight) to produce significant adaptation in specific performance parameters. Sound training develops all systems of the body while recognizing and respecting the body's wisdom, the demands of the sport, and the needs of the individual athlete. When implemented properly, this process produces a highly adaptable athlete who can perform without significant limitations in the competitive environment.

Developing Athletic Movement

In order for the body to execute efficient athletic movement, all parts and systems must work together in harmony. Movement is not a solo but a symphony, and it is impossible to truly isolate a body system. In fact, all systems of the body work at all times, and the demand on a particular system is determined by the intensity and type of the activity. To continue the symphonic metaphor, when a given section of the orchestra is featured or highlighted, the other sections are still playing, albeit in the background.

Let's also give credit to the conductor—that is, the brain. All systems of the body, including the muscles, are slaves of the brain, which drives, connects, and controls movements so that we can accomplish desired tasks. Therefore, if we are to understand the body's parts, we must keep sight of the whole. We must give the body credit for its inherent wisdom; its capacity to learn; and its ability to link, sync, connect, and coordinate in order to play the movement symphony we refer to as sport performance. Understanding this process requires us to take an eclectic approach that combines interpretation of sport science research, study of methods and concepts of rehabilitation, and practical experience as both coach and athlete.

The body is a link system or kinetic chain, and the linkages are emphasized and enhanced by sound training. When things go well, all parts of the chain work together in harmony, thereby producing smooth and efficient patterns of movement. Despite this reality, conventional academic preparation still focuses on studying individual muscles in terms of classical anatomy. We must remember, however, that we do not function in the anatomical position. Granted, this static position provides us with a mental convenience for easily observing and studying all of the body's individual muscles. But the brain does not recognize individual muscles; it recognizes patterns of movement, which consist of individual muscles working in harmony. Performance involves using the whole kinetic chain to produce and reduce force as needed.

We also cannot ignore gravity and its huge effect on movement. Indeed, this effect must be a prime consideration when we design and implement training programs to prepare an athlete's body for the forces that it must overcome. To this end, carefully analyze the movement you are trying to enhance. What forces are involved? What plane of motion is dominant? Sport takes place in a dynamic environment, which forces movement to occur in all planes of motion by using multiple joint actions to produce the desired mechanics. Because movement occurs simultaneously in all three planes—sagittal, frontal, and transverse—it must be trained in all three planes. More generally, we must understand desired movements and design training programs accordingly.

Movement, then, is a complex event that involves synergists, stabilizers, neutralizers, and antagonists working together to reduce or produce force. Therefore, the basic foundational principle is to train movements rather than muscles. Sport scientist Roger Enoka, a recognized authority on muscle activation and fatigue, has demonstrated the significance of task required and context. In other words, different movements use muscles differently. All movements, however, are controlled and directed by the same command station—namely, the central nervous system (CNS). The CNS calls for patterns of movement that can be modified in countless ways to react appropriately to gravity, ground reaction forces, and momentum. Each activity is subjected to further refinements and adjustments by feedback from the body's proprioceptors. This process ensures optimal neuromuscular control and efficiency of function.

The rest of this chapter focuses on what should be the ultimate goal in athletes' physical training: developing athleticism, or the ability to perform athletic movements (e.g., running, jumping, throwing) at optimal speed with technical proficiency, precision, style, and grace. Developing this quality requires a training program that addresses force production, force reduction, and stabilization in order to produce functional strength—that is, strength that athletes can use and apply beneficially in their sport.

Factors Affecting Athletes' Physical Development

Athlete growth and development is an organic process. It takes both time and proper timing of the appropriate stimuli for the athlete's stage of development. In addition, to some degree, athlete growth and development occur independent of training, and the most obvious consideration in this regard is biological age. Typically, development of young athletes is approached in terms of arbitrary age-group divisions or year in school, but these groupings serve only to accentuate actual developmental differences. They also tend to focus more attention on athletes who are more physically developed, to the detriment of those who are less developed.

A good program must also account for athletes' level of intellectual and emotional maturity. If an athlete is limited in cognitive ability, then adjustments must be made in the structure and complexity of the program. As for emotional development, the athlete must be able to handle the expected pressure and receive advice and criticism in a constructive manner.

The developmental process is also affected by gender differences. Specifically, females mature earlier than males; in fact, they are usually about two years more advanced in terms of biological age, and this earlier maturation carries profound implications for the makeup of training groups. Up to puberty, it is acceptable for boys and girls to train together. Then, during the pubertal growth spurt, males generally gain a physical advantage and therefore should train separately from females. In postpubescence, when males have completed their growth spurt, then it is once again possible for them to train with females in selected situations.

As an athlete progresses through the developmental process, the ratio of training to competition is crucial. In today's world, there is a tendency to overcompete and undertrain at the developmental stages; in other words, a distorted emphasis is placed on competition, to the exclusion of training. In effect, development programs tend to be performance programs rather than true development programs. However, in order to allow young athletes to proceed through the developmental process, the ratio of training to competition must be controlled.

Training Phases

An effective physical training program must consider not only the athlete's current developmental stage but also the long-term training progression that will ensure optimal development throughout the athlete's career. That long-term training plan should include three phases: basic training, build up, and high performance. These phases are not fully distinct; rather, they overlap, blend, and seamlessly flow from one to the next.

- *Basic training phase (4-6 years duration).* The goals of this phase are to facilitate general physical development and mastery of fundamental movements (i.e., high degree of physical literacy), establish the foundations of sport technique, and establish a sound training routine and training habits. The frequency of training during this phase increases from three sessions per week in the first years to as many as five sessions per week at the end of the phase. Sessions should be limited to one hour each.

- *Build-up training phase (3-4 years duration).* The goal here is to develop a high level of trainability, which is the ability to train effectively enough to stimulate appropriate adaptation. The overall workload must be related to the athlete's trainability—that is, the ability to handle work of sufficient intensity at a volume that is commensurate with the athlete's developmental level, both physically and in terms of the chosen sport. This phase also gradually shifts the emphasis to training loads that are more specific and of higher intensity. It also places more emphasis on competition, although the competitions are designed to provide objective feedback regarding training progress rather than high-level results. The number of sessions can be as high as 12 in a seven-day period, and session length is gradually increased. In the later stages, multiple daily training sessions may be added.

- *High-performance phase (undefined time frame).* The whole developmental process points toward this phase. Training in this phase is directed by the specific needs of the athlete in relation to competition goals; that is, training is now driven by the demands of key competitions. Training in this phase involves high intensity, more specificity, and multiple training sessions in the same day. Moreover, given the lucrative financial rewards now available in high-performance sport, training is often geared toward helping athletes compete well beyond what were formerly thought to be the age limits for elite performance.

Physiology 101

In order to plan a comprehensive athletic development program, we must consider basic physiological principles. And in order to understand those principles, we must understand the fundamental concepts of capacity, power, and efficiency:

- Capacity consists of the total amount of energy available to perform work; in simple terms, it is the size of the tank. In the build-up phase of athletic development, one primary goal is to build a big tank to hold reserves that can be used when needed. Thus specific work is directed toward increasing capacity, and this work is usually volume oriented.

- Power consists of the amount of energy that can be produced per unit of time. Training for power usually involves higher-intensity work.

- Efficiency, or economy, is the unifying element—namely, the optimal use of available energy. It is both metabolic and mechanical.

Work capacity accumulates and builds on itself from week to week, month to month, and year to year. It includes both power and aerobic capacity. However, once capacity is increased to a certain level and aerobic power is elevated, the time cost required to raise it even further is greater than the return. Therefore, for nonendurance athletes, time devoted to marginal improvement in aerobic capacity and power would be better invested elsewhere. The focus then needs to shift to efficiency, which is how the aerobic component can best contribute to further performance improvement. This need for developing efficiency carries profound implications for selecting both the means of training and the sequence of workouts.

The challenge lies in how to develop the necessary aerobic power to recover from the short, intense bursts of activity that occur in game play and speed and power events without compromising the explosive power necessary for optimal performance during the bursts. We know that slow, sustained aerobic work can compromise explosive power. Therefore, for athletes whose games demand repetitive sprinting and the ability to recover quickly from those bouts of high-intensity work, the effort could be better spent in other areas.

Energy for doing work can be derived either anaerobically or aerobically. The anaerobic system produces energy rapidly, which enables large but brief power outputs for intense activities. This system is particularly limited in the total amount of energy it can produce. The aerobic system, on the other hand, can produce large amounts of energy, but not rapidly. It is limited by the body's ability to break down carbohydrate and fat with the help of oxygen and to deliver the oxygen required by the muscles.

Together, the anaerobic and aerobic systems are capable of meeting the body's need for energy during exercise.

The body's systems are trainable to varying degrees. Therefore, it is necessary to focus on the efficiency and interaction of the systems rather than trying to target one system for development. This integration is achieved by developing a training plan that distributes work in a way that matches the conditioning demands of the athlete with the demands of the chosen sport.

COACHING SNAPSHOT

The physical fitness required in wrestling is one of the most appealing aspects of the sport to **Cael Sanderson**, who won an Olympic gold medal and was 159-0 in earning four national championships as a collegiate wrestler. Sanderson, shown here lifting one of his champion wrestlers, remains fit and fabulously successful as a coach, with his Penn State University teams winning eight national championships and counting.

Developing Athletes' Biomotor Abilities

Sound training emphasizes development of all biomotor abilities in a balanced and proportional manner throughout the training year. The relative emphasis given to each biomotor quality should reflect the demands of the chosen sport, the athlete's position or event, and the stage of the athlete's career. Biomotor abilities are interdependent and must be trained consistently in order to achieve desired results. Therefore, all components of training are addressed throughout the training year but with different emphases depending on the time of year and the athlete's developmental level.

Strength

Of all the biomotor qualities, strength is the most pervasive. Indeed, it is all encompassing, in that all forms of motion require some expression of force. Therefore, athletes in all sports can benefit from sport-appropriate strength training. Because of the importance of strength and the ease of measuring it, coaches may be tempted to train it independently. However, it is also a highly interdependent motor quality that interacts profoundly with all of the others, and this interaction must be accounted for in the overall training program. The benefits of a good strength training program are as follows:

- Improved ability to reduce and produce force
- Increased ability to express explosive power
- Increased joint stability
- Significant contribution to injury prevention and rehabilitation

Strength differs from power. By definition, strength is the ability to exert force without any time constraints. Power, on the other hand, involves a time element; in other words, it is the ability to express force in the shortest amount of time. Power can be subdivided into two main categories: strength dominated and speed dominated. Strength-dominated power is characterized by the need to express high force against external resistance, as in the shot put, the discus throw, and American football. In contrast, speed-dominated power is characterized by restricted resistance; examples include throwing a baseball and swinging a golf club or tennis racket.

Traditionally, strength training has emphasized force production through the movement of a body part. Contemporary thinking, however, has shifted to recognize that strength also plays an important role in resisting movement by a body part. Also known as the eccentric component of strength, this force reduction phase is where most injuries occur. Strength also contributes to another important performance factor—

that of stabilizing or fixating a body part. Therefore, a sound strength development program carefully directs training to address all three of these muscle-action functions in an integrated manner.

Strength acquisition is governed by neuromuscular, muscular, biochemical, structural, and biomechanical factors. Each factor should be taken into consideration when designing and implementing a strength training program. Ultimately, the neural component drives the system and enables the muscles to do work; more specifically, the nervous system governs recruitment order and sequence in response to the demands of a specific task. Naturally, then, the initial adaptation that occurs in strength training is neural. Essentially, this adaptation involves learning to engage the appropriate stabilizers in order to reduce and produce force as needed. The neural adaptations are manifested in the form of increased firing rate and motor unit recruitment and improved motor unit synchronization. These adaptations explain why beginners tend to experience dramatic initial gains in strength without appreciable gains in hypertrophy.

Maximum strength is the highest force that can be exerted during a single voluntary muscular contraction. Both practice and research tell us that once the necessary neural pathways have been opened for such a contraction, it is relatively easy to tap into them again. In other words, once a maximal strength base has been established, we do not have to repeat the same loading cycles in each training year. Instead, we can use cycles that are shorter and more intense to reopen the pathways.

In acquiring and expressing strength, the limiting factor is often not the strength of the large muscles themselves but the strength of the smaller stabilizing and synergistic muscles. These muscles guide and allow the development of functional strength, which is the ability to dynamically reduce and produce force through the full range of movement with speed and control. Functional strength contributes greatly to smooth, coordinated athletic movement; therefore, although it is less measurable, it is very observable.

Strength endurance is the ability to perform repetitive strength-oriented actions in a climate of fatigue. It can be trained once base-level strength has been developed (one must possess a base level of strength in order to sustain it!). Thus we derive the principle of strength before strength endurance, which is why the initial block in a training sequence is devoted to basic strength acquisition.

Strength training, then, amounts to coordination training with appropriate resistance to handle body weight, project an implement, resist gravity, and optimize ground reaction forces. In order to better understand and apply this definition, we need to understand each element of it. Intermuscular coordination provides the key to efficient movement and effective force application. Appropriate resistance, in turn, incorporates the following:

- *Handle body weight.* This aspect emphasizes relative strength by working with various percentages of body-weight resistance.
- *Project an implement.* In throwing events, the weight of the implement determines the resistance needed in order to develop the strength to move that implement at the desired release speed.
- *Resist gravity.* Sports that demand work against gravity require more eccentric and isometric emphasis to express the necessary force.
- *Optimize ground reaction forces.* Sports with high ground reaction forces demand reactive strength.

Thus this definition can inform a spectrum of training methods that address the varying strength and power demands of all sports.

Speed

Speed does not stand alone; to the contrary, it depends on strength, explosive power, posture, and body awareness. Moreover, it is a motor skill that can be enhanced by applying motor learning principles in training. In other words, it is trainable if approached systematically. At the same time, because it is a fine motor skill, it takes time to develop to its highest levels. This is especially true of absolute speed, or "fast coordination," which is more difficult to develop because it is so highly dependent on other biomotor qualities.

Speed demands differ for a specialist sprinter and an athlete preparing for a multidirectional sport. In multidirectional sports, very little movement involves going straight ahead for any significant distance; instead, most movement involves angles, curves, starts, stops, and direction changes. Therefore, it is a fundamental mistake to use traditional track-oriented drills and workouts in an effort to improve multidimensional speed.

Linear or straight-ahead speed (SAS) includes a distinct flight phase through which the legs must be allowed to cycle. In multidirectional movement, on the other hand, the flight phase is detrimental to performance because having one's feet far from the ground makes it is very difficult to stop or change direction. Therefore, game speed is closely related to multidimensional speed and agility (MDSA), which is the ability to recognize, react, start, and move in the required direction, change direction if necessary, and stop quickly—typically within two to five seconds.

The phases of straight-ahead speed are as follows (see also figure 9.1):

- Reaction—response to the primary stimulus
- Starting—overcoming of inertia from a stationary or moving position

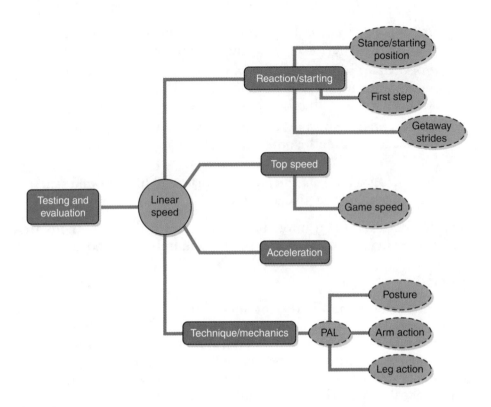

FIGURE 9.1 Components of linear speed.

- Acceleration—achievement of maximal velocity in minimal time
- Top speed (maximum speed)—highest speed of which an athlete is capable
- Speed endurance—ability to maintain speed in a climate of fatigue
- Deceleration—process of slowing down under control (critical for sport success)

In order to ensure optimal transfer from training, speed must be developed in close conjunction with the technical aspects of the chosen sport.

Multidimensional Speed and Agility

In order to fully understand MDSA, we must consider the following elements:

- Ability to complete a given sport-specific task in the shortest time possible
- Ability to change direction with minimal loss of speed
- Ability to change direction, position, or body orientation based on internal and external information

- Combination of physical, biomechanical, and decision-making abilities
- Maintenance of dynamic equilibrium
- Quick acceleration and deceleration (stops and starts)

In essence, then, MDSA involves a series of complex movements performed in the context of a specific sport. Agility is influenced mainly by factors related to perception, decision making, and changes in direction or speed; in other words, it includes both cognitive and motor-related components. In addition, agility can be either planned or reactive. Planned agility is used when the athletes know where they are going and can plan their movements. Reactive agility, on the other hand, is totally unplanned and accounts for most agility demands in sport situations.

MDSA training is not conditioning work but speed training. Therefore, we should begin by teaching the skill and helping the athlete master it. Then we can add reaction and help the athlete master that. Only then should we incorporate fatigue. The specific components of multidimensional speed and agility training are as follows (see also figure 9.2):

- *Balance, body control, and awareness.* This component involves ability to control the body and its parts and maintain a high level of awareness of those parts in relation to the goal of the movement. This is not necessarily trained separately but is an integral part of most drills.

- *Recognition and reaction.* Recognition falls into the domain of the specific sport skills involved. It consists of recognizing patterns and cues that prompt reaction—that is, quick responses to key stimuli. Reaction should be incorporated as soon as the athlete masters the movement.

- *Starting and first step.* Starting involves the ability to overcome inertia. In multidirectional sports, a start may be made from a stationary position, while moving, or a combination of the two. The position of the first step is crucial in terms of creating a positive shin angle. This step must be made in the intended direction, and the length of the step must be relatively short in order to allow control for a direction change if necessary. Effective starting demands a high level of concentric strength in order to overcome inertia; specifically, it requires extension of ankle, knee, and hip to push back against the ground and thereby propel the body in the intended direction.

- *Acceleration.* In MDSA, acceleration involves achieving optimal speed (as distinct from maximal speed in straight-ahead speed). As a result, it requires situational awareness, an element of control, and the ability to decelerate and reaccelerate as necessary.

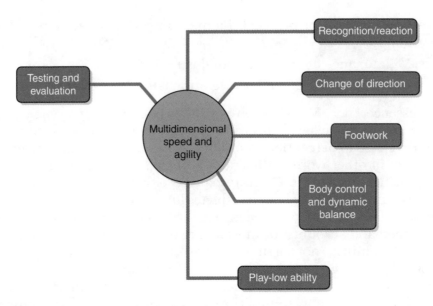

FIGURE 9.2 Components of multidimensional speed and agility.

Mechanically, acceleration demands triple extension of the ankle, knee, and hip.

- *Footwork.* Footwork focuses on the hip-to-foot relationship. It serves as the unifying thread in all agility work because agility is built from the ground up. Indeed, in sports where the hands are used, the feet get the hands to the ball.

- *Change of direction.* This type of change is initiated by shifting the center of gravity outside the base of support and then regaining control to enable movement in the intended direction. It also incorporates the ability to restart when necessary, regardless of body position.

- *Stopping.* Mechanically, this action demands proportional bending of the ankle, knee, and hip in order to control high eccentric loads, properly absorb shock, and make the needed play. Correct stopping not only enables the athlete to make the play but also helps prevent injury. It demands high levels of both eccentric and isometric strength.

- *Play-low ability.* This component involves playing with a low center of gravity in an effective athletic position.

Flexibility

Flexibility is defined as range of motion at a joint with control. If, on the other hand, range of motion is uncontrolled, the joint experiences hypermobility, which is undesirable because it increases the risk of injury. Like balance and posture, flexibility is not a static quality but a dynamic one. It is also highly specific to the chosen sport or event and to the individual athlete; indeed, every individual is unique in terms of muscle elasticity, ligament laxity, and body structure. As a result of these factors, flexibility is not subject to universal norms; instead, we must approach flexibility work in context.

To understand the role of flexibility in movement, it is helpful to think of it in terms of the correct amount of motion deployed at the correct joint, in the correct plane, and at the correct time. Given these demands, the development of flexibility requires an eclectic approach that applies what has been used for years in martial arts, dance, yoga, and physical therapy.

Flexibility work is necessitated in part by the fact that some muscles chronically shorten due to their location in the body and the function they perform. These muscles must be lengthened through functional movements; in fact, they require constant attention in order to maintain high-quality movement and prevent overuse injuries. Chronic shortening can also be caused by typical daily activities and repetitive sport motions. The muscle groups that require constant attention for lengthening include the gastrocnemius, soleus, psoas, hamstrings, adductors, iliotibial band, latissimus dorsi, pectoral group, and wrist flexors. Flexibility in these muscles should be addressed daily, depending on the sport and individual needs.

Flexibility training methods consist of the following:

- *Static stretching routines.* These traditional stretching exercises place a joint in a position that challenges range of motion, usually using gravity or other muscle groups to increase the tension.
- *Facilitated stretching routines.* These more sophisticated routines include proprioceptive neuromuscular facilitation (PNF), elastic band techniques, and yoga.
- *Dynamic flexibility exercises.* These simple movements move joints through large ranges of motion; examples include leg swings, trunk twists, and arm circles.

Work Capacity

Work capacity consists of the ability to tolerate a workload and recover from doing so. To enhance work capacity, we must choose the appropriate method based on the demands of the sport, the phase of training, the athlete's position or event, and the athlete's individual needs. Let's consider four approaches: traditional, fartlek (variation), interval, and repetition.

Traditionally, the aerobic component of work capacity has been addressed through continuous work designed to improve vascularization of the active muscles and enhance their physical, chemical, and metabolic characteristics. This type of training involves working in an aerobic zone for a prolonged period of time. It works well and is particularly appropriate for endurance athletes (e.g., swimmers, distance runners, cyclists) who are capable of pushing themselves and sustaining a sufficient tempo to achieve a training effect. It is much less effective, however, for athletes in sprint, intermittent, and transition sports who are used to giving uneven bursts of effort and do not have the ability to push themselves to get a significant training effect.

The variation method, also known as *fartlek* (Swedish for "speed play"), involves a high-level game or race simulation. Essentially, it uses a continuous workout in which intensity is varied until the target time or distance for the session is reached. This method can be either highly or loosely structured, depending on the objective. It can also be either inner directed (driven by the athlete) or structured to respond to demands from the coach during the workout. Fartlek workouts can also be made less movement specific but still metabolically demanding. To use this approach, pick a target time for the workout (e.g., 40 minutes), then devise a logical progression to get the athlete to that goal. As part of the progression, assign a specific number of hard efforts for each time period (e.g., 10 hard efforts lasting 30 to 90 seconds each in a period of 20 minutes), then let the athlete determine the distribution. This approach allows you to control workout density while the athlete controls intensity.

The third option is to use the interval method, which is highly quantifiable and can be made very specific. This is the best method for developing aerobic capacity with minimal sacrifice of explosiveness. As the name implies, this type of training focuses on intervals of work and rest and it allows you to alter the training effect by manipulating the length or intensity of work intervals in relation to rest intervals.

The most demanding and most intense method for training work capacity is the repetition method. Intended to improve economy of effort, this approach alternates high-intensity workload with complete rest to allow for full recovery between repetitions. It involves working in the range of 90 percent to 100 percent of full effort.

Coordinative Abilities

Coordinative abilities involve connecting, linking, and syncing efficiently in order to reduce force, produce force, or stabilize at the appropriate time and in the appropriate plane—all in a matter of milliseconds. These abilities include the following:[1]

- Balance—maintenance of the center of gravity over the base of support (both a static and a dynamic quality)
- Kinesthetic differentiation—ability to feel tension in order to achieve desired movement
- Spatial orientation—control of the body in space
- Reaction to signals—ability to respond quickly to auditory, visual, and kinesthetic cues
- Sense of rhythm—ability to match movement to time
- Synchronization of movements in time—synchronization of unrelated limb movements
- Movement adequacy—ability to choose movements appropriate to the task

Coordinative abilities are closely interrelated and provide the foundation for technical skills; in fact, technical execution is highly dependent on coordinative abilities. Therefore, development of general coordinative abilities should precede development of sport-specific abilities.

Key Training Program Principles

Every coach needs to grasp the key concepts of proper physical development of athletes. These concepts include progression, accumulation, variation, context, overload, recoverability, trainability, and SAID.

Progression

Training should advance from simple to complex, easy to hard, and general to specific. Like athletes themselves, training variables do not all progress at the same rate. To ensure proper progression, define each step and articulate specific goals and objectives for it. Begin with a clear vision of what you want the athlete to achieve or look like at the end of a training program, but remember that progression toward that ultimate objective will probably occur unevenly. In other words, steady progress should be made toward the goal, but it will include plateaus and occasional regression along the way.

In a given training year, as in an athlete's career, progression should involve the following steps:

1. *Basic conditioning.* Systematically develop global motor qualities.
2. *Basic technical model.* Master basic event techniques.
3. *Specific advanced conditioning.* Incorporate advanced training methods designed to meet the individual athlete's needs.
4. *Advanced technical model.* Refine and build on the basic technical model to improve the athlete's repertoire of technical skills.

Accumulation

Adaptation to the stress of training occurs cumulatively. Moreover, if training is approached in proper context, then training effects will accumulate and progress at a predictable rate (for further explanation, see the later section titled Context). At the same time, adaptation to different training demands occurs at different rates; therefore, overall training adaptation is determined by synergistic accumulation of the collective training responses. Remember, then, that one workout cannot make an athlete, but it can break an athlete. Be patient; allow time for training to take effect. Do not get caught up in seeking constant positive reinforcement from workouts, which is ultimately self-defeating.

Variation

In order to ensure continual adaptation, we must constantly vary the training elements of volume, intensity, frequency, and, in some cases, exercise selection. This variation should be planned systematically in order to measure the effect of each variation. If training is not varied, the body adapts quite rapidly, and the training effect is quickly dulled. Lack of variation also puts the athlete at risk of staleness and possible overtraining. The principle of variation, or variability, is grounded in the time course of biological adaptation. That is, the human body's response to training stress is predictable. During the first 7 to 14 days of a new training program, the body adapts quickly, and we often see rapid training gains and technical breakthroughs. After this initial period, however, the athlete typically levels off. Here are some of the variables that can be modified to ensure continued adaptive response:

- *Increase volume.* Volume may be the easiest and simplest variable to manipulate.
- *Increase intensity.* Change the quality of work; this approach is more viable in speed and power events.
- *Change frequency.* Increase or reduce the number of training sessions; also consider using multiple sessions per training day to address different components.
- *Change workout composition.* Consider making a change in rest intervals or in the sequence of exercises (workout monotony can dull the adaptive response).
- *Increase training difficulty.* Change the environment (e.g., from sea level to higher altitude, from moderate to hot climate) or the training structure (e.g., consecutive hard sessions).
- *Take a combined approach.* Any sensible combination of the preceding approaches will ensure continued adaptive response.

Context

Context establishes the relationship of the various components of training in a given system. If something new is incorporated into training, it needs to fit into the context of what is already being done and what is planned. In short, today's training should fit with yesterday's workout and flow into tomorrow's. Perhaps the biggest violation of the principle of context is to train one component (e.g., speed or strength) to the exclusion of all other physical qualities; as previously stated, this approach is fundamentally unsound. It is acceptable to design a program to emphasize a chosen component for a given phase, but this focus should be kept in proportion to other components and approached in the context of the whole training plan.

Overload

In order to progress, athletes must be subjected to loads beyond those to which they already have adapted. Overload is achieved by manipulating the training variables of volume (amount of work), intensity (quality of work), and frequency. Because volume and intensity share a reciprocal relationship, we must be careful about increasing them at the same time.

Recoverability

The ability to recover from workload, both short- and long-term, is crucial to positive adaptation to the training stimulus. If an athlete is unable to recover from training stress, then the load is not appropriate.

Trainability

Great athletes develop a high level of trainability—that is, the ability to train effectively enough to stimulate appropriate adaptation. As we have seen, in order to force adaptation and achieve a positive training response, it is necessary to overload. However, that overload must be related to the athlete's trainability. In other words, it must use a level of work intensity and volume commensurate with the athlete's development in terms of both physical and sport-specific concerns. The more effectively an athlete trains, the better the adaptive response; in turn, improved trainability increases the athlete's chance to compete at a higher level.

SAID

The SAID acronym summarizes a number of key factors: specific (S) adaptation (A) to imposed (I) demands (D). In short, you are what you train to be. As we have seen, training requires more than just doing work. The work must be specific to the individual and directed to fulfill a particular purpose related to a specific sport, event, or position. Training adaptation also depends on the type of overload imposed on the athlete. The highest degree of specificity is that of a particular sport event, and we can use knowledge of the biomechanics needed for that event to design drills and exercises that deliver maximal return for time invested.

COACHING SNAPSHOT

Andrea Hudy, once a college volleyball player, is now recognized as one of the top strength and performance coaches in all of sport. Named Strength Coach of the Year in 2012 by the National Strength and Conditioning Association, Hudy has been particularly lauded for her innovative methods and use of technology while seeking to maximize athletes' physical capabilities for the demands of their sport and position.

Training Program Design

Despite the synergistic relationships among biomotor qualities, they do not all get equal emphasis in a training program. Instead, emphasis varies from athlete to athlete, from event to event, and with the time of year and the stage of the athlete's career. To be sure, all components are trained during all phases of the year, but the proportion changes with training age and the priorities of a particular training period. The key to a good training program is found in progression. Articulate where you have been and where you are going. Then fill the gap with a logical, functional progression that moves forward only when the current step has been mastered.

Adaptation

Along the way, recognize that adaptation time changes with the particular quality being trained and the system being stressed. For instance, in order to achieve optimal adaptive responses, some training tasks require complete recovery before they can be repeated. These activities, which involve high neural demand, address maximum strength, speed, and speed strength. Other training tasks can be performed with incomplete recovery; these activities involve high metabolic demand and address basic endurance, alactic speed endurance, and strength endurance.

Different training components require different amounts of time for adaptation to occur. For instance, flexibility adapts and improves from day to day, strength from week to week, speed from month to month, and work capacity from year to year. We must also remember the principle of reversibility: Without emphasis, each of these qualities declines at the same rate at which it adapts.

Planning

Training should focus on the cumulative training effect. From this perspective, a workout is only one component of a very big picture. Therefore, it is imperative to carefully plan the sequence of training sessions (both from day to day and within a given day) and to project the potential effect of training on subsequent days. Where does today's workout fit within the short-term plan? Within the long-term plan?

Careful consideration of the complementary nature of training units is necessary to achieve positive training adaptations both within and between workouts. Complementary training units are just that—components that work together to enhance each other. For example, the following training units are complementary: speed and strength, strength and elastic strength, endurance and strength endurance, and speed and elastic strength. In fact, the units bear more than a complementary relationship; they should enhance each other to produce an ultimate effect that is synergistic! At the same time, we must bear in mind that certain units are contradictory. This reality can be summed up quite simply, in that activities with high neural demand contradict those with high metabolic demand.

Planning consists of the preparatory work that the coach must do in order to structure training systematically and align it both with chosen themes and objectives and with the athlete's level of conditioning. Here are the basic factors to consider when developing a plan:

- Demands of the chosen sport, position, or event
- Qualities of the individual athlete
- Injury patterns for the chosen sport
- 24-hour athlete concept (i.e., consideration of demands and stresses faced by the athlete outside of training)
- Gender (e.g., strength training more significant during all phases for female athletes)
- Available time frame (e.g., single competition, four-year scholarship)
- Specific plan goals (as detailed, specific, and measurable as possible in order to define the target)
- Athlete's developmental level (e.g., level of fitness and technical development)
- Competitive schedule (especially for high-performance athletes)
- Athlete's ability to recover from the work

Training Cycles and Periods

The long-term plan, or macrocycle, is a general guide that organizes training into periods or phases. A macrocycle can be as long as a year (in a single-periodized year) or as short as four to six months in a double-periodized year. Each macrocycle is divided into periods—typically a preparation period, a competition period, and a transition or recovery period.

The preparatory period includes no competitions. It emphasizes either general work to increase work capacity or specific work directed to address deficiencies. The competition period comes in two forms: competition I and competition II. Competition I focuses on developmental competitions that enable adaptation work based on what was done in a preceding preparatory block. Competition II encompasses the important and crucial competitions of the macrocycle. It focuses on highly specific application work based on what was done in the competition I block. The transition period is devoted to bridge competition and training blocks; thus it is an active period that prevents detraining. The goals here are to regenerate, rehabilitate, and remediate (i.e., address any fundamental deficiencies).

These periods—preparatory, competition, and transition—are divided into mesocycles, each of which is given a general theme and a priority list of major and minor emphases for training. A mesocycle usually lasts four to six weeks and is subdivided into microcycles that last 7 to 14 days each.

Daily training takes a thematic approach in which each day focuses on a very specific theme that determines its direction and content. Themes are carefully chosen to direct the flow of training from day to day, thus enabling the athlete to meet training and competition targets. To ensure a consistent approach, daily themes do not vary significantly from phase to phase.

The Training Session

The individual training session serves as the cornerstone of the training plan. To put it the other way around, the long-term plan consists of a succession of linked individual training sessions (each of which, in turn, is a collection of training units) in pursuit of specific objectives. Therefore, the individual training session should be given the greatest emphasis in planning and execution. In addition, each session must be carefully evaluated, and the following sessions should be adjusted accordingly. It is especially important to have contingency plans ready for individual training sessions to deal with issues like bad weather, injury, or unavailable facilities.

Always approach a given training session within the context of the whole plan. Within that framework, each training session should be given a general theme that is supported by objectives for each component of the training session; therefore, the components should be specific and measurable. A skill-based session should also account for the difficulty of the skill being taught. Of course, any planned session should fit comfortably within the time available for training that day, and the needed equipment should be prepared and checked for proper functioning.

In terms of specific workout organization, it is very helpful to address the following questions:

- What should I do? What equipment do I need?
- When in the workout should I do the activities that demand the highest neural intensity?
- Where am I in the training year? What is the total volume of training?
- What is the number of exercises or drills? What is the work-to-rest ratio?
- What is the planned intra-exercise and intra-segment recovery?

Each session should emphasize either teaching or training. When you emphasize teaching, make sure the skill is performed correctly the first time. Do not hurry; take time to attend to details and to individual needs. The ultimate goal is for athletes to master the skill. The training emphasis, on the other hand, focuses on refinement and therefore involves more repetition. It may not take more time, but it does demand constant attention to detail.

Session design should carefully consider the following elements:

- Progression and sequence
- Training time available and time allocation
- Integration with skill workouts
- Size of the facility or training area relative to the number of athletes training
- Equipment needed and available
- Coaching personnel available
- Number of athletes who will participate in the session

Every workout should include a component geared toward injury prevention, typically during the warm-up. This remedial element should take no more than 10 minutes and should be designed to meet the needs of individual athletes. Session design should also consider intra-workout recovery, which can take the form of self-massage, shaking, and stretching. Also remember that the most basic and practical form of recovery involves intra-workout nutrition in the form of hydration.

As an athlete progresses in training age, multiple workouts per day may be implemented to allow a narrower focus in each workout. Indeed, for elite athletes, multiple daily sessions are not an option but a necessity. Think of each session as flowing or leading into the next and structure the sessions so that the work is compatible. When taking this approach, session length should be limited to no more than 60 minutes with at least three hours between sessions to ensure quality.

Training Program Implementation

In order to implement a comprehensive program of physical preparation, coaches assemble all of the elements discussed in this chapter into an actionable plan. This process involves both assessment and action steps.

Program Assessment

Implementation begins with the types of evaluation discussed in the following subsections. The results are compiled to establish baseline performance standards that can be used to track improvement by each athlete. This longitudinal tracking addresses all physical performance parameters, as well as injury history, and provides both information and motivation along the way.

Sport Demands Analysis Profile

This profile can be used to develop a specific conditioning program that reflects the general demands of the chosen sport, any particular demands for certain positions or events, and any other elements necessary for success in the sport.

Sport Injury Profile

This profile reviews the most common injuries in each sport, how they occur, and the time frame for rehabilitation. Thus it enables the athletic development staff to develop specific prevention programs for each sport.

Comprehensive Athletic Profile

This three-tier process addresses the following elements:

1. Musculoskeletal assessment
2. Functional athletic competencies
3. Performance indicators

Program Action Steps

Program, process, and principles are based on scientific laws, functional movements, and practical experience and are all designed to develop the complete athlete. The training program addresses the needs of individual athletes, team and season goals, and any other objectives that the coaching staff wishes to accomplish in that season or training year. The development of the training program is a team effort involving input from sport coaches, athletic development staff, sports medicine staff, and, of course, the athlete. Program development follows a five-step process.

Step 1: The Sport

Conditioning requirements and game demands vary dramatically from sport to sport. For instance, if the sport is dominated by speed and power, then speed and power should be the dominant themes in the athletic development program. Training can also be affected by an athlete's position or event within the chosen sport. For example, a quarterback has different requirements than an offensive lineman, and those differing demands must be reflected in their training programs in terms of type of strength, movement speed and direction, and specific fitness requirements.

Step 2: The Athlete

The program must also account for the different qualities that each athlete brings to the sport. This kind of tailoring requires information such as speed, work capacity, basic strength, injury history, skill level, and motivation—all of which can be addressed through testing, routine evaluation, and observation.

Step 3: The System

A systematic approach helps all athletes achieve a higher level of performance. A good training system is multifaceted and multidisciplinary and includes the following components:

- Work capacity—ability to handle a workload and recover from doing so
- Speed—ability to perform a specific movement in the shortest period of time with efficiency (perhaps the most important of all athletic qualities)
- Strength—ability to exert force (i.e., measurable strength)
- Power—ability to express force in athletic movements
- Agility, balance, and coordination—taken together, the ability to start, stop, change direction, and control the body

These components are interrelated and can be developed systematically to enable optimum athletic performance.

Step 4: The Plan

No system can be implemented without a thorough plan. The plan should be based on specific, measurable goals and objectives in the context of a definite time frame for achieving them. An effective plan also takes into account the various blocks of the training year and distributes work accordingly. Here are the basic building blocks of a training plan:

- Introduction—short period to orient, teach techniques, and establish a training routine
- Foundation—base period that focuses on increasing work capacity
- Specific preparation—application period in which the base work is applied to the demands of the chosen sport
- Competition—fine-tuning of certain components and stabilization of others
- Peak competition—period of sharpening and peaking
- Transition—active rest phase in which fitness is maintained but the athlete is given a break

Planning should also include a long-term (multiyear) dimension to improve performance throughout the athlete's career.

Step 5: Testing and Evaluation

Testing essentially serves as a system of feedback, checks, and balances that allows the coaches and athletes to measure developmental progress. It establishes a baseline for beginning a training program and setting effective, fact-based goals.

All effective training programs include the following critical elements:

- Strong commitment from all parties to shift from the traditional paradigm of strength and conditioning to an athletic development approach
- Highly qualified staff committed to the program's mission and goals
- Strong staff commitment to continued learning
- Continual willingness to innovate and think creatively

Exercise

Take a few minutes to reflect on the types of movement and biomotor training that are essential and appropriate for athletes in your sport and at your level of participation or competition. Next, identify the key training principles (e.g., frequency, variation) involved in developing those physical abilities and consider what game-like activities your athletes could engage in to develop and build on them. Finally, review the guidelines presented in this chapter for designing and implementing a training program, then chart a sample training session for your athletes during each of the following three macrocycles: preseason, in-season, and off-season.

When you have finished, ask a certified strength and conditioning specialist—preferably, one who is experienced in working with athletes in your sport—to assess how well you did and where you may have missed the mark. Use the specialist's assessment to improve and build on your plan; in addition, try to maintain your relationship with this expert so that you can obtain further support in the future.

_____

_____

_____

_____

_____

_____

_____

_____

_____

_____

_____

_____

_____

_____

_____

_____

_____

_____

Chapter 10

Technical and Tactical Development of Athletes

Damian Farrow

Helping athletes develop technical and tactical skills is a critical role played by all coaches. However, though a great deal has been written about how coaches influence athlete development and conditioning, relatively little has been said about skills coaching. Consequently, in many facets of skill development, coaches rely strongly on tradition rather than scientific evidence. To help fill that gap, this chapter focuses on the science of coaching for skill and tactical development. While much of this content may be considered complementary to current practice, some of the evidence presented here directly challenges established coaching conventions.

Qualitative Analysis of Sport Skills

Coaches constantly assess their athletes' progress, whether during skill corrections in the practice environment or through routine monitoring in practice and competition settings. Whatever the context, it is useful to have a framework to follow. Figure 10.1 presents a particularly useful example known as the integrated model framework.[1] This model defines qualitative analysis as "the systematic observation and introspective judgement of the quality of human movement for the purpose of providing the most appropriate intervention to improve performance."[2] (p. 17)

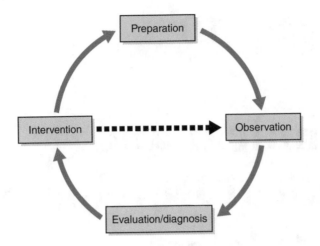

FIGURE 10.1   Integrated model of qualitative analysis.

Adapted by permission from D.V. Knudson and C.S. Morrison, *Qualitative Analysis of Human Movement,* 2nd ed. (Champaign, IL: Human Kinetics, 2002), 9.

As the figure indicates, this model involves integrated steps and is circular in nature; therefore, the quality of the coach's performance at each stage influences the quality of information available for use at the following stage. The model is also nonlinear. For instance, a coach can proceed immediately from intervention back to observation, which is consistent with what typically happens in many coaching sessions. For our purposes here, we focus mostly on the observation stage, with occasional references to the evaluation and intervention stages.

Observation and Evaluation

In the observation stage, the coach systematically gathers appropriate sensory information about performance—primarily through vision, of course, but also through other senses. For instance, information can also be gained from certain sounds, such as the crack of a bat hitting a ball or the thud of a runner's foot contacting the ground. These days, coaches can also employ any number of user-friendly digital tools for analysis (e.g., phone and tablet apps) to replay a skill performance and extract various kinds of quantitative information that may aid their observation and ensuing evaluation. For example, this can range from a coach simply filming an athlete with their phone and watching the movement back in slow motion, to comprehensively analyzing the captured footage frame by frame in an analysis package such as Kinovea (https://www.kinovea.org).

Despite the supporting role that technology can play, providing athletes with timely and accurate feedback depends on the coach's ability to rapidly understand and interpret the available biomechanical information related to skill performance (more on this later). That is, much in the same manner as a high-level tennis player can interpret the movement pattern (kinematics) of an opponent under severe time constraints to aid anticipatory decisions, skilled coaches can also observe performance in a systematic fashion.

Before discussing coaches specifically, however, it is worth considering the skills of another cohort of sport-related people who rely heavily on observational skill—namely, gymnastics judges. Research has found that expert judges were significantly better than novice judges at anticipating upcoming actions and errors regardless of the athlete's skill level.[3] Consequently, when the expert judge correctly anticipated a maneuver, a more accurate score resulted. The researchers proposed that expert judges were better at understanding the available biomechanical information and therefore better at determining the ensuing elements of the movement sequence. As a result, the researchers suggested, the information-processing demands placed on the expert judges were reduced, which enabled them to devote more attention to analyzing the performance.

By extension, these findings suggest that expert coaches may also possess greater ability to understand available biomechanical information and use it to determine changes in movement patterns. In fact, this possibility has been examined in research exploring the observational and diagnostic skills of experienced and novice tennis coaches as they viewed and analyzed a series of tennis serves with the goal of maximizing serve speed.[4] As you might expect, experienced coaches were better at evaluating the serve and identified more technical weaknesses. Analysis of the coaches' visual search behavior found that expert coaches spent more time viewing the torso and thus were more attuned to proximal or center-of-body kinematics, whereas novice coaches spent significantly more time viewing distal elements. More specifically, experienced coaches spent more time viewing the trunk and chest during the preparatory phase and the chest and torso during the follow-through phase, whereas novice coaches prioritized viewing the ball (see figure 10.2). Thus the experienced coaches demonstrated superior ability to use the most salient kinematic information to analyze and interpret overarm movement patterns.

Perhaps it is unsurprising that more experienced coaches exhibit more refined observational skills; after all, they have amassed a larger knowledge base and more observational practice. It may be even more important, however, for a coach to be sensitive to changes in a skill. Here again, we can turn to research evidence related to tennis coaches. Specifically, expert coaches were found to discriminate changes in a server's knee flexion as small as three degrees, whereas novice coaches did not reliably detect a change until six degrees.[5] While such results vary across body locations and also depend on whether the coach is focused

FIGURE 10.2 Differences in the regions fixated on by expert and novice coaches when analyzing a tennis serve.

on a specific joint or on observing technique more globally, this research highlights the incredible perceptual and observational sensitivity that many coaches develop over the course of their career.

At the same time, the coach's observation of small changes in an athlete's technique is not necessarily beneficial to the athlete. For instance, if the coach instructs a pupil to flex the knees another few degrees, what capacity does the athlete have to act on that instruction? In a study of skilled junior tennis players, the results demonstrated that they had considerable control over their movements but executed only some instructions with accuracy greater than the variability normally found in their movement pattern.[5] Given this variability, it was concluded that instructions requiring changes smaller than 5 percent of the target movement are unlikely to be volitionally controllable by athletes.

Nonetheless, the finding that coaches can develop great perceptual sensitivity to changes in a movement pattern is instructive on two levels. First, a considerable amount of the change that a coach observes can be attributed simply to natural repetition-to-repetition variation in an athlete's movement pattern. As a result, coaches need to be circumspect about whether the variation needs correction or can be ignored. Second, although perceptual sensitivity is certainly useful in analyzing and understanding the effectiveness of a movement pattern, the content of the coach's message to an athlete is critically important. In particular, evidence tends to suggest that less precise feedback is more valuable than overly precise instruction (see also the section of this chapter titled Providing Valuable Feedback).[6]

Intervention

The intervention stage begins once the coach has evaluated a performance and decided which key elements to address. Successful intervention depends on many factors. Two of the most influential factors that can be controlled by the coach relate to feedback and manipulation of practice conditions. Handling these two elements effectively helps to ensure that athletes can transfer skills smoothly to competition settings.

Getting the Message Across

As we have seen, skilled coaches can detect small differences in technical execution by their athletes. Converting these observations into effective instruction or feedback is a critical task. Fortunately, this process can be informed by a range of scientific principles (some understood better than others). Rather than provide an exhaustive review of the relevant literature, this section focuses on a couple of contemporary issues (see Schmidt and Wrisberg[7] for a more complete review).

As coaches and athletes both know, successful performance usually occurs when the athlete is *not* focused on skill execution but just "lets it happen." This fact can inform a coach's decision about whether to use internally or externally focused instruction to influence the performer's focus (see Wulf[8] for a detailed review). External focus results when instructions lead the performer to consider the effects of a movement on the environment, such as telling a golfer to "focus on the ball flight." In contrast, internal focus directs the athlete to the motion of the body itself, such as an element of technique (e.g., wrist position when hitting a golf ball). Research indicates that both highly skilled and less skilled performers benefit from instruction that leads to an external focus. The reason? Once a skill is automated—that is, controlled effortlessly and efficiently as a consequence of extensive practice—internal focus can disrupt the automatic process, thereby de-automatizing the skill so that it must be controlled by conscious processing, which is slower and less fluid.[8, 9]

Applying these findings in a practical coaching context may seem daunting given the importance placed on developing technique and the notion that this work requires internal focus. Two potential solutions have been proposed. First, some have argued that attentional focus is dynamic and that in the preparation stage of a movement, attention might be directed internally to an element of technique, such as establishing a good stance and gripping the golf club. However, as the golfer proceeds to the swing phase of the movement, attention is focused externally on the behavior of the ball in flight. For example, if the ball curves hard into a slice, the performer may be positioned too close to the ball. This information can be considered in the evaluation of the hit and attention can then be refocused more internally.[10]

The other solution, which is supported by substantial research with less skilled performers, employs implicit learning techniques (see Masters[9] for a review). This approach uses analogies or visual metaphors to synthesize a number of instructional elements into one vivid piece of information. It has been found effective not only in helping learners execute skills effectively but also in avoiding de-automatization (i.e., "movement reinvestment"). For example, rather than giving multiple setup instructions, a coach might ask a cricket batter to shape the arms and bat to form the numeral 9 or ask a tennis player to adopt the "trophy position" while serving (see figure 10.3). Moreover, research evidence tends to suggest that learners who are given such metaphors can identify and mimic the desired movement pattern without acquiring explicit knowledge of how they are doing it, thus freeing them from the pitfall of "paralysis by analysis."

Providing Valuable Feedback

The value of feedback provided by a coach is affected by many variables. One common way of teasing apart the key issues is to consider feedback timing and content. Traditionally, feedback took the form of verbal information communicated by coaches (and, to a lesser extent, sport scientists) based on their perceptions of performance or on data from a simple device such as a stopwatch. However, technology has evolved sufficiently that athletes and coaches can now access a wide variety of specific measurement tools that provide real-time information about key elements of skilled performance (e.g., coordination, force). These options represent both opportunities and challenges for coaches when viewed in the context of available evidence on giving effective feedback.

Although the influence of feedback on skill learning in sport has been investigated for many years, the research is subject to limitations that make it difficult to generalize to coaching settings. Specifically,

FIGURE 10.3   Example of the "trophy position" for tennis serving.

the majority of feedback guidelines have been derived from laboratory-based experiments involving simple movements performed by novices over a very short intervention period. This experimental context clearly differs from applied sport environments and the needs of coaches and athletes. Furthermore, investigation of modern feedback technologies has only just begun, which means that confirmatory evidence is not readily accessible.

With these caveats in mind, let us consider some of the more robust feedback principles as applied to sport coaching. First, feedback is meant to augment the information already available to the performer. For instance, a basketball shooter doesn't need to be told whether her shot went in or missed, but she may be unaware of how much knee bend she used in taking the shot. Consequently, feedback usually needs to focus on the information that performers cannot see, hear, or feel effectively for themselves. However, as an athlete's skill level develops, his capacity to interpret response-produced (intrinsic) feedback improves, and the coach needs to adjust feedback precision and frequency as appropriate (for more on precision, see the Observation and Evaluation section).

A second key principle holds that the coach must determine which aspects of an athlete's performance require feedback. More specifically, does the potential feedback address what the athlete is focusing on during the practice session? For instance, if a swimmer is focused on improving leg drive during a start but the coach comments on head position, this feedback distracts from what the athlete is trying to resolve. Despite the simplicity of this guideline, it requires constant reinforcement for both coaches and athletes alike.

As for the timing of feedback, the claims made about many modern feedback technologies seem to be at odds with existing research. In particular, many feedback tools are promoted on the basis that they can provide real-time feedback. One emergent technology in this regard consists of interactive garments that provide auditory feedback about angular displacement (see figure 10.4). While such devices may seem appealing, the search for empirical evidence to support their use remains in its infancy; moreover, earlier feedback literature suggests that the real-time nature of the feedback provided by these devices may be counterproductive for learning (e.g., guidance hypothesis).[11]

FIGURE 10.4 Example of an interactive garment that provides a netball shooter with feedback about joint angles during the shooting action.

The value of any augmented feedback whether it is technologically derived or from a coach observation is likely affected largely by the relative difficulty of learning the chosen skill and the availability and salience of the intrinsic information available to the athlete. For example, when learning a complex skill with response-produced feedback that is hard to interpret (e.g., a swim turn), the relative value of augmented feedback may be greater than it would be for a skill with more accessible feedback (e.g., ball flight after a golf hit).

COACHING SNAPSHOT

Baylor track-and-field coaching legend **Clyde Hart**, sometimes referred to as the King of Quarter-Miler U. because of his particular expertise in teaching and training champion 400-meter sprinters and 4x400 relay teams, appreciated more than most the significance of perfect technique in a sport where the slightest error can mean the difference between first and worst. Hart, who coached until he was 85, did so with passion and compassion to help his athletes succeed in their athletic careers and lives and subscribed to a favorite saying, *"Don't count days, make days count."*

Thus we likely need to establish guidelines for practitioners who wish to use real-time feedback. For instance, current research on cyclical tasks (e.g., running, cycling, swimming) shows that real-time concurrent feedback can improve learning because the performer can use the feedback in the next cycle of the movement. However, this benefit may not apply to a discrete skill (e.g., golf shot) in which the brevity of the movement reduces the athlete's ability to influence the skill execution of the current trial. In either case, the coach needs to observe the athlete's progression and attune the athlete to the most salient feedback sources, whether augmented or intrinsic to the athlete (see Phillips, Farrow, Ball, and Helmer[12] and Magill and Anderson[13] for reviews).

Creating Representative Practice

Coaches can choose from a wide variety of practice approaches. The selection of practice type is influenced by a range of factors, including the nature of the skill (technical or tactical), the complexity of the skill, the specific needs of the athlete (e.g., learning or confidence), the stage of athlete development, and the proximity of the practice to a competition. Of course, the ultimate goal of any practice intervention is to develop a skill or one of its component parts so that it translates to improved performance in competition (see Davids, Araújo, Vilar, Renshaw, and Pinder[14] for a review).

Transfer of skills from practice to performance is best achieved through "representative practice," or practice that provides opportunities for athletes to identify and perform functional skills based on the conditions encountered in the performance environment (e.g., the perceptual information available). Current evidence shows that athletes change their movement behaviors during nonrepresentative tasks,[15, 16] thereby effectively practicing something other than the intended skill. For example, the movement behavior of elite springboard divers was compared in dry-land skill drills (in a gymnastics-type setting) and in the usual aquatic environment (see figure 10.5).[15] Due to the nature of the dry-land environment, some aspects of diving skill were practiced in parts rather than as whole movements. When the dry-land and aquatic behaviors were subjected to biomechanical analysis, differences were found in how the skills were performed. For instance, in the aquatic practice, the athletes used greater step lengths, jump heights, and board depressions than they did in the supposedly same movement on dry land.

Examples abound in which coaches seeking to simplify a skill inadvertently change the nature of the skill so much that it no longer transfers effectively to the performance setting. For instance, in cricket, practicing batting against a projection machine (a less representative approach) rather than a live bowler (more representative) leads to significant changes in batting technique and timing; specifically, batters tend to adopt a more defensive, back-footed approach against the batting machine.[16]

FIGURE 10.5 Dry-boards and trampolines in the Australian Institute of Sport (AIS) dry-land training facility.

© Sian Barris. Used with permission. Reprinted from S. Barris, K. Davids, and D. Farrow, "Representative Learning Design in Springboard Diving: Is Dry-Land Training Representative of a Pool Dive?" *European Journal of Sport Science* 13, no. 6 (2013): 638-645.

Thus, in order to maximize skill transfer to performance, both intuitive logic and scientific evidence support the use of representative practice conditions—that is, simulations as close as possible to the typical competitive setting. However, this approach is not always found in current coaching practices. Indeed, a number of studies have broadly considered the representativeness of practice activities in a number of sports and found that "representative practice" is underused by coaches.[17-19] In fact, more than two-thirds of the observed total practice time was spent in low-representative activities, regardless of the competitive level or sport being observed.

The reason for this disparity is relatively unexplored, but we can consider a range of possible explanations. One potential issue stems from the difficulty that coaches (and scientists!) face in determining when a skill has been learned. That is, has the athlete made a permanent change in the technical or tactical skill being practiced, or is the improvement somewhat transient; in other words, do successful executions appear in some repetitions of the skill but disappear in others? Furthermore, it is not always easy to recognize what constitutes a successful skill execution that is indicative of skill learning. For instance, a skillful performance might reflect a player's capacity to adapt to changing constraints, and adaptability might be the key metric for defining skill learning. Or a coach might want to see consistency in a performance outcome (e.g., 80 percent accuracy from the basketball free throw line).

Understanding whether an athlete is in a learning mode and consequently engaging in trial-and-error practice or a performance mode where more consistent skill execution is expected can influence how a coach interprets the quality of a given practice activity. Imagine a coach who feels that an athlete's learning progress is too slow—for instance, that the athlete is engaging in too much trial and error (even though this is the usual course of learning). In response, the coach may simplify the practice in order to generate what appears to be learning or improvement. Yet in doing so, the coach may make the practice less representative. As a consequence, the observable practice performance of the athlete may seem to improve (e.g., hitting a target more consistently), but this type of short-term progress is usually not extended into a more permanent change in skill.

The scarcity of representative practice may also relate to the broader messaging to which coaches are exposed in relation to skill practice. Recent times have seen a focus on the quantity (i.e., volume) of practice rather than on the quality necessary to attain high levels of skill performance. Although the scientific literature is relatively clear on the importance of well-structured quantity and quality, this message seems to have been misconstrued in some of the more accessible general information available to coaches. This misconstrual is consequential because overfocusing on volume tends to oversimplify practice design in order to allow the desired volume to be completed. For example, large blocks of basketball free throws may be completed with little separation between practice attempts, and golf practice may be completed mostly on a practice range that lacks the environmental complexity of a full course. In both instances, the sheer volume of practice completed leads to some degree of performance improvement, but the legacy of this approach is relatively weak due to its low representativeness.

Testing Skill Progression

While a number of methods are used to assess skill learning in the scientific domain, the most effective methods in sport settings are retention testing, transfer testing, and dual-task testing (see Schmidt and Wrisberg[7] for a more detailed review). Retention testing requires that the skill be assessed after a period without practice, which can be quite impractical in settings where athletes are often constantly practicing their skills. Where practical, however, this approach is used to determine how well established a skill change has become when not directly influenced by short-term factors that might inflate the athlete's apparent skill level (e.g., having a block of practice immediately before a test). Thus it can help coaches make more conclusive decisions about skill development. Quite often, at the end of a training block, the coaching assessment is overly positive, and we often hear comments such as "they picked up the skill really well" or "they mastered that component." In reality, such conclusions should be drawn only after the effects of intensive practice have dissipated—hence the value of a retention test.

Transfer testing also assesses learning and is a very common form of assessment in sport. As the name suggests, this approach tests whether the skill performance holds up when transferred to a new context or different conditions. The most prevalent method is simply to use the weekly game performance as the ultimate measure of transfer. This method is particularly useful if this assessment is based on a combination of objective qualitative and quantitative measures. At the same time, coaches are understandably reluctant to rely only on assessing players in a competitive environment, where skill performance may be influenced by a wide range of factors. In this case, coaches can develop a representative game or activity within the training context to assess whether the skill has been learned.

The third type of skill assessment, which is also useful in the practice context, is known as a dual-task test. This approach is based on the assumption that as a skill develops, an athlete can devote less conscious attention to executing it. With this in mind, a dual-task test requires the athlete to perform the skill while also completing a secondary task. Such a test can be achieved in many and varied ways. For instance, the athlete might be asked to count backward in threes from one hundred, talking aloud, while performing the skill of interest. The logic underlying the test posits that if the primary skill (e.g., basketball free throw) has progressed into a more permanently developed pattern, then the player will have spare attentional capacity to use on counting backward. If the player cannot maintain the skill performance level while counting backward, then the coach knows that the skill requires further development. Because the aim is simply to demand the athlete's attention, any number of other secondary tasks could be used (e.g., rhyming words, basic math sums).

Dual-task testing can also be made sport specific. For instance, a skill that has generally been practiced only in an isolated context, with focus on technical elements, might be embedded into a task that also requires a decision-making focus, such as a soccer player who has been practicing their dribbling skills around cones may now have to practice dribbling around an opponent. In this way, the coach can assess whether the technique holds up under the additional demand to make a good decision.

COACHING SNAPSHOT

Synchronized swimming coach **Mayuko Fujiki** was a child prodigy in her sport, representing Japan at the Junior World Championships when she was only 14 years old. After finishing her competitive career as an athlete, Fujiki used her keen knowledge of techniques, exceptional capabilities as a choreographer, and teaching skills to become a very successful coach internationally.

Creating Practice Conditions That Promote Skill Acquisition

The most influential practice elements for skill acquisition are repetition and variability. Although both factors are necessary, the number of practice repetitions often lies beyond the coach's control because it depends largely on time and availability at the junior levels and is heavily influenced by physical conditioning in high-performance settings. Consequently, this section focuses on how to organize practice most effectively in order to enable a given volume and thereby enhance skill acquisition. In other words, how can we practice smart?

The answer is to manipulate practice variability. Whether the skill is technical and performed in a closed environment or tactical and performed in an open environment, the message remains consistent: Variable practice experiences lead to more effective skill acquisition. The concept and value of practice variability can be explained by multiple theoretical positions, but the practical outcomes are relatively similar from a coaching perspective.[20] In essence, skill acquisition is influenced considerably by the degree to which the coach organizes the available practice repetitions to create appropriate variability for the learner.

One reason offered for the benefits of practice variability is that it demands greater mental effort from the athlete. As with many skills, the more effort one puts in, the more benefit one gains. Perhaps the most-detailed and best-researched method of organizing practice variability is to use either random or blocked practice (see Patterson and Lee[21] for a review). Random practice involves alternating between two or more skills or variations on each practice attempt. For example, a tennis player hits one serve followed by one volley and then repeats this process in some fashion—for instance, serve, serve, volley, serve, volley, volley, and so on. In other words, while the overall volume of each skill is kept constant, the order in which they are practiced is relatively random.

Blocked practice marks the other extreme on a continuum because it involves practicing one skill continuously for a block of practice attempts before practicing another skill. In our current example, all serve repetitions would be completed before performing volley repetitions. Research has demonstrated that blocked practice leads to better performance of skills in the short term than does random practice. This finding seems to be consistent with many coaches' perceptions when asked which approach would lead to better skill performance (an important point that will be revisited). The reason typically suggested is that blocked practice allows a player to get into the "groove" while practicing a skill.

However, when it comes to longevity or permanency, as well as transfer to competition settings, random practice produces improved retention or learning of the skill. Therefore, simply by reorganizing the distribution of practice trials of two different skills to be more random (i.e., variable), coaches can generate different rates and effectiveness of skill acquisition.

This advantage of random practice is thought to derive from the fact that blocked practice requires the athlete to exert mental effort in order to shift focus from one skill to the other more frequently.

Another example of practice that embraces the concept of variability (albeit from a very different theoretical philosophy) has been termed *differencial learning* (in this usage, *differencial* is deliberately misspelled to stress the importance of differences).[22] In simple terms, this approach argues that skill learning in sport can benefit from adding "noise" to skill practice in the form of random, variable, and irrelevant movement components. For example, in an experiment aimed at improving the start performance of speed skaters, a differencial learning group practiced the start under a wide variety of repetition conditions, such as holding the skates parallel to the left with the hips to the front, positioning two hands on the ice with the skates in a V shape, holding the arms beside the body and making a jump before the start, placing all the weight onto the hind leg with the hips to the back, and stepping to the left before the start. Each of the 60 starts completed was practiced in a slightly different way.[23]

This practice approach may aid skilled performance and learning by forcing the learner to explore the stability of functional (preferred) coordination patterns. In other words, the learner is presented with a wide variety of techniques that may extend the range of possible ways in which the chosen skill may be performed.

The logic behind differencial learning is predicated on previous research demonstrating that even the highly practiced skills of elite athletes are never performed in the same way twice.[24] Rather, skills are always being performed in a slightly different manner due to the nature of our nervous system control and the dynamic nature of sport settings; therefore it is suggested that such a practice approach helps the athlete find new movement solutions as required.[25] In short, the learner is confronted with significant differences between two consecutive practice trials, which, through the process of differencial learning, encourages exploration and pickup of information about the stability of a skill. This learning, in turn, may enhance performance of the skill in competitive settings.[23] This approach is argued to be analogous to another theorist's mantra that practice should take the form of "repetition without repetition."[26]

Whichever theoretical perspective is adopted, the message for coaches is relatively straightforward: Providing variation in the practice setting is likely to enhance skill acquisition and performance. In contrast, allowing an athlete to try performing a skill in exactly the same manner in repetition after repetition does not. This view often contradicts both the coach's perception of how a skill is developing in a given practice session and the perception of athletes who see value in trying to repeat the same skill in exactly the same way.

At this point, we need to consider the art of coaching. If the performer is a skilled athlete who is low in confidence, or a beginner who is just trying to assemble a coordinated movement pattern, then it may be appropriate to provide practice conditions that are less variable. This approach allows the learner to get an idea of the movement and establish a basic movement pattern (and some confidence) before engaging in more variable practice conditions. In simple terms, the beginning learner brings enough variability to the setting that the coach doesn't need to add additional variability. To the contrary, early learning requires opportunities to reinforce desirable outcomes without the interference of having to change or adapt. This application seems logical if we consider the amount of mental effort that a beginner applies to learning a new skill. However, once a basic movement pattern has been established, the learner should then be exposed to greater practice variability.

Thus practices can be placed on a continuum, and different levels of demand or challenge can be applied to meet the needs of the athlete or coach in a specific circumstance (see table 10.1). The process of finding the sweet spot can be aided by identifying the challenge point, where

TABLE 10.1 Adjusting Practice Interference to Suit Skill Level in Field Hockey

Drill or activity name	Description	Level of mental effort
Block trials	Instead of switching from skill to skill after one practice repetition, do a small block of each (e.g., five hits, then five dribbles).	Low to moderate
Variable practice	Instead of switching between two totally different skills, practice variations of one skill (e.g., hit and then lift).	Moderate
Win shift—lose stay (around the world)	Goal-scoring practice: A player who scores a goal *wins and shifts* onto a different hit location. A player who doesn't score a goal *loses and stays* in place to repeat the same shot on goal.	Player-generated difficulty based on current skill level
Skill circuits	Rather than counting practice repetitions, use time—for instance, three min of practice at four stations, each focused on a different skill (e.g., goal hits, trapping, agility, lifted hits).	Moderate depending on amount of time and number of stations in circuit
Differencial learning	Practice the goal hit using a different starting posture on each repetition (e.g., one-hand hit, with step, without step, high-grip, low-grip).	N/A
Practice–rest	The secret to making every repetition count is to force the player to "forget" the previous repetition (e.g., intervening between hits at goal to "have a chat" about an unrelated issue).	Moderate

Adapted by permission from D. Farrow, "Teaching Sport Skills," in *Coaching Excellence*, edited by F. Pyke (Champaign, IL: Human Kinetics, 2013), 171-184.

practice is neither too demanding nor too undemanding—but just demanding enough.[27, 28]

Technical and Tactical Skill Instruction

Technical and tactical skill development are often separated, both in how they are discussed and in how they are practiced. However, when it comes to skill practice, the same key messages apply equally to both technical and tactical skill development. These messages relate to the practice environment, game awareness, and decision making.

Practice Environment

Whenever athletes perform a technical skill, they do so in an environment rich with information that helps them properly control the timing and execution of the skill. Although the amount and type of information may vary from one context to another, the key point for coaches is to understand the importance of maintaining the link between perceptual information and action.

A practice environment that is truly representative of the competitive setting does more than merely replicate the appropriate perceptual information.[14, 29] For instance, an athlete's overall performance also depends on technical and tactical execution of key skills and game plan, as well as the athlete's intentionality or purposefulness in execution and the contextual changes experienced in the competition environment.[14, 29] Accordingly, coaches need to consider each of these factors in determining how representative a given practice context is of the performance context.

For example, let us consider an observational analysis of international-level field hockey players who were practicing field goal shooting.[30] An analysis tool was developed to assess the representativeness of the kinds of practice deemed most important in replicating the performance environment. Practice representativeness was assessed in relation to pre-shot play, position in the shooting circle, number of players involved, types of shot, opportunities for decision making, and defensive role of attackers (see table 10.2). These criteria were useful in assessing the representativeness of field-goal-shooting activities in relation to the perceptual, technical and tactical, and contextual aspects of the performance context. While this observational tool wasn't scientifically validated and was developed for the specific purpose of goal-shooting practice in field hockey, it illustrates how this type of tool can be applied to numerous sport contexts.

This research revealed that the practice conditions established by this cohort of senior international coaches was highly representative and typically relied on the use of small-sided games. This arrangement provided opportunities for players to practice and improve their tactical

TABLE 10.2 An Example of a Representative Design Checklist for Field Goal Shooting in Hockey

Pre-shot play	Play before the actual shot needed to include aspects of pre-shot qualities; e.g., fast break, general team build up, turn-over of possession or break down in penalty corner set play.
Position in the shooting circle	Opportunities for shots from both the outer and inner areas of the scoring-circle.
Number of players involved	There needed to be different force ratios of attackers to defenders and there had to be at least two strikers and defenders plus the goalkeeper.
Types of shot	The practice structure constraints needed to demand different types of shots; e.g., forehand, reverse, deflection.
Decision making	The structure needed to have an element of free-play; i.e., players could change decisions about shots, type of play, and allow for play to continue if the initial attack was unresolved. There needed to be an opportunity for two or three shots.
Defense role	The defense needed to play the ball out of the scoring area thus providing an opportunity for the attackers to regain possession and initiate another attack.

Reprinted from D.G. Slade, "Do the Structures Used by International Hockey Coaches for Practising Field-Goal Shooting Reflect Game Centred Learning within a Representative Learning Design?" *International Journal of Sports Science & Coaching* 10, no. 4 (2015): 655-668, by permission of SAGE Publications, Ltd.

understanding and decision making in competition-like simulations. This approach is consistent with research in soccer, where the representativeness of basic practice drills was found to be improved by including a greater number of possibilities for action, such as the number of passing options available to a player.[31]

Game Awareness and Decision Making

Developing game awareness for team invasion sports requires particular attention. The most notable difference between these sports and many sports focused on individual skill (e.g., gymnastics, swimming) is the premium placed on good decision making. For example, soccer players must not only execute core skills (e.g., kicking) but also make decisions such as how to distribute the ball and where to run in order to defend against an attack by the opposition. Thus decision making requires the capacity to select the correct option at the right time from a range of possibilities.[32] In fact, on many occasions, a player must make such a decision before the ball is hit or kicked. Thus we must give special consideration to the question of how to practice this ability.

We can begin by considering what is known about how expert decision makers developed their skills. Happily, a robust body of research has examined decision-making skill by interviewing athletes who were elite decision makers from a variety of team sports. It is argued that common approaches or practice contexts shared by these athletes in their developmental years might highlight the nature of the practice that coaches should consider when seeking to develop decision-making skill. The main findings from a range of research indicated that expert decision makers could be identified by the following factors:

- They tended to have played or sampled a range of sports in their junior years. In fact, the number of sports participated in was inversely related to the number of practice hours required to become an expert player. For example, one Australian netball player reported engaging in only 600 hours of netball-specific practice before being selected for the Australian team.[33] Meanwhile, she participated in 14 other sports as a junior!

- The key is not just participating in any sport. Rather, participating in sports that are conceptually similar to the preferred one is more likely to enable the transfer of the pattern recognition skills thought to support superior decision making.[34] For example, expert decision makers in Australian football were found to participate in more secondary invasion sports than did nonexpert decision makers, such as soccer, hockey, and, in particular, basketball.

- Skilled decision makers perform better than lesser-skilled decision makers in pattern recognition skills—that is, the capacity to recognize the structure of a commonly occurring tactical situation (e.g., zone defense in basketball). It is thought that this capacity helps players forecast a pattern's likely outcome and thereby anticipate where to move in order to intercept or receive a pass or simply make a better choice of position off the ball.

These findings provide useful direction for coaches who want to help their players develop decision-making skills. First, consistent with this chapter's key message, practice must be representative. If a coach designs practices devoid of patterns that require players to solve problems, then players are unable to develop pattern recognition or awareness skills. Unfortunately, coaches often remove decision-making opportunities from team drills and practices in an effort to develop a particular playing style or establish a preferred pattern of ball movement. In doing so, they develop players who are unable to move the ball as desired when faced with choices they have not experienced or practiced in training. Examples of this type of training can be found in sports such as basketball, netball, and Australian football, where a predefined ball movement pattern is established and players are directed to work the ball from cone to cone around the court or field in the absence of defenders.

Many coaches believe this "system training" is useful in establishing a desired style of play but then express concern when players are unable to run the same system in a competitive situation because the opposition destabilizes the pattern. Clearly, then, the early introduction of defenders in the practice context is a critical step. The challenge for coaches is to determine the appropriate level of challenge for their players. For instance, the defenders might be outnumbered, limited to defending only a certain part of the playing area, or barred from applying full pressure to the ball handler. The important point is that players need to be forced to solve problems during training through the proactive use of visual scanning, pattern recognition, and decision-making skills in order to be able to transfer their training to game contexts.

In order to improve players' decision-making skills, coaches can manipulate a multitude of factors during practice sessions, thereby altering the decision-making complexity. Here are a few examples:

- *Speed of play.* Increasing game speed—in terms of ball or player movement or both—usually increases game complexity.

- *Player density.* Complexity can also be increased by increasing player density, either around the ball carrier or where the ball carrier intends to distribute the ball.

- *Time available to dispose of ball.* Reducing the time available generally increases complexity (though it could be argued that complexity is sometimes reduced when a situation demands a particularly fast response).

- *Similarity to other situations encountered.* The more similar two situations appear to be, the more difficult it is to resolve their differences and the associated decision-making options.

- *Number of decision-making choices available.* More choices available means greater decision-making complexity.

- *Prohibition of verbal (voice) communication.* Preventing players from calling for the ball or telling teammates what to do increases the need to visually scan the environment, which in turn increases the decision-making challenge.

- *Structured versus unstructured play.* Unstructured play can be more difficult to read than structured situations that have been experienced more often.

Small-sided games have been successfully used to highlight and exaggerate particular facets of game awareness. In fact, a considerable body of research has examined the influence of small-sided games and their degree of representativeness in relation to actual game contexts. In particular, research has explored how to resize the playing area (usually by making it smaller) and how many players are required to elicit the game-like demands in terms of physiological and technical or tactical elements.[35-37] For example, research in basketball and soccer found that small-sided games with more players increased the percentage of successful passes and decreased the number of technical actions (passes and dribbles).[37, 38] The number of technical actions completed was also decreased by small-sided games with more playing area per player.[37, 39] Thus, while the exact scaling of a small-sided game must reflect the full equivalent of the specific sport, the number of players and the resultant player density both affect game dynamics and mediate how effective a small-sided game will be in promoting technical and tactical skill transfer to performance in competition.

Exercise

Skill acquisition is enhanced by engaging in practice that requires athletes to make decisions in challenging activities associated with the sport. Some of those activities may, and should, be more structured—probably like most of your current practice drills. But the benefits of unstructured activities, or play, are also crucial to athletes' skill learning and development in sports that require game awareness and immediate decision making. Do you promote skill development by offering your athletes sufficient opportunities in practice to engage in activities (other than full-sides team scrimmages) in which they must anticipate, recognize, decide, and execute techniques and tactics in an instant?

Identify two skills that are essential for success in your sport and consider how you help your athletes learn and practice them. For both skills, list the structured and unstructured activities that you offer to your athletes.

Skill 1 _____

Structured

    1.

    2.

    3.

    4.

Unstructured

    1.

    2.

    3.

    4.

Skill 2 _____

Structured

    1.

    2.

    3.

    4.

Unstructured

    1.

    2.

    3.

    4.

If, like most coaches, your structured practice activities far outnumber your unstructured ones, consider options for bringing these two approaches more into balance.

From International Council for Coaching Excellence, *Sport Coaches' Handbook*, eds. D. Gould and C. Mallett. (Champaign, IL: Human Kinetics, 2021).

Chapter 11

Career Decision Making in Coaching

William Taylor and Mike Sheridan

In recent years, both the role of the coach and the profile of coaching have grown. As a result, the importance of professional, informed coaches who are motivated and well qualified has been increasingly recognized by governments, national sporting bodies and agencies, professional teams, regional and local sport clubs, school sport associations, and global organizations such as the International Council for Coaching Excellence.[1, 2] Coaches not only enhance playing standards but also enable high-quality experiences for performers at all levels, thus increasing participation and adherence rates.

The importance now placed on high-quality coaching has increased coaches' opportunities for employment and deployment throughout the world. Indeed, coaches are becoming part of the globalization of sporting practices. As a result, they need to be able to respond effectively to demands for their services and expertise, wherever those demands may originate. This increasing range of opportunities has led many coaches to be more active in planning and developing their career paths. Whether you are considering the coaching profession or already involved in it, this chapter will help you plan the next steps in launching or advancing your career.

Coach Preparation and Development

Until recently, the recruitment process for coaching has been a rather insular affair. At least on the surface, the move from being an athlete to becoming a coach seems to follow an intuitive logic, and in some sports it has worked for a number of former athletes. Approval of this transition is often based on the notion that "those who can (or could), do." In this case, possessing athletic skill and experience is viewed as qualifying an individual to work with those who need to learn. Moreover, by receiving coaching for hundreds of hours during their own playing years, former athletes have effectively served an observational apprenticeship in coaching.[3] In addition, their successful playing career allows them to enter coaching with a degree of respect, admiration, and at least short-term credibility among their athletes. This experience-based perspective may also grant other advantages, such as empathizing with a slumping athlete and offering players firsthand insights about the competitive arena.

However, though a playing career equips ex-athletes with some of the knowledge required by any aspiring coach, overemphasis on playing experience diminishes the significance of the pedagogical, interpersonal, and management skills required for effective coaching. In addition, some of the individual qualities associated with being an elite athlete—such as single-mindedness and even ruthlessness—do not necessarily mesh with being an inclusive, thoughtful, and progressive coach. Thus, experience as an athlete can bring both benefits and baggage, and it is a mistake to view playing experience as the primary qualification for becoming a coach.

Indeed, coaching is essentially an educational and management endeavor. Beyond teaching athletes and helping them develop sport skills and tactics, coaches also shape them into effective learners, decision makers, and valued team members. In other words, coaches are increasingly called on to fulfill the claims made about the moral and personal worth of sport and to embed this work into their practice.[4] Therefore, coaches need knowledge and competence in a number of areas in order to succeed; they also need both formal education and hands-on experience in learning their craft. Fortunately, multiple pathways are available for becoming a coach (see the sidebar titled Entry Into Coaching).

Although differing stages of development apply across the world, the coaching sector is now generally characterized by a discernible move toward professionalization.[2, 5-7] This trend is accompanied by increases in the expected qualifications and by the appearance of various certification structures and schemes for coach education informed by best practices and evidence-based research.[8] These developments have raised the standard and advanced the practice of coach education.

In some countries, these developments are not new. For example, in some parts of Europe, professional coaches are required to hold a college degree and obtain a license, and standards and coach education programs are overseen by central sporting agencies. In recent years, the movement toward more stringent coaching qualifications has advanced in the United Kingdom, which now operates a nationwide four-level educational system across most sports.[9] However, even though this development has increased the standard of coach education and practice in the

Entry Into Coaching: Three Common Pathways

The Accidental Coach

Bunny had always wanted her children to be active in sport. More specifically, she had wanted the same positive outcomes for John and Sissy that she had gained from her 11 years of playing volleyball at the district and state levels. Thus she was happy when both kids took readily to the game; in fact, from the age of five or six, they spent most of their summer days hitting a ball over a net in front of their house. Later, in their early teens, they joined a local volleyball club, and Bunny drove them to games and training sessions and watched from the parents' bench with pride. Then, one evening, after a casual conversation with the head coach, Bunny found herself taking on the assistant coach's role with the under-14 squad, for which she led occasional practice sessions and helped with preseason fitness training. Within two more years, she was volunteering on three or four nights per week and serving as head coach for the under-18 girls. Thus, Bunny had arrived as a supportive parent and ended up taking on a demanding position as head coach. She had not planned for this outcome; rather, in her words, it had "just crept up on her."

Forced Retirement

For Dave, ice hockey was life. It was all he had wanted to do ever since he could remember. But now the team doctor was saying that Dave's shoulder operation had failed and his playing days were over. Dave was sorely disappointed yet determined to stay in the game, and at 26 years old he felt that he had much more to give to the sport; as a result, he hung around the club for the rest of the season. However, when his former teammates talked about last night's game or made plans for the upcoming playoffs, he felt ill at ease and excluded. After thinking it over, Dave decided that coaching was the next best thing to playing, and his professional experience allowed him to find a junior coaching role with a lower-league team. It was not the same as playing, but it meant that he could stay involved in the game.

Planning to Be a Coach

Mielena had been inspired by her high school coach and her physical education teacher to prepare for a career of helping players develop to their full potential. Now, after a few years of hard work, she was well positioned to seek a full-time coaching role. Her degree in human movement and pedagogy was valued in the field, and her ability to relate to young elite swimmers made her popular with parents, athletes, and others in the sport. Having done a yearlong internship with a university swim team, she now looked forward to learning from senior coaching staff and gaining experience as a coach in her own right.

participating sports, coaches can still advertise and operate in the UK without such qualifications.

Still, for people who want to coach, these developments mean that the days of needing only a hat and a whistle are coming to an end. Broadly speaking, coach education is increasingly expected in one form or another. However, formal education is not enough. The latest research shows that coach learners need to "get their hands dirty" by seeing program delivery and other coaching competencies firsthand. They also need mentors to help guide them along the way. Learning in the coaching context does not just happen; rather, it should be accompanied by opportunities to reflect, experiment, and challenge what is observed in any particular workplace.

In fact, the learning pathways that enable an aspiring coach to develop expertise are likely to take a variety of forms. Certain opportunities aid the development of certain skills, whereas other competencies require different settings. Therefore, coaches who seek expertise in their craft need to become effective and proactive learners and seek out diverse opportunities not only to enhance their current practice but also to help them understand the possible demands involved in higher-level coaching positions.

The skill set expected of coaches today bears little resemblance to that of 30 years ago. In addition to advancements in sport science and training theory, we now have a battery of instruments and data-recording devices that can provide a bewildering amount of information. Session plans and seasonal targets are computer generated, and coaches at the performance level make decisions based on information such as an athlete's fat percentages, their heart rate profiles, and game tackle and ball retention quotas.

In addition, coaches are now required to curate an effective public image and relate in a positive manner with parents, support staff, members of the media, sponsors, and sport officials. Those who work in youth coaching are also encouraged to be particularly mindful of the social and personal responsibilities inherent in the role of a coach. Indeed, coaches now take on parental, mentoring, and other influential roles in many young people's lives through the sport experience.[10] Moreover, coaches are expected not only to do more but also to know more. The increased focus on researching the science of coaching means that coaches who are not effective learners are likely to be left standing still—and not serving as examples of best practice.

The notion of long-term coach development acknowledges that coaches work in dynamic and fluid environments where staying current, employable, and ahead of the game requires them to commit to lifelong learning. In doing so, coaches should view continuous professional development and continuous professional education as fundamental parts of their effort to maintain high standards. At the same time, developers of coach education programs now provide opportunities that are not necessarily related to the next level of award or certification but are intended instead to enhance existing practice and maintain high standards. These horizontal learning opportunities take a variety of forms—for instance, reading professional journals; attending conferences, updating events, and developmental workshops; and participating in web seminars, mentoring relationships, and communities of practice.

These relatively informal opportunities have moved coach learning away from being available only through attendance at the next level of award—that is, away from vertical learning, often in a formal setting—and toward modes that are more individualized, contextual, and readily available. This opening up of learning pathways has been accompanied by the use of educational logbooks. Educational logbooks provide opportunities for coaches to document their instructional experiences, personal reflections, and other important information related to their day-to-day coaching. These logbooks can be used to display the currency of the coach and may help when applying for a coaching position by demonstrating that one is up to date in the field and engaged in long-term learning. In fact, it is often required by employers and certifying agencies.

In summary, long-term coach development involves the following key elements:

1. Participation in appropriate levels of formal coach education and certification
2. Understanding the expanded duties of a coach and seeking both formal and informal educational opportunities to gain the needed knowledge
3. Identifying a mentor, peer learning group, or both to provide opportunities for regular reflection on coaching experiences

Job Considerations

Opportunities to enter the coaching profession vary as widely as the range of reasons that people choose to coach. For example, a study of 50 high school coaches from various sports in the United States found that more than half had decided to coach before entering college.[11] Participants in the study reported making decisions about their coaching career based on personal characteristics, personal experiences in sport, devotion to sport, and desire to work with young people. Many of them had participated in organized youth and high school athletics (usually as multisport athletes) and therefore had observed coaches firsthand. Similarly, another study found that "successful coaches accumulate thousands of hours of 'pre-coaching' experience while competing in sport as athletes."[12 (p. 121)]

Career Development

Career development is essential to success, both for coaches and for their teams and organizations. However, because sport coaching careers are multifaceted and often nonlinear, it takes some effort to fully understand the nature of the field.[13 (p. 479)] In addition, it is often unclear who should be responsible for a coach's career advancement, and the reality is that few organizations take responsibility for ongoing systematic development of coaches. As a result, it often falls to coaches themselves to figure out what is—and what is not—important in order for them to improve.[13]

One potential resource can be found in the national coaching standards developed by experts in coaching science in the United States.[1, 14] It is not at all clear, however, that these standards are widely used by coaches to assess their proficiency. Instead, they are used mostly by coaching educators to evaluate coaching education programs and provide a systematic framework for curriculums based on what experts agree to be the minimal coaching competencies.

Meanwhile, those in the profession itself often invoke the image of coaching as a family. Indeed, it is not uncommon for coaches to enter the profession because family members were also involved in coaching. Among the many examples at all levels of sport, New England Patriots head coach Bill Belichick was inspired by his father, Steve, who coached football at Navy for 33 years. In turn, Bill's son is also a Patriots coach, and his daughter coaches NCAA lacrosse. In other examples, Buddy Ryan was a longtime NFL coach whose lead was followed by sons Pat and Rex, and brothers Jim and John Harbaugh faced each other as head coaches in Super Bowl XLVII after seeing their father, Jack, coach at the high school and college levels.

Similar family connections can be found in NCAA Division I basketball. For instance, Sean Miller (University of Arizona) and Archie Miller (Indiana University) were inspired by the example of their father, John, whose teams won more than 600 games and four state high school championships in Pennsylvania. Bob Hurley, a legendary high school coach at St. Anthony High School in Jersey City, has watched his sons Bobby (Arizona State University) and Dan (University of Connecticut) follow in his footsteps. As these examples illustrate, coaching can "run in the family," as offspring see the appeal of the profession firsthand and are nurtured in a sport environment, often from birth.

Generational continuity, however, does not ensure high-quality coaching. In fact, the lack of a systematic approach to coaching development leaves wide open a wide range of methods and learning opportunities for coaches when they begin to plan for their own professional development. In this relatively unmapped terrain, how do coaches know what they need in order to climb the next rung on the coaching ladder? How do they learn what jobs are available and identify the ones they might

COACHING SNAPSHOT

As son of a football coach, **Bill Belichick** was exposed to game film at an early age and became enthralled by the sport's schemes and formations. Never a player himself, Belichick was nonetheless hooked on football for life, happy to start his career as a low-level aide to the NFL's Baltimore Colts coaching staff for only $25 a week. From there, Belichick moved up through the NFL ranks and applied his accumulated knowledge and *"Do your job"* credo to ultimately coach the New England Patriots to six Super Bowl titles.

actually be able to obtain? Granted, a clear set of teaching standards and benchmarks do exist,[15] along with a systematic path to professional development, for public school elementary and secondary educators in the United States. This infrastructure includes formal evaluation by a local professional development committee, submission by the educator of a professional deployment plan, and renewal of a teaching license.[16] Outside of public schools, however, the decentralized nature of coach development in the United States means that coaches are mostly left to themselves to determine what competencies they need to improve—and to hope that doing so enables them to secure the next position.

Self-Evaluation

We know that expert coaches continually reflect on their own coaching.[17] Therefore, it makes sense that coaches exploring the job market or professional advancement opportunities should first strive to understand themselves—that is, their personal philosophy and values, strengths and weaknesses, motivation to coach, and career goals. This awareness, which is central to career development, comes only through deliberate self-evaluation.

One way for coaches to perform a systematic self-evaluation is through journaling. In one example, an elite Olympic swimming coach with 20 years of experience used journaling to perform a self-evaluation after losing her job when the two-time world-record holder she took to the Olympics failed to make the finals.[18] As part of her self-examination, she asked herself challenging questions, such as the following: "Do I have the energy to continue? Am I motivated enough to commit this much time for another four years? Am I able to give a level of commitment on par with what my competitors are doing? Am I good enough? What did I do wrong? Could I have done anything differently."[18] (p. 318)

Such questions are essential to effective self-reflection, yet some coaches are uncomfortable with journaling. In that case, a different approach may work—for instance, assessing strengths and areas of need by means of a coaching evaluation checklist. Many such checklists have been published, ranging from the rather basic inventory developed by the Coaches Association of British Columbia[19] to the more thorough instrument created by Team USA Volleyball.[20] An even more detailed evaluation might entail using a tool similar to that of Team USA Volleyball in combination with assessments from athletes, administrators, peers, and perhaps even a mentor.

Whatever evaluation method is chosen, coaches can use the results to inform decisions about their coaching career path. The key is to answer the following question: What is a good fit for me? In the words of coach educator Wade Gilbert, "You will know when you have found your coaching purpose when your purpose is inseparable from who you are as a person."[21] (p. 5)

Job Market

Following this self-examination, another important step on the path of career advancement is for coaches to investigate job openings that meet their needs and interests. As in any profession, the number of jobs available to a given candidate depends on the individual's experience, performance record, references, interviewing skills, and flexibility in terms of salary and location. Generally, novice and less experienced coaches must be willing to accept entry-level positions that pay less and require them to do "grunt work" assigned by senior coaches in order to learn the ropes and prove their aptitude and dedication. Beyond this basic reality, job seekers in coaching will find various categories of job types and will need to overcome a variety of potential obstacles.

Categories of Coaching

Experts have categorized the various positions available to coaches in multiple ways. For instance, one model classifies coaching into three contexts: recreational, developmental, and elite.[22] A similar approach using different terms has been adopted in Canada (a world leader in coaching and coach education), where the National Coaching Certification Program (NCCP) divides coaching into three streams: community sport, instructional, and competition.[23] The community sport stream introduces young children to sport and focuses on fun, safety, and fundamental skills. The instructional stream serves beginners and intermediate-level athletes who want to refine their strategies. And in the competition stream, both children and adolescents are taught basic skills and participate in local competitions; in addition, high performers are prepared for national or international competition.

Another model classifies coaching as focused on either participation or performance,[24] a two-part division that is also used in the *International Sport Coaching Framework*.[1] The framework defines participation coaching as working with children, adolescents, or adults in recreational or community sport programs. It also subdivides performance coaching into work with emerging athletes, performance athletes, or high-performance athletes. See figure 11.1.

The *International Sport Coaching Framework* also outlines specific roles for coaches:[1]

- Coaching assistants help deliver sessions and meet program needs.
- Coaches possess a wider view of plans and reviews, deliver practice sessions, help manage competitions, and develop coaching assistants.
- Advanced or senior coaches plan and deliver the program, evaluate coaching sessions, and manage the development of coaches and coaching assistants.
- Master or head coaches oversee and help develop the entire program, including design and oversight of management structures for other coaches on staff.

Thus coaches may work in various positions at different levels and require diverse skills in order to fulfill their roles.

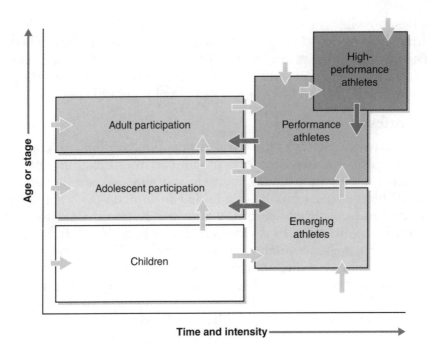

FIGURE 11.1   Sport participation spectrum.

Reprinted by permission from ICCE et al., *International Sport Coaching Framework, Version 1.2* (Champaign, IL: Human Kinetics, 2013), 20.

Potential Obstacles to Overcome

As we have seen, coaches have a multitude of career options from which to choose. Yet these paths are sometimes marked by both real and perceived barriers. For starters, coaching can be hard, and "first-time coaches are often confronted with a harder-than-expected experience."[25] For instance, a study of high school coaches from a variety of sports found that many were unprepared for the amount of time and effort required of new coaches; for these coaches, "reality shock . . . came in the form of understanding the importance [that] the coaching culture assigns to long hours and hard work."[11 (p. 88)] Indeed, long hours, dedication, and sacrifice are generally included in coaching doctrine and culture. Accordingly, many coaches take pride in 80-hour work weeks, and this devotion is revered by their peers and celebrated in the media.

At the same time, the expectation of long hours and sacrifice can present an obstacle to continuing and extending a coaching career. For example, a study of 10 female assistant coaches found that many "struggled to figure out how to juggle a coaching career with having a spouse and children; however, they saw this as a constraint that could be overcome, rather than a barrier that would prevent them from achieving their goals."[26] (p. 336) Obstacles can also come in other forms. For instance, a survey of 103 NCAA Division I football players found that African American student-athletes perceived fewer coaching opportunities and had less coaching interest than did their Caucasian peers because they saw fewer black coaches.[27]

To overcome such obstacles to advancement, aspiring coaches are encouraged to identify and establish a personal set of values that are critical to them (see chapter 3). For instance, "if discipline and winning defines a coach's personal approach, then that coach is more likely to be triggered by athletes who arrive late or do not adhere to training programs in comparison to a coach whose approach is defined by fun and personal growth and development."[28] (p. 11) In other words, if you openly articulate your core values, you will find it easier to navigate the inevitable times of adversity by aligning "what you believe, how you personally behave, and the way you design the sport environment" in order to engage in "authentic coaching."[29] Therefore, before you move on to the next step in the career journey, it is crucial to pause and reflect on what is, and what is not, important to you.

Compensation

From Little League to the Premier League, coaches work across multiple levels of competition in a variety of capacities—some as volunteers, others in full-time paid positions. Regardless of their compensation, coaches face high expectations in terms of the experiences they provide for their athletes, the manner in which they conduct themselves, and the results that athletes achieve under their tutelage. In fact, many coaches enter the profession with the goal of becoming a "people changer."[21] That is, they devote their lives to coaching because they want to help others fulfill their goals and dreams.

Of course, all coaches feel satisfaction when former players return to express gratitude, but for many coaches this type of response—rather than money earned—is what keeps them in the field. Conversely, coaches who leave the profession rarely miss the championships or the applause of the crowd. What they miss are the relationships they developed with their players and their coaching peers.

Like all professions, however, coaching requires more than just good feelings, and the monetary compensation must at least enable the basic standard of living sought by the individual. If coaches were unable to make a satisfying living for themselves and their families, then few would remain in the field just to be people changers. Aspiring coaches, then, should thoroughly investigate the financial compensation for the jobs they consider. They should also be aware of the very wide salary range that characterizes coaching—from unpaid volunteers in youth sport to professional and high-level collegiate coaches who can earn millions of dollars.

In North America, junior high school and middle school coaches are not likely to receive stipends greater than a thousand dollars, though some are paid more based on experience, school district, or location in the country. In contrast, head coaches at the high school level can bring in several thousand or even tens of thousands of dollars, depending on their sport, years of experience, and location. For example, a novice softball coach in a small Midwest town receives a mere fraction of what is paid to a veteran football coach at a powerhouse program in Texas. These stipends are considered to be supplemental contracts between the school and the employee. Therefore, if a coach is also a teacher, the pay for coaching is earned in addition to the teacher-coach's teaching salary.

However, the hundreds or thousands of dollars that interscholastic coaches earn do not fairly compensate them for the immense time and effort they expend in what has become a 12-month season for most high school sports. As a result, many coaches supplement their pay by hosting their own summer camps or working at camps sponsored by colleges and other organizations. For this reason, it is not uncommon to find school sport coaches who also coach a club or AAU (Amateur Athletic Union) team during the off-season, often for little pay.

Balancing salary demands with job satisfaction is a difficult juggling act in most professions, and coaching is no exception. A study of 179 South African coaches from a variety of team sports found that they derived satisfaction from performing the coaching task itself but experienced dissatisfaction related to compensation, administrative work, levels of media and community support, and job security.[30] The researchers concluded that sport coaches were not satisfied with their pay; however, this dissatisfaction may be counterbalanced by the satisfaction that most coaches seem to derive from doing their jobs.

With all of these factors in mind, aspiring coaches must balance their individual needs related to job satisfaction, life satisfaction, monetary compensation, and nonmonetary rewards. Similarly, practicing coaches should occasionally reflect on what motivates them to remain in the profession, what they find most rewarding about their role, and whether the investment they make in sport is sufficiently compensated for them. Closely monitoring life priorities as they evolve over time is well worth the effort for all coaches at any level.

Position Fit and Résumé Enhancement

Finding and securing a desirable coaching position depends on a number of factors.[31 (p. 26)] Two key measures that facilitate finding the right job and enhancing your chances of getting it involve:

1. Identifying a position fit
2. Adding to a résumé

Identifying a Position Fit

Identifying a position fit requires the coaching candidate to address factors such as choice of sport, age or level of sport, athlete gender, and, if relevant, school-related factors (e.g., size, location, particular choice of school or district).

Choice of Sport   Naturally, a given individual may have a preferred sport in mind, but aspiring coaches are well advised to keep an open mind in order to keep their options open. Indeed, some coaches enter the field by coaching a sport they did not play in high school or college. A candidate who is asked to coach an unfamiliar sport should be honest about his or her lack of experience while entertaining the possibility of saying yes. For example, administrators are often impressed when a candidate says something like the following: "I haven't coached baseball before, but I'm willing to help as an assistant and learn more about it." This type of response demonstrates willingness to learn, be a team player, and serve in positions of need. Therefore, demonstrating the willingness to be flexible can be an important part of a novice coach's job search.

Age or Level of Sport   Similarly, when exploring interscholastic positions, candidates should identify a preference for level of play (e.g., varsity, junior varsity, youth sport) but remain flexible. Coaches also need to be mindful of how these levels may differ. For example, coaching athletes in younger grades provides different challenges than coaching older adolescents due to developmental differences, transportation challenges, and wide discrepancies in abilities and skills. Therefore, coaches who work with younger players need to exhibit great patience, skillfully teach the fundamentals, and keep the game fun. They do not need to be as knowledgeable about game tactics because they focus on teaching athletes how to become players—not how to run plays.[32]

Coaches of younger athletes must also be prepared to navigate the expectations of parents and in some cases other coaches. In terms of parental involvement with younger athletes, coaches should formulate a plan to address rules, boundaries, and limitations of parental involvement. In addition, novice coaches who work with athletes in younger grades are often asked to run systems dictated by a varsity coach. In such cases, they should be prepared to be flexible in playing the athletes preferred by the varsity coach and using the prescribed teaching, training, and tactical systems. In other cases, the varsity coach may take more of a hands-off approach.

Athlete Gender Coach candidates are sometimes asked to coach a different gender from their own. For instance, in 2014, the San Antonio Spurs hired Becky Hammon as the first full-time paid female assistant on an NBA coaching staff.[33] Coaching a gender other than one's own may present challenges that a candidate has yet to consider, such as supervising the locker room or earning respect from players who are used to working with coaches of their own gender.

Candidates should also be mindful of potential differences between coaching boys and coaching girls. For example, leadership preferences have been shown to differ between boys and girls; specifically, some girls prefer a more democratic coaching style, whereas some boys prefer a more autocratic approach.[34] Research has also shown that males tend to have more of an ego orientation—that is, to be more concerned than females about comparisons with others in terms of their athletic performance.[35] Furthermore, high levels of team cohesion are highly correlated with performance on female teams, whereas cohesion is only moderately correlated with performance on male teams.[36] This finding implies that cohesion is important to both males and females but seemingly more important for team success when working with females.

Given these potential differences, coaching candidates should be honest about whether they have experience in coaching athletes of a given gender while being open to the possibility of coaching either gender.

School-Related Factors Coaches who are interested in working at the interscholastic level should also give some thought to school size, location, and type. For instance, expectations can vary greatly in regard to achievement in both sport and academics, depending on the school or the school district. In addition, some schools take a strict approach to behavior and discipline, whereas others are more relaxed. In many cases, the culture of a school, and more specifically that of the sport program, is based on the viewpoints espoused and the tone adopted by the school's principal or district superintendent. And in some cases, this framework may conflict with the views of the coaching candidate.

Some candidates may find that in rural school districts—where the school and community are smaller—the coach shares athletes with other sports. In fact, despite the national trend toward specialization in one sport,[37] athletes in many rural schools still diversify their athletic experiences. Therefore, coaches in these areas must be prepared to support their athletes' desire to participate in multiple sports. On the surface, this challenge may seem easy to overcome. However, if a basketball coach shares three or four starters with a football team that typically makes a deep run into the state playoffs, then the basketball team will likely be without most of its best players until late November or early December. This shortage doesn't make it easy on a young coach trying to develop a winning culture! Still, coaches who take a flexible approach to athlete sharing are more likely to thrive in a smaller school. On the other hand, coaches who promote sport specialization at such a school will likely be at odds with parents, athletes, members of the community, and fellow coaches.

In contrast, in a large urban school district, coaches may find student-athletes who desire to specialize in one sport and want to be deeply involved in a local AAU or club team during the interscholastic season. In addition, it is not uncommon in urban environments for parents to be either overly involved or not involved at all in their children's sport participation (this range of parental involvement may also be found in some rural and suburban districts).

COACHING SNAPSHOT

Demonstrating a passion for tennis long before winning a match at Wimbledon at 14 years of age, **Kathy Rinaldi-Stunkel** has channeled her lifelong love of the sport into helping subsequent generations of athletes enjoy similarly positive experiences through her coaching. Current U.S. Fed Cup captain, Rinaldi-Stunkel is sometimes referred to as the "Tennis Mom," as her self-described approach with players is *"being in their corner."*

Adding to a Résumé

Factors that add to a coach's résumé include experience, specialized knowledge, relevant skills, and certifications.[31] For instance, aspiring coaches who have playing experience in a given sport may also have access to an impressive list of contacts. At the same time, candidates who lack experience in the sport may remain open to the possibility of coaching in it with the understanding that they would need to demonstrate commitment and devotion to learning it.

As for specialized knowledge, candidates in the United States might demonstrate this qualification through certification from an organization such as the National Athletic Trainers' Association or the National Strength and Conditioning Association. Such qualifications can demonstrate a breadth of experience that may appeal to administrators and head coaches who need to fill more than one vacancy. Similarly, candidates who seek both a coaching position and a teaching position can benefit from possessing a teaching certificate (elementary, secondary, or both). Moreover, administrators take a big-picture view of hiring and staff movement in their district and often anticipate upcoming retirements, intra-district transfers, and departures for any number of other reasons. Therefore, coaching candidates who are flexible and credentialed in more than one area look more attractive as potential employees.

Professional Advancement

In the coaching field, professional advancement rarely follows a linear path. Instead, it is characterized by fluidity and variable movement— sometimes forward, at other times backward or lateral. The bottom line is that coaches must be willing to move when a new position becomes available. For example, Lane Kiffin moved down a level to transition from offensive coordinator at Alabama to head coach at Florida Atlantic. In contrast, within six weeks, Steve Sarkisian, who succeeded Kiffin as (interim) offensive coordinator at Alabama, moved up a level to become offensive coordinator for the NFL's Atlanta Falcons.

In the NCCA Division I Football Bowl Subdivision (FBS), a typical career path for a coach begins with a graduate assistant position, followed by a more formal assistant coach role and then another new position every two or three years. Along the way, if a head coach is fired (at the FBS or professional level), the entire staff may also be replaced. Therefore, in order to stay in the coaching ranks, some coaches must move to a lower level or take a position that pays less or assigns less responsibility.

Throughout this process, much of what coaches learn comes through experience rather than formal coaching education.[38] In fact, most coaches prefer informal methods of development and agree that finding a mentor is critical to advancement, especially in the early stages of a career. Indeed, learning from a successful coach through mentoring or apprenticeship remains one of the most effective methods of gaining expertise, though its success depends in part on the ability of the master coach to serve in that role by sharing relevant information.[12 (p. 21)]

Networking

The old saying that "it's not what you know but who you know" doesn't always hold true, but having access to key contacts in sport and coaching can certainly grease the wheels in a job search. Networking involves connecting with administrators, teachers, and others involved in coaching who might assist in some way. For example, an influential contact might agree to serve as a reference or put in a good word to a member of the hiring committee, and this type of credibility can give a candidate an advantage over other applicants. Therefore, coaching candidates are well advised to make a list of the people in their network and contact them systematically to inquire about position openings and make reasonable requests for assistance in the job search process.

Candidates should also attend gatherings of coaches and sport administrators, such as camps, clinics, and professional meetings. It's been said that every conversation is an interview waiting to happen, and candidates who take the initiative to meet prospective employers gain an advantage over those who are content to rely on phone calls, emails, and social media. This is not to say that electronic communication is unnecessary; to the contrary, it is essential in this digital age. Candidates are in fact encouraged to call and email other coaches, athletic directors, and administrators about potential openings. In addition, a college career services department may be able to provide contact information for people in hiring positions at schools of interest.

One of the most important ways to network with other coaches is to join professional organizations. For example, a candidate should investigate the Society of Health and Physical Educators (SHAPE America), as well as state high school coaches' associations and state education associations. The cost associated with joining an association or attending a meeting is outweighed by the chance to meet many coaches and administrators who seek to fill their job openings. For example, in the United States, the annual national soccer and football conferences held in January typically draw several thousand coaches, and similar numbers are found at the annual meetings of some state high school coaching associations. These events provide educational, social, and career-enhancing opportunities.

Another possible network can be found in the rise of AAU and club teams. Some of coaches involved with these teams interact frequently with interscholastic coaches while coaching their players in the school sport's off-season.

Finally, it was once a rite of passage for many aspiring coaches to enter the profession or move up through the ranks by doing summer work at residential camps hosted by colleges. However, with the advent of major recruiting camps, team camps, and camps hosted by coaches, the traditional summer camp option may not offer as many networking opportunities as it did in the past.

Interviews

When interviewing for an open position, coaching candidates should be fully prepared to demonstrate their interest in that particular job. Doing so requires detailed preparation before arriving for the interview. Candidates should also prepare a list of questions to ask the interviewer in order to determine whether the hiring organization shares their values and coaching philosophy.

Most administrators in hiring positions devote many hours to interviewing candidates. As a result, they can identify an applicant who is disorganized or unprepared within the first few minutes of the interview. Proper preparation includes being ready to answer certain types of interview questions commonly asked of coaching candidates. The following list provides a sampling:

- What are your reasons for applying for this position, and what do you feel you can bring to the role?
- What is your experience of coaching in this environment, and what key skills do you possess to manage the job capably?
- What additional learning have you done to bolster your experience (e.g., reading books on coaching, taking coaching courses, attending coaching clinics)?
- In your personal experience, who has impressed you most as a coach, and why?
- Coaches are often advised to remember that they "coach people, not a sport." What does this advice mean to you?
- As a lead coach, you would be responsible for the well-being of the athletes under your supervision. What measures would you take to ensure their health and safety?
- What does the term LTAD mean to you? How does it affect your coaching?

- In what ways have you seen athletes develop due to your coaching?
- Good communication skills are essential for this role, which involves interacting with a variety of individuals and groups. How would your communication skills help you succeed in this position?
- How do you use technology to communicate and conduct coaching activities more effectively?
- What factors do you think are important when planning a practice session, and why?
- Tell us about a coaching session that went very well.
- Tell us about a coaching session that did not go so well and what you did to resolve it.
- Suppose that an athlete is repeatedly difficult and disruptive during a practice session. What course of action would you take?
- Tell us about a practice session you conducted with a group of athletes with mixed abilities. How did you ensure that all participants were engaged in and benefitted from the experience?
- How do you know when you have delivered a high-quality practice session?
- How do you monitor and evaluate the success of your coaching?
- Your role may involve mentoring less experienced coaches. What would you do to support such a coach?
- Your role may involve doing some administrative tasks, such as record keeping and reporting. Tell us about your experience in carrying out such tasks.
- Which areas of your coaching would you like to develop, and why?

Prepared candidates also bring a portfolio or other organized documentation indicating how they would run the program or serve in the desired role. This material should address coaching philosophy, policies and procedures for staff and players, plans (practice, seasonal, and yearly), and methods of evaluation. Candidates need to demonstrate that they have devoted considerable thought to conceiving and organizing off-season training for strength and conditioning as well as skill improvement. Furthermore, on request, they should be able to outline how they intend to improve athletes' mental skills and how they will evaluate their own coaching behavior (e.g., establishing targeted outcomes for their own development).

In many cases, printed material will be enough to demonstrate preparation and readiness for the interview. However, it is also beneficial to create a brief digital presentation (using an app such as Prezi or PowerPoint) that includes video of coaching interactions and referrals from others. In addition, given the digital explosion in recent years, coaches should be prepared to provide examples of how they will use technology to enhance their coaching and discuss any restrictions or limitations they might place on athletes' use of social media.

Teaching and Coaching

As in many professions, coaches enter the field in a variety of ways. Some decide as early as adolescence that they want to coach, whereas others decide only after attending college. Some coach first, then acquire a teaching license or certificate; others begin coaching at the same time that they obtain a teaching position. In fact, it is not uncommon for an administrator to convince a teacher candidate to take on an additional duty of coaching in order to fill two needs at once.

Teacher-coaches often seek a job primarily as a coach and give only secondary consideration to the teaching position.[11] However, there has been a dramatic shift in how school districts hire coaches. For example, in Ohio, more than 50 percent of secondary interscholastic coaches are nonteachers who have no formal training in education.[39] This trend is likely common to school districts in other states as well. In fact, as compared with twenty years ago, far fewer coaches are physical education teachers: Many coaches who also teach possess certifications or teaching licenses in social studies, math, and other areas.[40]

Some coaches start out in an assistant role, whereas others become a head coach immediately. Still others prefer the role of assistant and never seek a head coaching position. For example, Larry Harrison, assistant men's basketball coach at West Virginia University, has been an assistant to head coach Bob Huggins for more than 20 years.[41] NBA coach Johnny Bach was a longtime assistant coach for the Chicago Bulls and Los Angeles Lakers under the guidance of head coach Phil Jackson.[42] In the NFL, assistant coach Rob Ryan spent more than 20 years without moving into a head coaching position.[43]

Thus a coach's professional preparation is quite unlike the training required for most professional careers in that there is typically no extended period of formal education or apprenticeship. With the exception of a few college programs that offer a major or minor in coaching, much of the training for becoming a coach occurs outside of formal academic settings. Without formal extended training, many aspiring coaches are provided with relatively limited opportunities to acquire the skills and develop the philosophy and values that are basic to the practice of coaching.

Culture of Coaching

Developing an understanding of the coaching environment requires observation, conversation with coaches, and immersion in the culture of coaching. One of the key concepts of the coaching culture is that of "social loops," or what coaching researchers refer to formally as communities of practice.[44-46] In other words, the profession is characterized by a variety of connected, unspoken social circles through which coaches both learn and network. In fact, researchers assert that learning occurs more effectively in these circles than it does in formal coach education.[46]

These unspoken circles also delineate levels within the profession's membership. They do not prevent coaches from moving outside of their groups and into new ones, but one must pay a sort of informal dues in order to enter a new circle. Moreover, many coaches choose to stay within their own circles. For example, there are connected circles within which only head coaches move and others in which only assistant coaches move. In order to move up into a circle of head coaches, an assistant coach must advance by paying the necessary dues to obtain a head coaching position.

These circles are dynamic and ever changing. Although no formal process exists for entering another circle, coaches must pass through unspoken barriers in order to meet and connect with other coaches. Breaking through perceived or real barriers within these coaching loops requires understanding how people behave in each community of practice. Head coaches feel connections with other head coaches due to the shared adversity they face in their daily work. It is difficult to understand the pressures and sacrifices that head coaches make unless one has held that position. Thus shared experiences breed connections between coaches.

The same types of circles exist at different levels of coaching; that is, varsity coaches move within their own circles, separate from junior varsity and junior high coaches. The same is true in relation to gender; for example, women's college basketball head coaches and men's college basketball head coaches each tend to move within their own circles. Furthermore, Olympic and professional coaches often move within their own communities of practice and social networks. Gaining access to these networks can pose a challenge, and aspiring coaches should learn about the culture of a given network before trying to move through the informal but very real boundaries surrounding it.

Coach Burnout

In order to fully understand the coaching culture, aspiring coaches must also become aware of the work ethic that is expected of coaches. As mentioned earlier, many novice coaches are shocked by the extent to which hard work and long hours are embedded into the coaching culture. To a considerable degree, coaches also lack control over the primary measurement of their own success—that is, their win–loss record—because it is affected by various factors that depend on others (e.g., officiating mistakes, transportation breakdowns, overzealous fans, parent interference). As a result, an unspoken rule in the profession dictates that coaches must work longer and harder than their opponents.

This intense work ethic, combined with coaches' limited control over their own professional success, can lead to frustration, resentment, and burnout. Coaches are also at risk due to the helping nature of their occupation, in which they are continually giving to others. Burnout is common in people-oriented occupations in which the client is the primary focus of concern for the practitioner (other examples include counseling, nursing, and teaching). Therefore, coaches who can create a healthy life balance are more likely to sustain a long and successful career.

Many articles have been written about burnout, and the majority of this research has been dedicated to athlete burnout. In recent years, however, the topic of coach burnout has been given more attention in the literature of sport psychology and coaching science. For our purposes here, we adopt the following description of burnout: "a psychological syndrome that is characterized by emotional exhaustion, cynicism and detachment from one's job, and reduced personal accomplishment characterized by a feeling of professional inefficacy and incompetence" (Goodger, Gorely, Lavalee, & Harwood, as cited in Raedeke and Kenttä[47 [p. 425]]).

External Pressure

Long hours, intense scrutiny from others, and inability to control some of the factors that enable success make coaches likely candidates for burnout. As noted earlier, the culture of coaching celebrates coaches for being dedicated to their craft and making sacrifices in other areas of their lives, including stress-related health risks and time away from family. However, these same factors can lead to emotional and physical exhaustion and eventually burnout. Indeed, coaches face constant demands. These stresses include pressure from alumni and other fans to perform, scrutiny from parents about playing time, and expectations from administrators to win while promoting academic and social success.

Internal Pressure

Coaches also generate considerable internal pressure to do their best and sometimes lose sight of what they control and what they do not.

For example, if asked, many coaches would assert that they have control over winning, but if this were the case then no coach would ever lose a game! Many coaches also believe that they have control over their players' actions during competition. In reality, although coaches exert considerable control over practice sessions—for instance, blowing a whistle to stop or start play—primary control of athletes' actions during competition resides in the athletes themselves. Coaches may find it difficult, however, to shift from the control mindset of practice to the management mindset of handling personnel and tactics during competition.

If coaches hold misguided beliefs about their control (or lack thereof) over winning and player behavior, they may experience frustration, self-doubt, and anger when their expectations go unmet. In turn, if not properly addressed, long periods of frustration and anger can lead to burnout. Therefore, it is important for coaches to learn how to achieve balance in their lives—an especially challenging task for coaches who take pride in being the first to arrive at work and the last to leave. Many successful coaches go to bed and wake up thinking about their team and find it hard to take a break from these thoughts. However, coaches who take breaks from the day-to-day grind are rewarded with the ability to persevere over the long haul. For example, when Urban Meyer was the head football coach at the University of Florida, he experienced health issues that affected his personal life. After stepping away from coaching for a time, he returned to the sidelines as head coach at Ohio State, but this time he decided to spend more time with his family and dedicate himself to achieving more balance in his life.[48]

Balance does not happen without effort. In fact, for hard-driving coaches, the project of achieving balance requires daily attention. Equilibrium must be achieved through methodical scheduling and dedication to attaining a balanced state of mind and body. In fact, coaches must plan for balance in the same way they make plans for their team—by systematically setting goals, subgoals, and targeted outcomes on a daily, weekly, seasonal, and yearly basis.

Few coaches who feel burned out would admit to it. Burnout involves exhaustion and feelings of incompetence and emptiness, which many coaches would view as signs of weakness—something that most sport participants would rather not acknowledge. Therefore, the first step in preventing or overcoming exhaustion is to develop self-awareness. Coaches who resist, ignore, or deny feelings of burnout are likely to be harder to help. However, those who will admit to feeling drained can help themselves through the following strategies: addressing work overload; processing feelings about lack of control, insufficient rewards, or the absence of fairness; building a sense of community in the work group; and resolving any value conflicts.[47]

Priorities

Coaches who feel overloaded by their work may benefit from making a list of life priorities.[49] For example, some coaches might list the following:

1. Winning a championship
2. Achieving hall of fame status
3. Placing three players on the all-district or all-regional team
4. Spending time with family

With the exception of spending time with family, these priorities lie outside of the coach's direct control. Nonetheless, failure to meet them is likely to cause frustration, resentment, and hostility toward others in the coach's inner circle. A more balanced set of priorities might look something like this:

1. Setting a regular date night with one's significant other
2. Spending two (instead of six) hours per day watching film
3. Devoting 30 to 45 minutes to exercise (e.g., walking, bicycling) on three or four days per week
4. Recruiting for 90 minutes (instead of four hours) per night

This plan is more balanced and more measurable, and an overworked coach can adapt behaviors accordingly to prevent burnout and lead a more balanced life.

"Controlling the controllables" is an overused phrase in sport but a meaningful one if understood properly. For example, coaches who learn that they control only so much during competition are usually more relaxed, thus freeing them to use their energy for analyzing trends and making adjustments (e.g., in matchups or tactics). In contrast, coaches who think they can control the game often engage in histrionics and overcoach their players, which can lead athletes to perform tentatively, indecisively, and without flow—all of which is frustrating both for themselves and for the coach. Truly great coaches (e.g., John Wooden, Bill Belichick) know that their players control the game and therefore devote their own energies to things that they can control—namely, their own thoughts and actions.

Values

Coaches who experience burnout are often at odds with their employer about values. For instance, a coach who values player development, teaching, and good sporting behavior over winning is likely to bench the best player if he or she is late to practice, misbehaves, or breaks a team rule.

However, if the employer's primary goal is to win, then an administrator may downplay inappropriate behavior and force the coach to keep the player active. This kind of conflict can lead to frustration, resentment, discouragement, and, if left unaddressed, burnout.

Therefore, coaches must be willing to address conflicts about values with their employer. A coach whose personal values fail to align with those of the employer may have to look for another job—one where those values are shared—or be forced out by the employer.

Coaches devote their lives to athletes, families, and communities. They also have families of their own, and the constant possibility of having to uproot one's family due to job loss looms large for many in the profession. One way to avoid this outcome is to ensure a good alignment in values between coach and administration.

Most experts view burnout as difficult to treat and therefore recommend adopting strategies to prevent it.[47] Coaches who fail to do so may drop out of the profession or experience other trials and tribulations in their lives, such as personal health issues and family discontent. Burnout is a serious condition that must be addressed through a systematic, preventive approach.

Post-Coaching Career Planning

Considerable research has been done on the termination of athletic careers, the transition process that follows, and the fact that some athletes experience this change as a traumatic event resulting in loss of identity and periods of insecurity.[50, 51] Research is scarce, however, on the transition from coaching into other occupations or retirement. Those few researchers who have investigated this process have cautioned about consequences for the sport itself due to loss of the coach's knowledge and expertise, which are embedded in their very practice.[52] Therefore, the transition into post-coaching life requires planning and thought on the part of both the individual and the sport.

In a number of sports, however, the post-coaching occupational pathway is neither systematic nor well established; in other words, there is no traditional means of progressing from coaching to other leadership roles.[53] To help fill this gap, this section of the chapter addresses the following post-coaching possibilities: sport administration, coach education, coach mentoring, and coaching research.

Sport Administration

Coaches who wish to seek a position in sport administration may have already experienced an observational apprenticeship much like that experienced by players who closely observe their coaches. In this case, working closely with administrators allows coaches to witness firsthand the skills and competencies required for serving in such a position. In fact, many of the team management skills that coaches develop over the course of their careers would also apply to the position of sport program director.

The transition from coaching to administration involves both a logical occupational step and a shift in culture. Although administration resembles coaching insofar as it requires the management of people and systems, some coaches may find it hard to be distanced from the heat of competition. For these individuals, being trackside or poolside or on the sidelines gives them a sense of excitement and involvement that managing people and systems may not provide.

Coach Education

Alongside the international movement to professionalize coaching and raise standards across the coaching sector, the position of coach educator has emerged as a distinct occupation. Research has identified coach education as a central component in the effort to raise coaching standards and generally increase competency levels among coaches.[8, 54] To achieve these goals, coach educators need to apply some skills that differ from those employed by coaches. Therefore, just as the transition from athlete to coach is not always seamless, the process of becoming a coach educator is not a simple transition.

What Use Is Experience?

The following quotation is excerpted from an interview with Mike Devlin, coaching director of the British Canoe Union, who has interviewed numerous coaches and read hundreds of résumés. When asked about the importance he places on a coach's experience, he offered the following perspective:

Of course, having experience is of central importance, . . . but I always ask about this experience. . . . What they have done and where? Having 10 years' experience in the sector can mean a number of things. I would prefer to employ coaches who have had a range of experiences and can show diversity in what they have done and who they have worked with. One of the myths of our industry is that experience is a great teacher. . . . Well I disagree! It can be, but it depends on what the coach . . . does with that experience. If they have reflected on the experience, . . . have been honest with success and failure, sought other opinions, changed, challenged, and developed their skill set because of what they have learned, . . . that makes a difference. Those coaches who have coached the same way for 10 years because they believe it is the only way . . . tend not to get the position. So, yes, experience is important, but only if it is seen as an opportunity to learn.

In addition, emerging evidence from the coaching research literature suggests that formalized coach education programs exert only limited influence on the day-to-day practice of individual coaches.[55, 56] Therefore, we may need to explore alternative forms of pedagogy and novel educational approaches.[57] One criticism of existing coach education programs is that they lack contextual relevance. In other words, individuals who transfer from the coaching domain to that of the coach educator should be able to bring with them practice-based examples and scenarios. These points of reference resonate with coach learners in terms of their individual practice.

At the same time, coach education is fundamentally a pedagogical role. As such, it may need to strike a balance between individualizing the interaction in order to advance each coach's understanding of the craft and delivering a certain curriculum and covering the contents of a given syllabus. Fortunately, a number of sporting bodies recognize this inherent complexity in coach education and address it by hiring educational experts to train coach educators, help them design curriculum, and facilitate best educational practices.

COACHING SNAPSHOT

Once a ballet dancer and ballet coach, **Valorie Kondos Field** never became a gymnast, yet she became a hall of fame gymnastics coach. Her UCLA women's gymnastics teams won seven national championships, and she was named National Coach of the Year four times. Yet "Miss Val," as she became known, was appreciated as much for her leadership and dynamic personality as she was for her winning record and became a successful public speaker following her coaching career.

Coach Mentoring

Due to concerns about the effectiveness of formal coach education, methods that focus on workplace-based learning have come to the fore. This approach, known as contextual education, may seem more familiar to coaches because it makes substantial use of mentoring, something in which most coaches have participated during their career. Indeed, it is an established practice in most sports to spend some time learning from others who possess greater insight, experience, and knowledge. Therefore, these methods give coaches who are transitioning into new roles a natural way to aid in the development of other coaches.[58]

In light of lessons learned in the education, business, and medical professions, the notion of mentoring has advanced from that of simply passing down canons of knowledge to enabling learning in the practice environment. Serving as a mentor can be quite rewarding as one develops a deep professional relationship with the mentee—one that may in fact resemble the bond between a coach and an athlete who complement each other in an individual sport. Research indicates that the compatibility of the two parties is crucial; that is, mentoring involves more than just "add two or more coaches and stir."

Mentoring programs can be either paid or voluntary, and they come in a number of forms. Schemes such as the United Kingdom Coaching Certificate view the mentor role as a key ingredient in the development of coaches at all levels. For instance, the Elite Coaching Apprenticeship Programme run by UK Sport uses cross-sport mentors as well as mentors from the business world.[59] In this program, mentors are expected to help mentees reflect, review, and critically appraise their practice in order to develop critical consciousness and approach continuous improvement as their own responsibility.

Effective mentors are often in short supply, and any offer to serve in this role is likely to be met with approval. Therefore, retiring coaches are well positioned to nurture and support junior coaches; moreover, with adequate training, they can share their knowledge so that it remains available to be adapted and absorbed by the next generation of coaching professionals.

Coaching Research

Increasingly, the practice of coaching, including the programs and systems that coaches put in place, is informed and underpinned by research. Although this knowledge has traditionally been generated by the university sector, more people are realizing that the research agenda needs to be driven by coaches and others directly involved in sport. As a result, considerable research is now commissioned and conducted by sporting bodies and government agencies, and these inquiries often address issues of immediate concern to the sport community. In parallel with these developments, a small but increasing number of organizations now employ staffers to manage or conduct research from within the sporting world. Coaches who are open to these new opportunities can contribute by applying their insights both about their chosen sport and about the profession of coaching.

On the other hand, coaches may lack the academic credibility and skills to conduct academic research on their own or to work in concert with those in academia. However, universities acknowledge that the drift from research to practical application can be mediated by employing individuals with recent experience in coaching and by working more closely with current coaches. For now, employment opportunities in academia remain limited for coaches without a higher degree of some sort. However, as the relationships between universities, coaches, and sporting organizations grow stronger, the resulting "intellectualization of the practice of coaching" will continue to expand the possibilities for coaches to transfer into this exciting area of growth.

Exercise: Preparing an Effective Résumé and Cover Letter

The following is a sample job advertisement that should be used to complete this exercise, which asks you to create your own résumé, or curriculum vitae (CV), and cover letter.

Sample Job Advertisement

Director of Tennis

The University of Southfields is looking for a full-time Director of Tennis and Head Men's Tennis Coach. An attractive benefits package is included.

Position Overview

The University of Southfields is an NCAA Division II member of the Intercollegiate Athletic Conference accepting applications for a full-time Director of Tennis and Head Men's Tennis Coach to be compensated with an attractive salary and benefits package in the region of $30,000 to 40,000 (depending on the individual hired).

Position Description

This position will oversee both the men's and women's university tennis programs and serve as Head Tennis Coach for the men's team. The responsibilities will include, but not be limited to, the following: practice organization, contest preparation, budget management, player and junior coach development, fundraising, sponsor recruitment, recruitment of a diverse population of successful student-athletes from within the university cohort, commitment to character development, and other duties as assigned by the Director of Athletics.

The university offers 31 varsity programs in which more than 40 percent of the student body participates and is a four-year residential liberal arts university located in the heart of Southern California, between Los Angeles and beautiful Orange County. Southfields University is distinguished by its inclusive atmosphere, pioneering faculty, and nationally recognized and inventive curriculum. Facilities rival those at large public institutions, but ours is an intimate setting where students and professors unite in an ongoing pursuit of knowledge.

Position Qualifications

Bachelor's degree required, master's degree preferred. National Tennis qualification essential. Experience working in an educational institution desirable. Minimum four years of successful coaching experience at this level along with varied playing experience. Excellent oral, written, and interpersonal skills. Ability to both work in a team and self-manage.

How to Apply

To apply, either mail or email a résumé and cover letter, including names and email addresses of three professional references.

Writing Your Résumé

The résumé or curriculum vitae (CV) is the traditional way of displaying and detailing your qualifications and experience for any prospective employer. Indeed, this type of document is important enough that you can employ a specialist to create one for you. That said, here are some key points that are common to all effective résumés.

- Keep in mind that this document may serve as your first contact with a future employer. Make sure that it is up to date, has been thoroughly proofread, and is easy to read and clearly related to the position for which you are applying.

- An effective résumé strikes a balance between detail and brevity. Although certain things about yourself are evident to you, they may not be apparent to a potential employer. Make sure that key information is clear, easy to locate, and sufficiently detailed.

- Provide contact information for references. Relying on the standard line "references available on request" makes it harder for people to find out about you.

- Increasingly, people are using two types of résumés—a short version limited to one sheet of paper (both sides if necessary) and the other a lengthier version that details all of your education, experience, certifications, awards and honors, and evidence of continuing professional development (CPD), as well as personal information and references. This information should include dates. For instance, recent engagement in CPD indicates currency; on the other hand, if your last professional training was 20 years ago, that suggests something else.

- Presentation quality is crucial. Use high-quality paper and select an easy-to-read (i.e., serif) typeface and a font size of 12 to 14.

Writing Your Cover Letter

Whereas your résumé profiles your education, experience, and personal and professional qualities, your cover letter focuses on how you would fulfill the requirements of a particular position. Therefore, in constructing your letter, identify the qualifications detailed in the job posting and divide them into those considered essential and those viewed as merely desirable. In the sample posting for this exercise, the essential requirements include four years of experience, a bachelor's degree, tennis coaching qualifications, interpersonal and communication skills, and the ability to both work as a team member and self-direct. Desirables, on the other hand, include a master's degree and experience working in education.

Then, in your letter, indicate where and when you have met the requirements of the position; in doing so, use terms included in the job posting. Here is an example: "Between 2006 and 2013, I served as assistant coach at the University of Northfield, where we competed in NCAA Division II, gaining promotion to the next division in 2007." This short sentence indicates clearly

(continued)

(continued)

that you have met three of the requirements stated in the details—the minimum length of experience, coaching at an appropriate level, and working in an education setting.

Here is another example: "As a level 3 qualified assistant coach, I managed three junior coaches and oversaw the recruitment of four new sponsors who contributed a total of $5,000 per year over a five-year period. These contributions were added to the annual departmental budget, in which I had sole budgeting responsibility for all tournament events, such as Northfield's involvement in the Pan-Canadian Universities Cup." This sentence indicates where and when you met a number of explicit and implied conditions—namely, post-contest preparation, budget management, tennis coaching qualification, junior coach development, fundraising, sponsor recruitment, and self-direction.

The following are tips to use while writing your cover letter:

- A letter of application should be no longer than two sides of a standard sheet of paper. Use short, detailed sentences that allow the reader to easily identify how you meet the requirements of the post.

- Employers are likely to see dozens of applications, so take your time in writing your letter. Relate it directly to the required profile of the advertised post and make it easy for potential employers to select you for an interview.

- Practice this process before applying for your next position. Get online, download a job posting that interests you, and work though the suggestions made here.

Job Interview Tips

Preparing for a coaching job interview entails much more than anticipating what questions might be asked. To prepare fully, work through the following list of key steps and gather as much up-to-date documentation as possible ahead of time. Mock interviews are useful to help you iron out issues and ease the nerves.

- *Job advertisement.* Obtain a written copy of the advertisement for review. It should include information such as salary range, key requirements, and the role that the coach will be expected to perform.

- *Job description.* Obtain a document that clearly outlines expectations for the job, including responsibilities and tasks. More complete job descriptions also identify specific skills, types of knowledge, and attributes needed for the position.

- *Application form.* This form gathers both general and more job-specific information about candidates. Use it to highlight your instruction, training, and experiences that are most relevant for this job. Include references who can make the case for your abilities and achievements.

- *Formal interview.* Most interviews involve questions similar to those presented earlier in this chapter. Employers compare each candidate's responses with those of others. Candidates do best when they give answers that are honest, clear, and concise while presenting a professional yet personable demeanor.

- *On-site observation.* Not often, but sometimes, employers ask to see a prospective coach perform in a practice setting. This assessment is intended to gauge an applicant's real-world ability and skill in working with athletes. Even when not asked for this type of performance, candidates should consider providing a video that shows them conducting a practice session.

- *Preemployment checks.* Most employers, and sometimes the governmental agencies that oversee them, require screening of job applicants. Here are just some types of screenings that you might encounter:

  - *Pupil Activity Permit.* Many U.S. states require this documentation for anyone who works in a public education institution. It certifies that the holder has passed basic courses in working with children under the age of 18 years.

  - *Qualification check.* The United States has not established a universal certification program for coaches, but most employers require completion of a recognized course in CPR and first aid. Many sport governing bodies also require specific kinds of certification. These requirements typically entail coursework; some also involve passing an on-field practicum. Candidates should stay current with the certifications available in their chosen sport for the types of jobs they might pursue.

  - *Medical and immigration clearance.* Outside of the United States, a valid passport and documentation of medical clearance are often required prior to employment. While not necessary for some jobs in the United States, both of these items are good to have on hand when seeking a position.

From International Council for Coaching Excellence, *Sport Coaches' Handbook*, eds. D. Gould and C. Mallett. (Champaign, IL: Human Kinetics, 2021).

Chapter 12

Continuing Education in Coaching

Cliff Mallett, Steven Rynne, and Pierre Trudel

As shown throughout this book, the many potential benefits of sport participation are much more likely to be realized when athletes are coached by qualified, competent coaches. For this reason, the ongoing education of coaches is considered important at all levels of sport around the world. Too often, however, coach education is regarded as sufficient if participants merely complete a short online course or even a single workshop. While such activities can be useful as initial elements in formal coach education, they do little good if coaches fail to build on them throughout their careers.

Therefore, this chapter emphasizes opportunities for ongoing coach education and explores how these learning experiences (whether formal or informal) can enrich and enhance coaches both personally and professionally. These benefits are supported by the latest research and by our own work as coaches and coach educators. We have worked with and interviewed some of the top coaches in the world, and one thing they share is that they are continually learning.[1-3] In other words, they emphasize the notion of coaches as learners in their own right—indeed, as lifelong learners in the pursuit of becoming better coaches.

If you are a coach or aspiring coach, you might use this chapter to help you understand how your past has influenced your desire to coach as well as your thoughts about how to coach. The chapter gives you opportunities to think about ways in which you can learn continually and keep up with the latest developments in coaching practice. You can explore the fundamentals of learning and development as a basis for your craft and your own self-improvement. All of this work will allow you to create or access a better learning environment—one that will challenge your current thinking and stretch your knowledge to its maximum.

Learning as a Coach

Learning is a process that shapes change. It leads to more sophisticated cognitive understandings and behavioral outcomes. The catalyst for this change is experience, which increases one's potential for improved performance and subsequent learning. Here are some key points about this definition:

1. *Learning is not an end in itself (i.e., a product) but a process.* We can only infer learning has taken place (via observation of coach behaviors or self-reports) because this learning process initially takes place in the mind.

2. *Learning involves changes in both cognition (knowledge, beliefs, attitudes) and behavior.* These changes are dynamic, evolving over time, and exert enduring influence on how coaches think, feel, and act.

3. *Learning is a personal responsibility.* Just as coaches cannot make athletes learn, coach developers cannot make coaches learn. They can create conditions that are conducive to learning, but coach learning ultimately depends on how coaches engage, interpret, and respond to their lived experiences (past and present), both implicitly and explicitly.

The ways in which coaches respond to learning situations are influenced by their experiences, self-efficacy (confidence), openness to trying something different, and personal qualities.[4] These factors carry implications for facilitating coaches' learning related to autonomy, practical application, experience, and collaboration. In most cases, coaches are autonomous learners; that is, they are mature learners who freely choose to learn. Thus, in contrast with, say, young children engaged in compulsory schooling, they are self-directed, self-empowered, and therefore well positioned to be heavily involved in planning their own learning. Essentially, coaches seek learning opportunities because they want to become better coaches.

Second, the heart of a coach's learning is found in praxis, or in the application of skill. Certainly, most coaches want a solid theoretical foundation and a good grasp of basic coaching concepts—but always with an applied focus. In other words, learning for coaches tends to be goal directed, in that their learning is driven by specific desired outcomes or critical incidents. As a result, coach learning may appear to be far more individualized than learning in other settings.

Third, veteran coaches come to any learning situation with a richness of experience that can provide a basis for generating new understandings and capabilities. At the same time, these experiences, which may be associated with ways of being, are often challenged through learning, and coaches may find this process to be limiting, confronting, upsetting, or some combination thereof. The goal, then, is to encourage open-mindedness and decreased defensiveness about established ways of thinking and being—an aspirational goal that can be challenging to achieve in practice.

Finally, opportunities are available for coaches to learn collaboratively, and this approach may resonate with the goal-directed nature of coach learning in that coaches' goals almost always involve others (e.g., athletes, athletic trainers). In addition, most adult learning occurs outside of formal situations—for instance, through social networking or engagement in coaching tasks—thus downplaying individual achievement and performance and emphasizing the pursuit of agreed-on (i.e., collaborative) objectives. Of course, this dynamic may run against the grain in the competitive environment of sport.

Research has highlighted seven core principles that underpin learning and are relevant for coaches.[5 (p. 6)] Think about how these principles relate to the ways in which you have learned and continue to learn your coaching craft:

- New knowledge is built on existing knowledge; yet existing knowledge can either help or hinder learning.

- The ways in which we organize knowledge influence how we learn and how we apply what we learn.

- Our motivation to learn determines and sustains what we do in order to learn.

- Mastery depends on developing essential skills, regularly integrating them into practice, and knowing when to apply what we have learned.

- Learning is enhanced by goal-directed practice coupled with specific and constructive feedback.

- Learning is shaped both by one's current level of development and by the social, emotional, and intellectual climate in which we live and work.

- As self-directed learners, we should develop self-regulatory skills, such as monitoring and evaluating how we learn.

In brief, while learning is an individual process influenced by the learner's prior knowledge and motivation, it happens in a social context. Therefore, sport organizations and coach developers play an important role by proposing various learning situations based on a coach's stage of development in a specific context and setting.[6]

One way to conceptualize how we learn to coach divides the coaching journey into three phases: broad early learning, certification or accreditation, and postcertification. The first phase involves learning that takes place before assuming a coaching role. In fact, research suggests that coaching philosophies are considerably influenced by childhood experiences in family, school, and sport.[7] Granted, the importance of athletic experience as a source of coaching knowledge has sometimes been overestimated, but it has also been well documented and widely acknowledged.[8]

Ideally, the second phase of the journey involves training or coach education programs that lead to certification or accreditation. Although it has not been easy to rigorously demonstrate the effectiveness of such programs,[9] they provide an efficient way to ensure that everyone who coaches in a specific context has been exposed to minimal coaching standards for core competencies defined by coach developers. One key question here asks how we can know what participants have learned. Even so, certification is important considering that professionalization has been on the global coaching agenda for some time. Although the drive to make coaching into a fully developed and fully recognized profession is far from complete, it is widely agreed that the vocation at least needs to be made more professionalized.

This brings us to the third phase of the journey: postcertification. Certification is assumed to indicate what a person knows at a specific moment. Thus, as the years accumulate, a coach's initial certification often becomes less relevant as the field develops new knowledge. For this reason, most professional organizations ask their members (e.g., coaches, teachers, medical doctors) to participate in learning activities known collectively as continuing professional development. These activities generally occur in the form of professional in-service training, conferences, workshops, seminars, short courses, postgraduate study, study leave, and study tours.

Influences on Coach Education

The need to continually update our knowledge in sport coaching is strongly influenced by the globalization of the industry and ongoing advances in technology. These influences have increased individuals' access to new information, which continues to grow exponentially and is now available 24 hours a day.

COACHING SNAPSHOT

Sergio Lara-Bercial, strategy and development manager for the International Council for Coaching Excellence, shown here presenting at a UEFA coaching conference, presents educational sessions for coaches online and in person around the world. The ICCE and many other organizations and institutions provide a variety of coach education and development resources and courses.

Globalization

The globalization of coaching can be seen most readily in the context of high-performance positions in professional and Olympic sport. For example, in pursuit of championships and gold medals, foreign coaches (as well as performance directors) have been hired by many clubs in the English Premier League and by numerous national sporting organizations in Olympic sports such as rowing, swimming, and track and field.

Often, these coaches bring excellent technical and tactical knowledge but struggle on a number of other fronts. In many cases, they need to learn a new language, and even those from a seemingly similar country must develop understanding of a culture different from their own. For example, a coach may move from a culture in which athletes never question a coach's authority to one in which they constantly ask why. In these instances, coaches face a learning curve both before and during their coaching tenure in areas such as language skill and cultural awareness.[10]

Globalization can also be seen at other levels of sport coaching. For example, a cycling coach in Australia might have direct contact with cycling coaches in Canada, perhaps when watching training sessions, accessing planning documents, interacting with head and assistant coaches, and seeing competition performances in real time. Moreover, the unprecedented access that individual coaches have to a range of potential learning sources about all levels of sport across the world carries positive implications for their potential learning. However, while globalization may necessitate new kinds of learning in order for coaches to perform optimally, the sheer fact of being in novel situations and having access to new levels of information does not always result in learning.

Finally, many Western countries have become more diverse as their immigrant populations have grown. For example, in the United States, Hispanic and Latino Americans now make up 17 percent of the population and have the highest birth rate. Therefore, coaches at all levels need to be culturally competent in order to work with a diverse population of athletes.

Technology

Much of the globalization of coaching has been facilitated by the growing availability of increasingly sophisticated technology, which in itself has necessitated ongoing learning on a number of levels. Consider the case of sporting equipment. At the highest levels of sport, technological advancements in equipment have contributed to performance improvements and sometimes conferred a competitive advantage. For example, the sport of swimming is not often thought of as depending on equipment, but technological advances in recent years have changed swimsuit fabrics and design, as well as swimming pool construction and operation (e.g., diving blocks), thus contributing to the fall of a great many world records. Even at the developmental and participation levels of sport, advances in materials and manufacturing have resulted in equipment modifications that greatly affect the training and game environments created by coaches—for instance, variations in ball, racket, net, and court specifications in junior tennis.

Technology has also affected the ways in which we view sport performance itself. We can now gather more information about the sports we coach than ever before. For example, sport coaches and officials are investing heavily in data analytics (data collection and analysis) at all levels, from participation to high performance and from individual to team to entire sport. In some cases, this flood of information has overwhelmed coaches, who struggle to handle the large data sets. At the same time, technological advancements provide more processing power (e.g., working with "big data" while also engaging in fine-grained analysis) and greater ease of access (e.g., GPS-enabled data collection via smart devices). In short, coaches and athletes can easily access more information about athletic performance (their own and others') than ever before.

Finally, technology has fundamentally changed the ways in which coaches communicate with each other, their athletes, and others in the coaching domain. The advent of social media (e.g., Facebook, Twitter, Instagram) and communication apps (e.g., WhatsApp, Messenger, Viber, Skype, Snapchat) has created communication possibilities that were nearly inconceivable just a decade or two ago. These developments have also created communication gaps between coaches of different generations. Therefore, learning is essential for coaches who hope to maintain a level playing field with the competition. Aside from any financial limitations, the key—whether in terms of data, communication practices, or equipment—is how coaches use technology. The best coaches not only stay at the forefront of existing technology but are also well positioned to innovate, often in collaboration with other experts such as manufacturers and software or web designers. Not all expert coaches are early adopters of technology, but the best ones tend to be informed users or at least surround themselves with people who are.

Drive and Direction in Coach Learning

Determining what to learn in order to become a better coach depends on context, especially on who you coach. In other words, what you need to know depends on the current and future needs of your athletes and the sport setting in which you work. For example, the needs of athletes in participation contexts, which emphasize sustained engagement and enjoyment, are likely to differ from the needs of athletes in performance settings that focus on competition and achievement.[11]

As discussed earlier in this book, coaching practice in all contexts is underpinned by coaches' knowledge in three broad domains: professional, interpersonal, and intrapersonal.[12] In brief, professional knowledge relates to the specific sport, the athletes, sport science, coaching theory and methodology, and foundational skills (i.e., content and how to coach it). For example, can the coach plan for skill development and design activities that promote it in an appropriate way? Interpersonal knowledge, in contrast, relates to the social context of the sport and the relationships involved (e.g., connectedness; emotional intelligence, especially empathy). For instance, how good is the coach at reading the team's emotional state before a major competition? Finally, intrapersonal knowledge pertains to one's coaching philosophy and lifelong learning orientation (e.g., reflection, self-awareness). For example, how does a high-performance coach make time in a hectic schedule for reflection and build a staff culture that allows for honest feedback?

COACHING SNAPSHOT

Shown here during her volleyball coaching days at Florida State University, **Cecile Reynaud** is the epitome of a coach with a thirst for learning and teaching. During her hall of fame coaching career she earned her doctorate in athletic administration, served as president of the National Coaching Association, was a top coaching instructor for many years, and has written multiple instructional books for coaches.

The mere fact that coaches are presented with myriad opportunities to learn does not necessarily mean that they will learn. Ultimately, each coach determines whether, what, and how to learn. The best coaches know that in order to succeed over any period of time, they must keep learning. Lifelong learners are self-driven and curious.

For instance, in a study involving 14 of the world's most successful coaches,[1] one common theme was their insatiable thirst to know more. They were driven to be the best they could be and to sustain their excellence through ongoing learning in order to get ahead and stay ahead of other coaches to advantage their athletes. For many, their pursuit of the latest knowledge was driven in part by fear of not knowing enough and by having experienced uncomfortable situations (e.g., their beliefs about coaching practice were challenged) and coming to uncomfortable realizations that might have caused them some sense of embarrassment or anxiety, thus involving what other authors have referred to as disjuncture or cognitive dissonance. In response, they viewed learning as a way to enable themselves to provide their athletes with the best possible coaching for their particular time and place.

Several studies have highlighted the trajectories of high-performance coaches.[1, 8, 13] In one example, researchers found that highly successful international coaches were university educated, had played the sport they coach, had managed a short transition from playing to coaching at the high-performance level, and possessed highly developed intrapersonal skills such as self-awareness and self-reflection.[1] More generally, this line of research has provided insight into how these coaches became effective practitioners with the goal of informing coach development activities. The results suggest that anyone who supports coach learning should take into account the following factors: coaching context, learning situation, and level of expertise. Indeed, these factors are treated as key elements of the *International Sport Coaching Framework*.[11]

These elements are also highlighted in figure 12.1, which presents a model for picturing how individuals learn to coach in a lifelong perspective (Trudel and Gilbert[14], revised in Trudel, Gilbert, and Rodrigue[6]). In this particular formulation, level of expertise is expressed as coach identity evolution. The dotted lines are used to stress that the elements must be seen as continuums rather than distinct categories. For instance, in the evolution of coach identity, the three components (coaching contexts, learning situations, and level of expertise) make variable contributions over time for any given coach. Also, the transition from, say, competent to supercompetent occurs not at a discrete point but over a period of time. Finally, a coach might be a newcomer in one area (e.g., strength development) but an innovator in another (e.g., tactics).

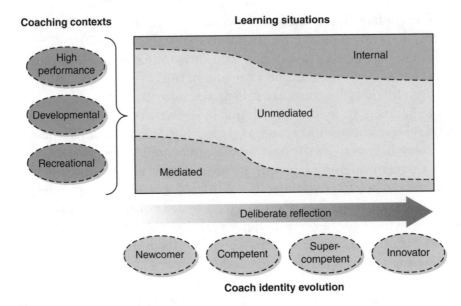

FIGURE 12.1 How sport coaches learn to coach.

Reprinted by permission from P. Trudel, W. Gilbert, and F. Rodrigue, "The Journey from Competent to Innovator: Using Appreciative Inquiry to Enhance High Performance Coaching," *AI Practitioner* 18, no. 2 (2016): 40-46.

Learning and Coaching Contexts

Coaching context is a key variable that influences coach learning. One model classifies coaching contexts into three categories—recreational, developmental, and high performance—but this classification can be adapted to reflect whatever is used in a given sport federation or country.[6] For instance, some national governing bodies might simply use participation and performance. Whatever model is used to categorize contexts, the key is to consider the motives, needs, and goals of the participants.

Learning context relates to the setting in which learning takes place; in turn, setting can be described in terms of the central figures involved, the supporting structures, and the prevailing conditions. The learning situation, on the other hand, can be thought of as the learner's unique perspective on the learning context. Thus, while we can provide the same learning context to a group of coaches (e.g., courses, websites), we cannot assume that each coach will engage in that context as a learning situation. The latest research and theorizing suggest that coaches have the opportunity to change their cognitive structure (e.g., in terms of knowledge or motivation) by engaging in any of three types of learning situations: mediated, unmediated, and internal (Trudel and Gilbert[14], drawing on a distinction made by Moon[15]; also see figure 12.1).

Mediated Learning Situations

In mediated learning situations, the learner's perspective is that someone else is directing the learning. The most common example can be found in large-scale coach education programs. In these situations, someone other than the coach—either an individual (e.g., coach developer) or an organization (e.g., national governing body)—directs the learning through content selection (curriculum), delivery (course organization and structure), and assessment (content, format, and timing). For instance, in a university degree program, academic staff and program conveners determine the offerings and set requirements for successful graduation.

Research shows that when formal university study is appropriate and authentic for meeting the specific needs of coaches (in terms of sport, setting, and performance level), it is viewed favorably as a way for coaches to develop their craft.[16] In fact, for many coaches, formal university study in a related field (e.g., sport science, physical education) has been valued as much as on-the-job learning.[8, 17] Thus university-based learning in a related field has been viewed as a key element of coach development[2, 8, 18] and successful performance.[1] While this conclusion may run somewhat contrary to the established practices in a variety of nations, university-based education for coaches has been commonplace in Eastern Europe since the 1940s. Similarly, in the United States, universities have offered undergraduate minors and master's degrees in coaching for a number of years.

Unmediated Learning Situations

In unmediated learning situations, the coach's perception is that he or she has decided what needs to be learned and how to go about it. This avenue has often been viewed as providing the bulk of coaches' knowledge, particularly in countries and in sports that lack a formal education tradition. This type of learning has been subdivided into two subcategories: unconscious and conscious.[19] Unconscious learning relates to the subculture of a sport. For example, this form of learning may initially enable coaches to behave, unknowingly, in ways that allow them to fit in with others in their chosen sport and context. Over time, it enables them to understand and navigate potentially tricky social and political arrangements in their team or sport.

The second subcategory relates to the far more conscious efforts that a coach might make in solving problems or developing new areas of expertise. Examples include reading relevant books, watching videos, or searching the web for specific information. However, the most popular methods in this category involve engaging in discussions with colleagues and observing them at work. At the same time, the competitive nature of high-performance sport may limit potentially generative dialogue and debate between coaches in the same sport. In addition, this type of learning is more likely to lead to uncritical reproduction of existing practices than it is to foster innovation or creative thinking.

Internal Learning Situations

This final category is closely associated with the notion of personal reflection. However, while coaches report almost universally that they understand, value, and engage in reflection, they often do so only at a superficial level and therefore gain only limited benefit for their coaching practice. As a result, we prefer to view internal learning as a kind of "cognitive housekeeping" in which coaches reorganize what they already know.[20] This kind of learning is more likely to be achieved when a coach schedules a specific time to reflect on personal practice or write in a personal reflective journal. Alternatively, a coach might reflect deliberately on a clinic presentation by another coach, or a book or article about coaching, and realize that the material presented reinforces his or her own current practice and thus breeds enhanced confidence.

Again, the dotted lines in figure 12.1 indicate that it can be difficult to differentiate the three types of learning situations because of how a learning context is structured. For example, during a weekend course of coach training, coaches listen to the instructor and do the prescribed exercises, which constitutes a mediated learning situation. However, during breaks and meals, they may discuss coaching topics unrelated to the course content, thus establishing unmediated learning situations. In addition, if the instructor asks the participants to draw a concept map of what they know about a coaching topic, that activity may create an internal learning situation embedded in the mediated one.

Finally, the question often arises of how to classify one's experience as an athlete. The key point is that athletes generally concentrate on how to improve their athletic skills, not their coaching skills. Only when they move into a coaching position do they go back in their memory and select examples of things that coaches have done. These recollections probably happen in situations where they are free from distractions and are writing or reflecting on their own—in other words, internal learning situations.

Roles of Others in Coach Learning

As we have indicated, learning can be viewed as an individual process that happens in a social context. Accordingly, in all three types of learning situations—mediated, unmediated, and internal—other people play important roles. In mediated learning situations, interactions should be based on sound teaching principles (i.e., not merely lecturing), and the quality of coach engagement influences the learning climate. In unmediated learning situations, other people play crucial roles—for instance, athletes, coaching peers, academic publishers, and representatives from the coaching departments of national sport organizations. Other people can even play a role in internal learning situations such as brainstorming activities.

Again, coaches report learning best when they observe and engage in discussion with others. As a result, they are likely to seek out others (e.g., coaching peers, trusted mentors) when trying to work through issues that arise in their coaching practice. These interactions are also highly valued by coaches for their ongoing development. The quality of these learning situations has been analyzed through a variety of lenses, including the following concepts: communities of practice,[8] dynamic social networks,[21] and workplace learning.[18]

A community of practice (CoP) has been defined as a group of people "who share a concern, a set of problems, or a passion about a topic" and seek to "deepen their knowledge and expertise" through ongoing interaction.[22 (p. 4)] Thus it is easy to see why this approach can be appealing. More specifically, the potential for highly generative relationships in a coaching CoP is suggested by multiple components: mutual engagement (active connections; e.g., regular meetings of head and assistant coaches to discuss practices and develop game plans), joint enterprise (negotiation of the purpose for participation; e.g., promotion of fair play across a league), and shared repertoire (shared culture that distinguishes one CoP from another; e.g., team anthem sung after a victory).

The research on CoPs in sport coaching is a bit more mixed.[23-25] It has shown that under certain circumstances, coaches in a CoP may benefit from interacting with each other and negotiating meaning related to their coaching practice; they may also be able to develop the field more generally by distributing relevant and authentic knowledge. At the same time, it has also been suggested that engagement between coaches may be stifled by the importance placed on winning, especially in high-performance sport environments but also in many youth settings.[21, 26, 27] The notion that high-performance coaches often find it difficult to engage generatively with their peers is supported by Australian research showing that head coaches in high-performance contexts report a strong sense of isolation. These feelings were attributed to the highly contested nature of high-performance sport,[21] and the resulting lack of a highly functioning social community was found to thwart potential learning. At the same time, however, it led to the development of a dynamic social network that fostered individual coach learning and development.

These findings have motivated us to regularly ask our coaching colleagues in high-performance sport who (if anyone) they go to when addressing the issues that inevitably rise in their complex coaching practices. Their answer, though perhaps not considered ideal for learning and development, is that they actively seek out confidantes whom they respect and trust to discuss their coaching issues. The composition and arrangements of an individual's social network are dynamic and generally take several years to form; in addition, the network continues to evolve in relation to the coach's day-to-day work practices and overall career arc. In other words, the membership of the network changes as the coach's identity develops and evolves (a point that is also addressed in the next section).

The day-to-day work practices of coaches have themselves received attention as a focus of learning research. Coaches at all levels of sport have regularly reported value in learning from experience—that is, learning on the job through trial and error. From this perspective, learning can be viewed as the creation of knowledge through social participation in everyday work. Coach learning in the workplace (the coaching setting) involves interplay between the coach's personal qualities, the degree of access to learning opportunities, the specific nature of the coaching work undertaken, and the amount of guidance available from others. For instance, research has shown that some high-performance coaches were not well prepared by their previous learning experiences to complete some of the tasks required of them (though they were generally well prepared for the tasks considered most central to their work).

As a result, coaches seek to learn from a variety of sources both within and outside of their workplace environment. For example, they may seek the counsel of the team sport scientist when planning recovery sessions between events with a short turnaround. Alternatively, high-performance coaches in particular may access professionals outside of sport surreptitiously to avoid revealing any perceived weakness or vulnerability to others in the organization.

Coach learning in the workplace is affected by a range of structural factors, such as working climate and physical environment. However, situational factors alone do not enable full understanding of the workplace as a learning environment. To the contrary, the learning that occurs, or does not occur, in the coaching workplace also hinges on the individual coach's agency. Individual agency involves aspects such as passion for the sport and drive to be the best. As considered in the next section, the nature of personal agency changes over time and corresponds closely with the evolution of a coach's identity.

Evolution of Coach Identity

Imagine a parent with a very limited coaching background who decides to coach her daughter's team at the recreational level. She is a newcomer, and her association will probably ask her to take a training course (a

COACHING SNAPSHOT

Called "The Professor" by many in his home country of Finland, **Erkka Westerlund** was tasked with rebuilding Finland's ice hockey program. Then head of coaching and education at the Vierumäki Sport Institute, Westerlund implemented an entirely new system that emphasized quality coaching at all levels of the sport. The results have since paid off in a big way, with huge participation figures and multiple World Junior Ice Hockey Championships.

mediated learning situation). At the same time, she will probably search on her own for additional information, perhaps by talking with other coaches (in unmediated learning situations). If she persists in her new role, she will become a competent coach, meaning that after completing the compulsory courses she can adequately reproduce the competencies covered in the curriculum.

As she continues, she will be increasingly able to develop her own coaching style, become more knowledgeable based on her own coaching experiences, and coach more fluently. In other words, she will have arrived at supercompetence—the final step before beginning to innovate in how one should coach, in this case at the recreational level. At this point, there may be fewer formal courses for her to take part in. As an alternative, she may look for any information that can help her adopt new perspectives and make time for reflection in order to imagine how she might do things differently. With this progression in mind, the arrowed line in figure 12.1 that is labeled "deliberate reflection" indicates that as we move from competence to supercompetence to innovation, it is essential that we get consciously involved in internal learning situations.

Now imagine an experienced coach who obtains a new position at the helm of a national team. For a time, he will be a newcomer. No doubt he has undertaken a variety of formal courses as required by his association (mediated learning situations), and he may have exhausted all of the relevant offerings. He is, of course, deemed competent in many areas, or he would not have been hired; still, he has little experience in a variety of tasks that come with his new position. Therefore, he seeks advice and support from trusted colleagues (his community of practice) and old confidantes (his dynamic social network) about the new issues he is encountering (unmediated learning situations). Perhaps these issues relate to increased media exposure (e.g., regular press conferences) or increased scope of work (e.g., providing leadership and guidance for the entire coaching system in his sport). He also learns on the job by completing novel work tasks and accessing resources both within and beyond his new workplace.

Thus, over time, he may become supercompetent in all of the coaching tasks required of him. However, his position also dictates that he be an innovator. The problem is that he perceives that he has less time now for deliberate reflection than at any other point in his coaching career. His solution? Amid the seeming chaos of his daily coaching work, he schedules short periods of quiet time at a local café. There, in addition to getting something wholesome to eat, he can catch his breath, consider the bigger picture, and organize his thoughts—thus creating an internal learning situation that enables deliberate reflection.

Deliberate Reflection

In sport coaching, we know that experience shapes learning; in other words, coaches construct knowledge through coaching practice. In and of itself, however, coaching practice is insufficient to learn and develop. Coaches must also engage in deliberate analysis (i.e., reflection) in relation to their coaching behavior and performance. This work goes beyond the kind of reflection that coaches often engage in about what is working and what is not, which tends to be unstructured and ad hoc. In contrast, deliberate reflection involves scheduling time to think substantively and uses a structured approach based on key questions such as the following:

- When might I reflect?
- On what do I reflect?
- How do I reflect?

This deliberate reflective practice is central to professionalization. Coaches are encouraged to reflect at various times: when designing practice (reflection-for-action), during practice or competition (reflection-in-action), immediately after practice or competition (reflection-on-action), and after a period of time has passed (e.g., few weeks) or at the end of a season (retrospective reflection-on-action).[28] For instance, a track-and-field coach might consider the number of reps and sets to use in a specific speed session (reflection-for-action); assess an athlete's performance status and reduce the number of reps in a set during a specific session (reflection-in-action); think about the quality of the session undertaken and whether the objectives were met (reflection-on-action); and, finally, after several weeks of preseason training, think about the athlete's progress in translating power training into speed development as desired (retrospective reflection-on-action).[28]

Test Your Deliberate Reflection Ability

Consider the following questions about a time when you were challenged in your coaching.

- What happened? What were your thoughts, feelings, and behaviors?
- When did it occur?
- Who was involved? What happened to who was involved?
- What was learned?
- Did it change your coaching practice? If not, why not? If so, how, and what resulted from the changes?

As coaches evolve in their identity, they are likely to engage in reflective practice more often and at a deeper level. Reflective coaches deliberately schedule time to take a step back when their emotional climate is conducive to rational thought and they are free from distractions and the emotions associated with competition.

Exercise

Reflect on your learning journey. To guide your refection, consider the following questions:

- Who (if anyone) has influenced your coaching, whether positively or negatively?
- What (if anything) have others done to help your learning?
- What (if anything) have you done to help your own learning?
- What (if anything) have you changed in your coaching?
- What (if anything) are you aware that you don't know (i.e., what have you missed out on)?
- How do you believe you learn best?

Now answer the following questions:

- List some key events in your life and how they may have shaped how and what you learn—for example, how a particular coach taught you a specific skill when you were struggling.
- As it relates to your coaching work, what and how have you learned by doing as an athlete? As a coach? As an employee? As a student? In other contexts?
- Consider a high point in your coaching. What did you learn from the experience?
- Consider a low point in your coaching. What did you learn from that experience?
- Consider a turning point in your coaching journey. What did you learn from it?

Based on figure 12.1, fill out the following tables to help you begin developing a plan for continuous learning as a coach. In the first table, indicate your main coaching context, then develop a list of key learning topics based on the coaching knowledge that is relevant to your work in the professional, interpersonal, and intrapersonal dimensions. In the second table, list each topic from the first table and indicate your current stage of coach identity: newcomer, competence, supercompetence, or innovator. Next, for each topic, indicate ways in which you might develop your coaching through mediated, unmediated, and internal learning; you could also indicate whether a given approach is of greater or lesser importance for that topic. In the rightmost column, indicate when you will develop that aspect of your work. This specificity is important in order to foster action. After completing the tables, elaborate on your plan to organize how you will work to develop your coaching craft.

Your coaching context: _____

COACHING KNOWLEDGE (INFORMATION, UNDERSTANDING, OR SKILL OBTAINABLE THROUGH EXPERIENCE OR EDUCATION)

Professional (sport specific)	Interpersonal (involving interaction with others)	Intrapersonal (e.g., through self-awareness, reflection)
(Example) Techniques and tactics	(Example) Athletes	(Example) Pressure and fatigue
(Example) Anti-doping rules	(Example) Assistants	(Example) Time to reflect
(Example) Sport science (e.g., physiology, biomechanics)	(Example) Referees, media	(Example) Level of adaptability

(continued)

(continued)

| Topic | Stage of coach identity[*] | TYPE OF LEARNING | | | When |
		Mediated	Unmediated	Internal	

[*]Indicate newcomer, competence, supercompetence, or innovator.

From International Council for Coaching Excellence, *Sport Coaches' Handbook*, eds. D. Gould and C. Mallett. (Champaign, IL: Human Kinetics, 2021).

REFERENCES

Introduction

1. Day, D. (2013). Historical perspectives on coaching. In P. Potrac, W. Gilbert, & J. Denison (Eds.), *Routledge handbook of sports coaching* (pp. 5-15). Routledge.

2. International Olympic Committee. (2015). Athens 1896. www.olympic.org/ athens-1896-summer-olympics

3. Wikipedia. (2019, August 29). List of participating nations at the Summer Olympic Games. https://en.wikipedia.org/wiki/List_of_participating_nations_ at_the_Summer_Olympic_Games

4. Gilbert, W.D., & Trudel, P. (2004). Analysis of coaching science research published from 1970-2001. *Research Quarterly for Exercise and Sport, 75*, 388-399.

5. Rangeon, S., Gilbert, W., & Bruner, M. (2012). Mapping the world of coaching science: A citation network analysis. *Journal of Coaching Education, 5*(1), 83-108.

6. Gallimore, R., & Tharp, R. (2004). What a coach can teach a teacher, 1975-2004: Reflections and reanalysis of John Wooden's teaching practices. *The Sport Psychologist, 18*, 119-137.

7. Gilbert, W., Nater, S., Siwik, M., & Gallimore, R. (2010). The Pyramid of Teaching Success in Sport: Lessons learned from applied science and effective coaches. *Journal of Sport Psychology in Action, 1*, 86-94.

8. Nater, S., & Gallimore, R. (2010). *You haven't taught until they have learned: John Wooden's teaching principles and practices.* Fitness International Technology.

9. Becker, A.J. (2013). Quality coaching behaviors. In P. Potrac, W. Gilbert, & J. Denison (Eds.), *Routledge handbook of sports coaching* (pp. 184-195). Routledge.

10. Cassidy, T., Jones, R., & Potrac, P. (2016). *Understanding sports coaching: The pedagogical, social, and cultural foundations of coaching practice* (3rd ed.). Routledge.

11. Erickson, K., & Gilbert, W. (2013). Coach–athlete interactions in children's sport. In J. Côté & R. Lidor (Eds.), *Conditions of children's talent development in sport* (pp. 139-156). Fitness Information Technology.

12. Huber, J.J. (2013). *Applying educational psychology in coaching athletes.* Human Kinetics.

13. Schempp, P.G., & McCullick, B. (2010). Coaches' expertise. In J. Lyle & C. Cushion (Eds.), *Sports coaching: Professionalisation and practice* (pp. 221-231). Routledge.

14. Côté, J., & Gilbert, W.D. (2009). An integrative definition of coaching effectiveness and expertise. *International Journal of Sports Science & Coaching, 4*, 307-323.

15. Gilbert, W.D., & Côté, J. (2013). Defining coaching effectiveness: A focus on coaches' knowledge. In P. Potrac, W. Gilbert, & J. Denison (Eds.), *Routledge handbook of sports coaching* (pp. 147-159). Routledge.

16. Hedlund, D.P., Fletcher, C.A., Pack, S.M., & Dahlin, S. (2018). The education of sport coaches: What should they learn and when should they learn it? *International Sport Coaching Journal, 5*, 192-199.

17. Cushion, C., & Nelson, L. (2013). Coach education and learning: Developing the field. In P. Potrac, W. Gilbert, & J. Denison (Eds.), *Routledge handbook of sports coaching* (pp. 359-374). Routledge.

18. Ewing, T.K. (2019). Rethinking head coach credentials: Playing experience, tertiary qualifications, and coaching apprenticeships. *International Sport Coaching Journal, 6*, 244-249.

19. Taylor, W.G., & Garratt, D. (2013). Coaching and professionalization. In P. Potrac, W. Gilbert, & J. Denison (Eds.), *Routledge handbook of sports coaching* (pp. 27-39). Routledge.

20. The Football Association. (2015). FA education courses 2015/2016. www.thefa.com/st-georges-park/fa-learning/fa-national-courses

21. Martel, K. (2015). USA Hockey's American Development Model: Changing the coaching and player development paradigm. *International Sport Coaching Journal, 2*, 39-49.

22. National Association for Sport and Physical Activity. (2006). *National standards for sport coaches: Quality coaches, quality sports* (2nd ed.). Author.

23. United States Olympic Committee. (2017). USOC quality coaching framework. Human Kinetics. https://www.teamusa.org/About-the-USOPC/Programs/Coaching-Education/Quality-Coaching-Framework

24. International Council for Coaching Excellence, Association of Summer Olympic International Federations, & Leeds Beckett University. (2013). *International sport coaching framework* (Version 1.2). Human Kinetics.

25. Kidman, L., & Keelty, D. (2015). Coaching and coach development in New Zealand. *International Sport Coaching Journal, 2*(2), 330-338.

26. Segwaba, J., Vardhan, D., & Duffy, P. (2014). Coaching in South Africa. *International Sport Coaching Journal, 1*, 33-41.

27. Malcolm, D., Pinheiro, C., & Pimenta, N. (2014). Could and should sport coaching become a profession? Some sociological reflections. *International Sport Coaching Journal, 1*, 42-45.

28. Roetert, E.P., & Bales, J. (2014). A global approach to advancing the profession of coaching. *International Sport Coaching Journal, 1*, 2-4.

29. Sheridan, M.P. (2014). "Could and should sport coaching become a profession? Some sociological reflections." A commentary. *International Sport Coaching Journal, 1*, 46-49.

30. U.S. Bureau of Labor Statistics. (2019, September 16). *Occupational outlook handbook: Coaches and scouts.* www.bls.gov/ooh/Entertainment-and-Sports/Coaches-and-scouts.htm

Chapter 1

1. *Coaching.* (n.d.). Wikipedia. http://en.wikipedia.org/wiki/Coaching

2. Stern, L.R. (2004). Executive coaching: A working definition. *Consulting Psychology Journal: Practice and Research, 56*, 154-162.

3. International Council for Coaching Excellence, Association of Summer Olympic International Federations, & Leeds Beckett University. (2013). *International sport coaching framework* (Version 1.2). Human Kinetics.

4. Côté, J., & Gilbert, W. (2009). An integrative definition of coaching effectiveness and expertise. *International Journal of Sports Science and Coaching, 4*(3), 307-323.

5. Côté, J., Bruner, M., Erickson, K., Strachan, L., & Fraser-Thomas, J. (2010). Athlete development and coaching. In J. Lyle & C. Cushion (Eds.), *Sports coaching: Professionalisation and practice* (pp. 63-84). Elsevier.

6. Trudel, P., & Gilbert, W.D. (2006). Coaching and coach education. In D. Kirk, M. O'Sullivan, & D. McDonald (Eds.), *Handbook of physical education* (pp. 516-539). Sage.

7. Young, D.C. (2014). Professionalism in archaic and classical Greek athletics. In T. Scanlon (Ed.), *Sport in the Greek and Roman Worlds, Vol. 2* (pp. 82-94). Oxford University Press.

8. Watkins, R. (1997). *Gladiator.* Houghton Mifflin Harcourt.

9. Hickman, K. (2008). *Hundred Years' War: English longbow.* Thoughtco. http://militaryhistory.about.com/od/smallarms/p/englongbow.htm

10. Robinson, P.E. (2014). *Foundations of sports coaching.* Routledge.

11. Ritchie, M. (1990). Counseling is not a profession—yet. *Counselor Education and Supervision, 29*, 220-227.

12. Gano-Overway, L., Thompson, M., & Van Mullem , P. (2021). National standards for sport coaches: Quality coaches, quality sports. SHAPE America.

13. United States Olympic and Paralympic Committee. (n.d.). *Coaching ethics code.* https://www.teamusa.org/USA-Karate/Officials-and-Coaches/Coaches-Resources/USOC-Coaching-Ethics-Code

14. Coaching Association of Canada. (n.d.). National Coaching Certification Program. www.coach.ca/files/NCCPModel_en_skin.swf

15. North, J., Lara-Bercial, S., Petrovic, L., Livingstone, K., Oltmanns, K., Minkhorst, J., & Hamalainen, K. (2016). *Project CoachLearn—Report #3—The context and motivations for the collection and application of sport coaching workforce data in 5 European countries.* CoachLearn.

16. De Bosscher, V., Shibli, S., Westerbeek, H., & Van Bottenburg, M. (2015). *Successful elite sport policies.* Meyer & Meyer.

17. Martens, R. (2012). *Successful coaching* (3rd ed.). Human Kinetics.

18. Olusoga, P., Butt, J., Hays, K., & Maynard, I. (2009). Stress in elite sports coaching: Identifying stressors. *Journal of Applied Sport Psychology, 21*(4), 442-459.

19. Purdy, L., & Jones, R. (2011). Choppy waters: Elite rowers' perceptions of coaching. *Sociology of Sport Journal, 28*, 329–346.

20. Gould, D., Guinan, D., Greenleaf, C., & Chung, Y. (2002). A survey of U.S. Olympic coaches: Variables perceived to have influenced athlete performances and coach effectiveness. *The Sport Psychologist, 16*, 229-250.

21. Mallett, C.J., & Lara-Bercial, S. (2016). Serial winning coaches: People, vision, and environment. In M. Raab, P. Wylleman, R. Seiler, A.-M. Elbe, & A. Hatzigeorgiadis (Eds.), *Sport and exercise psychology research: From theory to practice* (pp. 289-322). Elsevier.

22. Lara-Bercial, S., & Mallett, C.J. (2016). The practices and developmental pathways of professional and Olympic serial winning coaches. *International Sport Coaching Journal, 3*(3), 221-239.

23. Vealey, R.S., Udry, E.M., Zimmerman, V., & Soliday, J. (1992). Intrapersonal and situational predictors of coaching burnout. *Journal of Sport & Exercise Psychology, 14*(1), 40-58.

Chapter 2

1. Lyle, J. (2002). *Sports coaching concepts: A framework for coaches' behaviour.* Psychology Press.

2. Bandura, A. (2002). Selective moral disengagement in the exercise of moral agency. *Journal of Moral Education, 31*(2), 101-119.

3. International Council for Coaching Excellence, Association of Summer Olympic International Federations, & Leeds Beckett University. (2013). *International sport coaching framework* (Version 1.2). Human Kinetics.

4. International Council for Coaching Excellence. (2012). Codes of conduct for coaches. www.icce.ws/projects/ethics-in-coaching

5. Brackenridge, C., Pitchford, A., & Wilson, M. (2011). Respect: Results of a pilot project designed to improve behaviour in English Football. *Managing Leisure, 16*(3), 175-191. https://doi.org/10.1080/13606719.2011.583406

6. De Waegeneer, E., Van De Sompele, J., & Willem, A. (2015). Ethical codes in sports organizations: Classification framework, content analysis, and the influence of content on code effectiveness. *Journal of Business Ethics*, 1-12. http://doi.org/10.1007/s10551-014-2531-y

7. National Collegiate Athletic Association. (2015, October 1). 2015-2016 NCAA Division I Manual. www.ncaapublications.com/p-4420-2015-2016-ncaa-division-i-manual-october-version.aspx

8. Cassidy, T.G., Jones, R.L., & Potrac, P.A. (2015). *Understanding sports coaching: The pedagogical, social and cultural foundations of coaching practice.* Routledge.

9. Victor, B., & Cullen, J.B. (1988). The organizational bases of ethical work climates. *Administrative Science Quarterly, 33*(1), 101-125.

10. Cullen, J.B., Parboteeah, K.P., & Viktor, B. (2003). The effects of ethical climates on organizational commitment: A two-study analysis. *Journal of Business Ethics, 46*(2), 127-141.

11. World Anti-Doping Agency. (2019, November 25). *World anti-doping code 2021.* https://www.wada-ama.org/sites/default/files/resources/files/2021_code.pdf

12. Ungerleider, S. (2001). *Faust's gold: Inside the East German doping machine.* Thomas Dunne Books.

13. Bandura, A. (1986). *Social foundations of thought and action.* Prentice Hall.

14. Dubin, C. (1990). *Commission of inquiry into the use of drugs and banned practices intended to increase athletic performance.* Canadian Government Publishing Centre.

15. World Anti-Doping Agency. (2015). Independent commission report. https://wada-main-rod.s3.amazonaws.com/resources/files/wada_independent_commission_report_1_en.pdf

16. Moston, S., Engelberg, T., & Skinner, J. (2015). Perceived incidence of drug use in Australian sport: A survey of athletes and coaches. *Sport in Society, 18*(1), 91-105. https://doi.org/10.1080/17430437.2014.927867

17. Sajber, D., Rodek, J., Escalante, Y., Olujić, D., & Sekulic, D. (2013). Sport nutrition and doping factors in swimming; parallel analysis among athletes and coaches. *Collegium Antropologicum, 37*(Suppl. 2), 179-186.

18. Mandic, G.F., Peric, M., Krzelj, L., Stankovic, S., & Zenic, N. (2013). Sports nutrition and doping factors in synchronized swimming: Parallel analysis among athletes and coaches. *Journal of Sports Science and Medicine, 12*(4), 753-760.

19. Fung, L., & Yuan, Y. (2006). Performance enhancement drugs: Knowledge, attitude and intended behaviour among community coaches in Hong Kong. *The Sport Journal, 9*(3).

20. Patterson, L., & Backhouse, S.H. (2018). "An important cog in the wheel," but not the driver: Coaches' perceptions of their role in doping prevention. *Psychology of Sport and Exercise, 37,* 117-127.

21. Allen, J., Morris, R., Dimeo, P., & Robinson, L. (2017). Precipitating or prohibiting factor: Coaches' perceptions of their role and actions in anti-doping. *International Journal of Sports Science and Coaching, 12*(5), 577-587. https://doi.org/10.1177/1747954117727653

22. Goncalves, C., Coelho e Silva, M., Cruz, J., Torregrosa, M., & Cumming, S. (2010). The effect of achievement goals on moral attitudes in young athletes. *Journal of Sports Science and Medicine, 9,* 605-611.

23. Donahue, E., Miquelon, P., Valois, P., Goulet, C., Buist, A., & Vallerand, R. (2006). A motivational model of performance-enhancing substance use in elite athletes. *Journal of Sport & Exercise Psychology, 28,* 511-520.

24. Barkoukis, V., Lazuras, L., Tsorbatzoudis, H., & Rodafinos, A. (2011). Motivational and sportspersonship profiles of elite athletes in relation to doping behavior. *Psychology of Sport & Exercise, 12,* 205-212.

25. Ntoumanis, N., Gucciardi, D., Backhouse, S., Barkoukis, V., Quested, E., Patterson, L., Smith, B., Whitaker, L., Pavlidis, G., & Kaffe, S. (2018). An intervention to optimize coach motivational climates and reduce athlete willingness to dope (CoachMADE): Protocol for a cross-cultural cluster randomized control trial. *Frontiers in Psychology, 8,* 2301.

26. Mazanov, J., Hemphill, D., Connor, J., Quirk, F., & Backhouse, S. (2015). Australian athlete support personnel lived experience of anti-doping. *Sport Management Review, 18*(2), 218-230. https://doi.org/10.1016/j.smr.2014.05.007

27. Sullivan, P.J., LaForge-MacKenzie, K., Feltz, D., & Heung, S. (2015). The preliminary development and validation of the Doping Confrontation Efficacy Scale. *Psychology of Sport and Exercise, 16,* 182-190. https://doi.org/10.1016/j.psychsport.2014.04.011

28. Mazanov, J., Backhouse, S., Connor, J., Hemphill, D., & Quirk, F. (2014). Athlete support personnel and anti-doping: Knowledge, attitudes, and ethical stance. *Scandinavian Journal Of Medicine and Science in Sports, 24*(5), 846-856. https://doi.org/10.1111/sms.12084

29. TrueSport. Retrieved June 1, 2020. http://truesport.org/about-us/

30. Engelberg, T., & Moston, S. (2016). Inside the locker room: A qualitative study of coaches' anti-doping knowledge, beliefs, and attitudes. *Sport in Society, 19*(7), 942-956.

31. Patterson, L., Backhouse, S.H., & Lara-Bercial, S. (2019). Examining coaches' experiences and opinions of anti-doping education. *International Sport Coaching Journal, 6*(2), 145-159.

32. Laure, P., Thouvenin, F., & Lecerf, T. (2001). Attitudes of coaches towards doping. *Journal of Sports Medicine & Physical Fitness, 41*, 132-136.

Chapter 3

1. Vealey, R. (2005). *Coaching for the inner edge*. Fitness Information Technology.

2. Lyle, J. (2002). *Sports coaching concepts: A framework for coaches behavior*. Routledge.

3. Kassouf, J. (2014, July 14). *Ellis stressing connection with US players, coaches*. The Equalizer. https://equalizersoccer.com/2014/07/14/jill-ellis-stressing-connection-for-uswnt-players-coaches/

4. American Program Bureau. (n.d.). Bob Ladouceur. www.apbspeakers.com/speaker/bob-ladouceur

5. Martens, R. (2012). *Successful coaching* (4th ed.). Human Kinetics.

6. Australian Sports Commission. (n.d.). www.ausport.gov.au

7. Gilbert, W., Nader, S., Siwik, M., & Gallimore, R. (2012). The pyramid of teaching success in sport: Lessons from applied science and effective coaches. *Journal of Sport Psychology in Action, 1*, 86-94.

8. *For the Dad behind the greatest Little League pep talk of all time, coaching is parenting*. (2017, June 19). Fatherly. https://www.fatherly.com/play/dave-blisle-little-league-world-series-coach-motivation/

9. K. Tortolani (personal communication, July 25, 2015).

10. Positive Coaching Alliance. (2019, April 24). *First ever PCA grand prize winner announced: Charlean Crowell*. https://positivecoach.org/the-pca-blog/first-ever-pca-grand-prize-winner-announced-charlean-crowell/

11. Hoffman, K. (2014, March, April). *Fear the Irish: Muffet McGraw talks Notre Dame hoops*. Winning Hoops. https://winninghoops.com/article/muffet-mcgraw-notre-dame-hoops

12. Collins, K., & Barcelona, R.J. (2014). Youth sport coaches' perceptions of the usefulness of a statewide coach training program. *Applied Recreational Research and Programming Annual, 4*, 1-30.

13. Collins, K., & Barcelona, R.J. (2018). Keep 'em playing: Strategies for building positive sport experiences. *Strategies: A Journal for Physical and Sport Educators, 31*(5), 8-14.

14. Camiré, M., Werthner, P., & Trudel, P. (2009, January). Mission statements in sport and their ethical messages: Are they being communicated to practitioners? *Athletic Insight*, 75-86.

15. Forneris, T., Camiré, M., & Trudel, P. (2012). The development of life skills and values in high school sport. Is there a difference in stakeholders' expectations

and perceived experiences? *International Journal of Sport and Exercise Psychology, 10*(1), 9-23.

16. Gilbert, W., Côté, J., & Mallett, C. (2006). Developmental paths and activities of successful sport coaches. *International Journal of Sports Science and Coaching, 1*, 69-76.

17. Collins, K., Barber, H., Moore, K., & Laws, A. (2011). The first step: Assessing coaching philosophies of pre-service coaches. *The ICHPER-SD Journal of Research, 6*(2), 21-29.

18. Camiré, M., Trudel, P., & Forneris, T. (2012). Coaching and transferring life skills: Philosophies and strategies used by model high school coaches. *The Sport Psychologist, 26*, 243-260.

19. Collins, K., Gould, D., Lauer, L., & Chung, Y. (2009). Coaching life skills through football: Philosophical beliefs of outstanding high school football coaches. *International Journal of Coaching Science, 3*(1), 29-54.

20. Gould, D., & Carson, S. (2008). Life skills development through sport: Current status and future directions. *International Review of Sport and Exercise Psychology, 1*(1), 58-78.

21. Gould, D., Collins, K., Lauer, L., & Chung, Y. (2006). Coaching life skills: A working model. *Sport and Exercise Psychology Review, 2*(1), 4-13.

22. Gould, D., Collins, K., Lauer, L., & Chung, Y. (2007). Teaching life skills through football: A study of award-winning high school coaches. *Journal of Applied Sport Psychology, 19*(1), 16-37.

23. Chase, M. (2010). Should coaches believe in innate ability? The importance of leadership mindset. *Quest, 62*(3), 296-307.

24. Dweck, C. (2006). *Mindset: The new psychology of success.* Random House.

25. Balyi, I., Way, R., & Higgs, C. (2013). *Long-term athlete development.* Human Kinetics.

26. Lemyre, F., Trudel, P., & Durand-Bush, N. (2007). How youth sport coaches learn to coach. *The Sport Psychologist, 21*, 191-209.

Chapter 4

1. Martens, R. (1987). *Coaches guide to sport psychology: A publication for the American Coaching Effectiveness Program: Level 2 sport science curriculum.* Human Kinetics.

2. Collins, J.C., & Porras, J.I. (1996). Building your company's vision. *Harvard Business Review, 74*(5), 65-77.

3. Camiré, M., Werthner, P., & Trudel, P. (2009). Mission statements in sport and their ethical messages: Are they being communicated to practitioners? *Athletic Insight, 11*(1), 75-85.

4. Martindale, R.J.J., Collins, D., & Abraham, A. (2007). Effective talent development: The elite coach perspective in UK sport. *Journal of Applied Sport Psychology, 19*, 187-206.

5. Henriksen, K., Stambulova, N., & Roessler, K.K. (2010). Holistic approach to athletic talent development environments: A successful sailing milieu. *Psychology of Sport & Exercise, 11*, 212-222.

6. Henriksen, K., Stambulova, N., & Roessler, K.K. (2010). Successful talent development in track and field: Considering the role of environment. *Scandinavian Journal of Medicine & Science in Sports, 11,* 122-132.

7. Larsen, C.H., Alfermann, D., Henriksen, K., & Christensen, M.K. (2013). Successful talent development in soccer: The characteristics of the environment. *Sport, Exercise, and Performance Psychology, 2*(3), 190.

8. Mallett, C.J., & Lara-Bercial, S. (2016). Serial winning coaches: People, vision, and environment. In M. Raab, P. Wylleman, R. Seiler, A.-M. Elbe, & A. Hatzigeorgiadis (Eds.), *Sport and exercise psychology research: From theory to practice* (pp. 289-322). Elsevier.

9. Duda, J.L., & Balaguer, I. (2007). Coach-created motivational climate. In S. Jowette & D. Lavallee (Eds.), *Social psychology in sport* (pp. 117-130). Human Kinetics.

10. Duda, J.L., & Treasure, D.C. (2006). Motivational processes and the facilitation of performance, persistence, and well-being in sport. In J. Williams (Ed.), *Applied sport psychology: Personal growth to peak performance* (pp. 57-81). McGraw-Hill.

11. Flett, M.R., Gould, D., Paule, A.L., & Schneider, R.P. (2010). How and why university coaches define, identify, and recruit "intangibles." *International Journal of Coaching Science, 4*(2), 15-36.

12. Schroeder, P.J. (2010). Changing team culture: The perspectives of ten successful head coaches. *Journal of Sport Behavior, 33*(1), 63-87.

13. Smith, R.E., Smoll, F.L., & Curtis, B. (1979). Coach effectiveness training: A cognitive behavioral approach to enhancing relationship skills in youth sport coaches. *Journal of Sport Psychology, 1,* 59–75.

14. Smoll, F.L., & Smith, R.E. (2001). Conducting sport psychology training programs for coaches: Cognitive-behavioral principles and techniques. In J.M. Williams (Ed.), *Applied sport psychology: Personal growth to peak performance* (4th ed., pp. 378–400). Mayfield.

15. Fry, M.D., & Gano-Overway, L. (2010). Exploring the contribution of caring climate to the youth sports experience. *Journal of Applied Sport Psychology, 22,* 1-11.

16. Fry, M.D. (2010). Creating a positive climate for young athletes from day 1. *Journal of Sport Psychology in Action, 1*(1), 33-41.

17. Jowett, S. (2007). Interdependence analysis and the 3+1Cs in the coach-athlete relationship. In S. Jowett & D. Lavallee (Eds.), *Social psychology in sport* (pp. 15-27). Human Kinetics.

18. Lorimer, R. (2013). The development of empathetic accuracy in coaches. *Journal of Sport Psychology in Action, 4,* 26-33.

19. Whitmore, J. (2009). *Coaching for performance* (4th ed.). Nicholas Brealey.

20. Gould, D., Dieffenbach, K., & Moffett, A. (2002). Psychological characteristics and their development in Olympic champions. *Journal of Applied Sport Psychology, 14*(3), 172-204.

21. Jones, R. (2006). How can educational concepts inform sports coaching? In R. Jones (Ed.), *The sports coach as educator: Reconceptualising sports coaching* (pp. 4-13). Routledge.

22. Balyi, I., Way, R., Cardinal, C., Norris, S., & Higgs, C. (2008). Canadian sport for life: Long-term athlete development resource paper V2. Canadian Sport Centres.

23. Way, R., & Balyi, I. (2007). *Competition is a good servant, but a poor master.* Canadian Sport Centres.

24. Gould, D., Greenleaf, C., Guinan, D., Dieffenbach, K., & McCann, S. (2001). Pursuing performance excellence: Lessons learned from Olympic athletes and coaches. *Journal of Performance Excellence, 4,* 21-43.

25. Gilbert, W. & Trudel, P. (2006). The coach as reflective practitioner. In R. Jones (Ed.), *The sports coach as educator: Reconceptualising sports coaching* (pp. 113-127). Routledge.

26. Kidman, L. (2005). *Athlete-centered coaching: Developing inspired and inspiring people.* Innovative Print.

27. Penney, D. (2006). Coaching as teaching: New acknowledgements in practice. In R. Jones (Ed.), *The sports coach as educator: Reconceptualising sports coaching* (pp. 4-13). Routledge.

28. Knowles, Z., Gilbourne, D., Cropley, B., & Dugdill, L. (Eds.). (2014). *Reflective practice in sport and exercise sciences: Contemporary issues.* Routledge.

29. Weinberg, R.S., & Gould, D. (2019). *Foundations of sport and exercise psychology* (7th ed.). Human Kinetics.

30. Cushion, C., & Jones, R.L. (2001). A systematic observation of professional top-level youth soccer coaches. *Journal of Sport Behavior, 24*(4), 354-377.

31. Weinberg, R.S., & Gould, D. (2015). *Foundations of sport and exercise psychology* (6th ed.). Human Kinetics.

32. Loehr, J., & Schwartz, T. (2001). The making of a corporate athlete. *Harvard Business Review, 79*(1), 120-129.

33. Loehr, J.E., & Schwartz, T. (2005). *The power of full engagement: Managing energy, not time, is the key to high performance and personal renewal.* Simon and Schuster.

34. Dale, J., & Weinberg, R.S. (1990). Burnout in sport: A review and critique. *Journal of Applied Sport Psychology, 2,* 67–83.

35. Hjalm, S., Kenttä, G., & Gustafsson, H. (2007). Burnout among elite soccer coaches. *Journal of Sport Behavior, 30,* 415–427.

Chapter 5

1. Côté, J., & Gilbert, W. (2009). An integrative definition of coaching effectiveness and expertise. *International Journal of Sport Coaching and Science, 4*(3), 307-323.

2. International Council for Coaching Excellence, Association of Summer Olympic International Federations, & Leeds Beckett University. (2013). *International sport coaching framework* (Version 1.2). Human Kinetics.

3. Kidman, L., & Hanrahan, S.J. (2011). *The coaching process: A practical guide to becoming an effective sports coach.* Routledge.

4. Schwarz, R. (2013). The sandwich approach undermines your feedback. https://hbr.org/2013/04/the-sandwich-approach-undermin/

5. Stevenson, P., & Black, K. (2011). The inclusion spectrum framework. www.icsspe.org/documente/Ken_Black_-_Inclusion_Spectrum_summary.pdf

6. Weinberg, R.S., & Gould, D. (2019). *Foundations of sport and exercise psychology*. Human Kinetics.

7. Abraham, A., Collins, D., & Martindale, R. (2006). The coaching schematic: Validation through expert coach consensus. *Journal of Sport Sciences, 24*(6), 549–564.

8. Prentice, W.C. (2004). Understanding leadership. *Harvard Business Review, 82*(1), 102-109.

9. Bandura, A. (1979). *Social learning theory*. Prentice Hall.

10. Lave, J., & Wenger, E. (1991). *Situated learning: Legitimate peripheral participation*. Cambridge University Press.

11. Smoll, F.L., & Smith, R.E. (2002). Coaching behavior research and intervention in youth sports. In F.L. Smoll & R.E. Smith (Eds.), *Children and youth in sport: A biopsychosocial perspective* (pp. 211-233). Kendall Hunt.

12. Lara-Bercial, S., & Mallett, C.J. (2016). The practices and developmental pathways of professional and Olympic serial winning coaches. *International Sport Coaching Journal, 3*(1), 221-239.

13. Lara-Bercial, S. (2013). *Developing multi-skills in sport award*. Sportscotland.

14. Coleman, A. (2008). *A dictionary of psychology* (3rd ed.). Oxford University Press.

15. Chan, J.T., & Mallett, C.J. (2011). The value of emotional intelligence for high performance coaching. *International Journal of Sport Science & Coaching, 6*(3), 315-328.

16. Gilbert, W., & Côté, J. (2013). Defining coaching effectiveness: Focus on coaches' knowledge. In P. Potrac, W. Gilbert, & J. Denison (Eds.), *Routledge handbook of sports coaching* (pp. 147-159). Routledge.

17. Mallett, C.J., & Lara-Bercial, S. (2016). Serial winning coaches: People, vision, and environment. In M. Raab, P. Wylleman, R. Seiler, A.-M. Elbe, & A. Hatzigeorgiadis (Eds.), *Sport and exercise psychology research: From theory to practice*. Elsevier.

18. Lorimer, R., & Jowett, S. (2013). Empathic understanding and accuracy in the coach–athlete relationship. In P. Potrac, W. Gilbert, & J. Denison (Eds.), *Routledge handbook of sports coaching*. Routledge.

19. Jones, R., Armour, K., & Potrac, P. (2004). *Sport coaching cultures: From practice to theory*. Routledge.

20. Lyle, J. (1999). Coaching philosophy and coaching behaviour. In N. Cross & J. Lyle (Eds.), *The coaching process: Principles and practice for sport*. Butterworth-Heinemann.

21. Jowett, S. (2007). Interdependence analysis and the 3+1Cs in the coach–athlete relationship. In S. Jowett & D. Lavallee (Eds.), *Social psychology in sport* (pp. 15-27). Human Kinetics.

22. Kidman, L. (2005). *Athlete-centred coaching: Developing inspired and inspiring people*. Innovative.

23. Galipeau, J., & Trudel, P. (2006). Athlete learning in a community of practice. In R. Jones (Ed.), *The sports coach as educator: Re-conceptualizing sport coaching* (pp. 77-94). Routledge.

24. Rhind, D.J.A., & Jowett, S. (2010). Relationship maintenance strategies in the coach–athlete relationship: The development of the COMPASS model. *Journal of Applied Sport Psychology, 22*, 106-121.

25. Nicholls, J.G. (1984). Conceptions of ability and achievement motivation. In R. Ames & C. Ames (Eds.), *Research on motivation in education* (Vol. 1, pp. 39-73). Academic Press.

26. Deci, E.L., & Ryan, R.M. (1985). *Intrinsic motivation and self-determination in human behavior.* Plenum.

27. Dweck, C.S. (2006). *Mindset: The new psychology of success.* Ballantine Books.

28. Isoard-Gautheur, S., Guillet-Descas, E., & Duda, J.L. (2013). How to achieve in elite training centers without burning out? An achievement goal theory perspective. *Psychology of Sport & Exercise, 14*(1), 72–83.

29. Mallett, C.J., Rabjohns, M., & Occhino, J. (2015). Challenging coaching orthodoxy: A self-determination theory perspective. In P. Davis (Ed.), *The psychology of effective coaching and management.* Nova.

30. Occhino, J.L., Mallett, C.J., Rynne, S.B., & Carlisle, K.N. (2014). Autonomy-supportive pedagogical approach to sports coaching: Research, challenges, and opportunities. *International Journal of Sport Science and Coaching, 9*, 401–416.

31. Franks, I.M., & Miller, G. (1991). Training coaches to observe and remember. *Journal of Sports Sciences, 9*(3), 285-297.

32. Cassidy, T., Jones, R., & Potrac, P. (2009). Reflection. In T. Cassidy, R. Jones, & P. Potrac (Eds.), *Understanding sports coaching* (pp. 17-29). Routledge.

33. Schempp, P.G., Webster, C., McCullick, B., Busch, C., & Mason, I.S. (2007). How the best get better: An analysis of the self-monitoring strategies used by expert golf instructors. *Sport, Education & Society, 12*, 175-192.

Chapter 6

1. Bowes, I., & Jones, R.L. (2006). Working at the edge of chaos: Understanding coaching as a complex interpersonal system. *The Sports Psychologist, 20*, 235-245.

2. Lyle, J., & Cushion, C. (2017). *Sport coaching concepts: A framework for coaching practice* (2nd ed.). Routledge.

3. Côté, J., & Gilbert, W.D. (2009). An integrative definition of coaching effectiveness and expertise. *International Journal of Sports Science and Coaching, 4*, 307-323.

4. Siwik, M., Lambert, A., Saylor, D., Bertram, R., Cocchiarella, C., & Gilbert, W. (2015). Long-term program development (LTPD): An interdisciplinary framework for developing athletes, coaches, and sport programs. *International Sport Coaching Journal, 2*, 305-316.

5. Cross, N., & Lyle, J. (1999). *The coaching process: Principles and practice for sport.* Butterworth Heinemann.

6. Mallett, C.J. (2010). Becoming a high-performance coach: Pathways and communities. In J. Lyle & C. Cushion (Eds.), *Sports coaching: Professionalisation and practice* (pp. 119–133). Elsevier.

7. International Council for Coaching Excellence, Association of Summer Olympic International Federations, & Leeds Beckett University. (2013). *International sport coaching framework* (Version 1.2). Human Kinetics.

8. Manny. (2012, January 31). Brief history/mission statement. *Blogspot*. http://housethatbossbuilt.blogspot.com/2012/01/ch1-brief-history-mission-statement.html

9. National Basketball Association. (2018). *Our calling and values*. https://careers.nba.com/our-calling-and-values

10. Capalaba Warriors District Junior Rugby League Football Club. (2018). *Vision/mission statement*. SportsTG. http://websites.sportstg.com/club_info.cgi?c=1-2471-22503-0-0&sID=162564

11. New Zealand Rugby. (2019). *Our vision and priorities*. www.nzrugby.co.nz/about-us/governance/our-vision-and-priorities

12. Hodge, K., Henry, G., & Smith, W. (2014). A case study of excellence in elite sport: Motivational climate in a world champion team. *The Sport Psychologist, 28*, 60-74. http://dx.doi.org/10.1123/tsp.2013-0037

13. Davidson, P., & Griffin, R.W. (2006). *Management: An Australasian perspective* (3rd ed.). Wiley.

14. Lee, J., & Price, N. (2016). A national sports institute as a learning culture. *Physical Education and Sports Pedagogy, 21*(1), 10-23. doi:10.1080/17408989.2015.1072507

15. Karpin, D.S. (1995). *Reviewing Australia's managers to meet the challenge of the Asia-Pacific century*. Enterprising Nation: Report of the Industry Task Force on Leadership and Management Skills. Commonwealth of Australia.

16. Lyle, J. (2010). Planning for team sports. In J. Lyle & C. Cushion (Eds.), *Sports coaching: Professionalisation and practice* (pp. 85-98). Churchill Livingstone.

17. Mallett, C.J. (2005). Self-determination theory: A case study of evidence-based coaching. *The Sport Psychologist, 19*, 417-429.

18. Lyle, J. (2002). *Sports coaching concepts: A framework for coaches' behaviour*. Routledge.

19. Woodman, L. (1993). Coaching: A science, an art, an emerging profession. *Sport Science Review, 2*(2), 1-13.

20. Schein, E.H. (2004). *Organizational culture and leadership* (3rd ed.). Jossey-Bass.

21. Coulter, T.J., Mallett, C.J., & Singer, J. (2016). A subculture of mental toughness in an Australian Football League Club. *Psychology of Sport and Exercise, 22*, 98-113.

22. Johnson, T., Martin, A.J., Palmer, F.R., Watson, G., & Ramsey, P.L. (2013). Artefacts and the All Blacks: Rites, rituals, symbols, and stories. *Sporting Traditions, 30*(1), 43-59. https://search.informit.com.au/documentSummary;dn=405649600896879;res=IELHSS> ISSN: 0813-2577

23. Balyi, I., & Hamilton, A. (2004). Long-term athlete development: Trainability in childhood and adolescence—Windows of opportunity, optimal trainability. National Coaching Institute British Columbia & Advanced Training and Performance.

24. Côté, J., Young, B., North, J., & Duffy, P. (2007). Towards a definition of excellence in sport coaching. *International Journal of Coaching Science, 1*(1), 3-17.

25. Ericsson, K.A., Krampe, R.T., & Tesch-Römer, C. (1993). The role of deliberate practice in the acquisition of expert performance. *Psychological Review, 100*, 363–406.

26. Rynne, S.B. (2013). Culture change in a professional sports team: Shaping environmental contexts and regulating power: A commentary. *International Journal of Sports Science & Coaching, 8,* 301-304.

27. Frontiera, J. (2010). Leadership and organizational culture transformation in professional sport. *Journal of Leadership & Organizational Studies, 17*(1), 71–86. https://doi.org/10.1177/1548051809345253

28. Schroeder, P.J. (2010). Changing team culture: The perspectives of ten successful head coaches. *Journal of Sport Behavior, 33*(1), 63-88.

29. Elbe, A., & Wikman, J.M. (2017). Psychological factors in developing high-performance athletes. In J. Baker, S. Cobley, J. Schorer, & N. Wattie (Eds.), *Routledge handbook of talent identification and development in sport* (pp. 169-180). Routledge.

30. Ross, A.J., Mallett, C.J., & Parkes, J. (2015). The influence of parent sport behaviours on children's development: Youth coach and administrator perspectives. *International Journal of Sport Science and Coaching, 10,* 605-621.

31. Knight, C.J. (2017). Family influences on development in sport. In J. Baker, S. Cobley, J. Schorer, & N. Wattie (Eds.), *Routledge handbook of talent identification and development in sport* (pp. 181-191). Routledge.

32. Quarmby, T. (2016). Parenting and youth sport. In K. Green & A. Smith (Eds.), *Routledge handbook of youth sport* (pp. 209-217). Routledge.

33. Parkin, D., Bourke, P., & Gleeson, R. (2004). *What makes teams work.* Pan MacMillan Australia.

34. Kehoe, D., & Godden, S. (1998). *You lead, they'll follow: How to inspire, lead, and manage people.* BKC.

35. Pyke, F.S. (2000). Introduction. In C.J. Gore (Ed.), *Physiological tests for elite athletes* (pp. xii-xiv). Human Kinetics.

36. Coutts, A.J., & Cormack, P. (2014). Monitoring the training response. In D. Joyce & D. Lewindon (Eds.), *High-performance training for sports* (pp. 71–84). Human Kinetics.

37. McFarland, M., & Bird, S.P. (2014). A wellness monitoring tool for youth athletes. *Journal of Australian Strength and Conditioning, 22*(4), 22-26.

38. Noon, M.R., James, R.S., Clarke, N.D., Akubat, I., & Thake, C.D. (2015). Perceptions of well-being and physical performance in English elite youth footballers across a season. *Journal of Sports Sciences, 33,* 2106-2115.

39. Saw, A.E., Kellmann, M., Main, L.C., & Gastin, P.B. (2017). Athlete self-report measures in research and practice: Considerations for the discerning reader and fastidious practitioner. *International Journal of Sports Physiology and Performance, 12*(S2), 127-135.

40. Kellmann, M., & Kallus, K.W. (2001). *Recovery-stress questionnaire for athletes: User manual.* Human Kinetics.

41. Schinke, R.J., Stambulova, N.B., Si, G., & Moore, Z. (2018). International Society of Sport Psychology position stand: Athletes' mental health, performance, and development. *International Journal of Sport and Exercise Psychology, 16*(6), 622-639. doi:10.1080/1612197X.2017.1295557

42. Baca, A., Dabnichki, P., Heller, M., & Kornfeind, P. (2009). Ubiquitous computing in sports: A review and analysis. *Journal of Sports Sciences, 27*, 1335-1346. doi:10.1080/02640410903277427

43. Novatchkov, H., Bichler, S., Tampier, M., & Kornfeind, P. (2011). Real-time training and coaching methods based on ubiquitous technologies—An illustration of a mobile coaching framework. *International Journal of Computer Science in Sport, 10*(1), 26-50.

44. Ride, J., Ringuet, C., Rowlands, D., Lee, J., & James, D. (2013). A sports technology needs assessment for performance monitoring in swimming. *Procedia Engineering, 60*, 442-447. https://doi.org/10.1016/j.proeng.2013.07.072

Chapter 7

1. Koz, D., Fraser-Thomas, J., & Baker, J. (2012). Accuracy of professional sports drafts in predicting career potential. *Scandinavian Journal of Medicine & Science in Sports, 22*, e64-e69.

2. Barreiros, A.N., & Fonseca, A.M. (2012). A retrospective analysis of Portuguese elite athletes' involvement in international competitions. *International Journal of Sport Science and Coaching, 7*, 593-600.

3. Wattie, N., Schorer, J., & Baker, J. (2015). The relative age effect in sport: A developmental systems model. *Sports Medicine, 45*, 83-94.

4. Baker, J., & Wattie, N. (2018). Innate talent in sport: Separating myth from reality. *Current Issues in Sport Science, 3*, 006. doi:10.15203/CISS_2018.006

5. Davids, K., & Baker, J. (2007). Genes, environment and sport performance. *Sports Medicine, 37*(11), 961-980.

6. Till, K., Cobley, S., Cooke, C., & Chapman, C. (2014). Considering maturation status and relative age in the longitudinal evaluation of junior rugby league players. *Scandinavian Journal of Medicine & Science in Sports, 24*(3), 569-576. doi:10.1111/sms.12033

7. Gagné, F. (2004). Transforming gifts into talents: The DMGT as a developmental theory. *High Ability Studies, 15*, 119-147.

8. Côté, J., & Fraser-Thomas, J. (2016). Youth involvement and positive development in sport. In P.R.E. Crocker (Ed.), *Sport and exercise psychology: A Canadian perspective* (pp. 256-287). Pearson.

9. Côté, J., Baker, J., & Abernethy, B. (2003). From play to practice: A developmental framework for the acquisition of expertise in team sports. In K.A. Ericsson & J.L. Starkes (Eds.), *Expert performance in sports: Advances in research on sport expertise* (pp. 89-110). Human Kinetics.

10. Ericsson, K.A., Krampe, R.T., & Tesch-Römer, C. (1993). The role of deliberate practice in the acquisition of expert performance. *Psychological Review, 100*, 363-406.

11. Chow, J.Y., Davids, K., Button, C., Shuttleworth, R., Renshaw, I., et al. (2007). The role of nonlinear pedagogy in physical education. *Review of Educational Research, 77*, 251-278.

12. Henriksen, K., Stambulova, N., & Roessler, K.K. (2010). Holistic approach to athletic talent development environments: A successful sailing milieu. *Psychology of Sport and Exercise, 11*(3), 212-222.

13. Gagné, F. (2003). Transforming gifts into talents: The DMGT as a developmental theory. In N. Colangelo & G.A. Davis (Eds.), *Handbook of gifted education* (3rd ed., pp. 60-74). Allyn and Bacon.

14. Ericsson, K.A. (2013). Training history, deliberate practice, and elite sports performance: An analysis in response to Tucker and Collins review—What makes champions? *British Journal of Sports Medicine, 47*, 533-535.

15. Baker, J., & Young, B. (2014). 20 years later: Deliberate practice and the development of expertise in sport. *International Journal of Sport and Exercise Psychology, 7*, 135-157.

16. Gladwell, M. (2008). *Outliers: The story of success*. Little, Brown.

17. Colvin, G. (2008). *Talent is overrated: What really separates world-class performers from everybody else*. Portfolio.

18. Coyle, D. (2009). *The talent code*. Bantam.

19. Syed, M. (2010). *Bounce: Mozart, Federer, Picasso, Beckham, and the science of success*. Harper.

20. Epstein, D. (2013). *The sports gene*. Penguin.

21. Baker, J., Côté, J., & Abernethy, B. (2003). Learning from the experts: Practice activities of expert decision-makers in sport. *Research Quarterly for Exercise and Sport, 74*, 342-347.

22. Deakin, J.M., & Cobley, S. (2003). An examination of the practice environments in figure skating and volleyball: A search for deliberate practice. In J. Starkes & K.A. Ericsson (Eds.), *Expert performance in sports: Advances in research on sport expertise* (pp. 90-113). Human Kinetics.

23. Newell, A., & Rosenbloom, P.S. (1981). Mechanisms of skill acquisition and the law of practice. In J.R. Anderson (Ed.), *Cognitive skills and their acquisition* (pp. 1-55). Erlbaum.

24. Baker, J., Cobley, S., & Fraser-Thomas, J. (2009). What do we know about early sport specialization? Not much! *High Ability Studies, 20*, 77-89.

25. Ford, P.R., & Williams, A.M. (2017). Sport activity in childhood: Early specialization and diversification. In J. Baker, S. Cobley, J. Schorer, & N. Wattie (Eds.), *Routledge handbook of talent identification and development in sport* (pp. 117-132). Routledge.

26. Côté, J., Baker, J., & Abernethy, B. (2007). Practice and play in the development of sport expertise. In R. Eklund & G. Tenenbaum (Eds.), *Handbook of sport psychology* (3rd ed., pp. 184-202). Wiley.

27. Whitehead, M. (2001). The concept of physical literacy. *European Journal of Physical Education, 6*, 127-138.

28. Balyi, I., Way, R., & Higgs, C. (2013). *Long-term athlete development*. Human Kinetics.

29. Gulbin, J.P., Croser, M.J., Morley, E.J., & Weissensteiner, J.R. (2013). An integrated framework for the optimisation of sport and athlete development: A practitioner approach. *Journal of Sports Sciences, 31*, 1319-1331.

30. Bullock, N., Gulbin, J.P., Martin, D.T., Ross, A., Holland, T., & Marino, F. (2009). Talent identification and deliberate programming in skeleton: Ice novice to Winter Olympian in 14 months. *Journal of Sports Sciences, 27*(4), 397-404.

31. Legg, D. (2011). Athletes with disabilities—Moving forward. *Canadian Sport for Life*. http://canadiansportforlife.ca/blog/athletes-disabilities-moving-forward-dr-david-legg

32. Handford, C., Davids, K., Bennett, S., & Button, C. (1997). Skill acquisition in sport: Some applications of an evolving practice ecology. *Journal of Sports Sciences, 15*, 621-640.

33. Williams, A.M., Davids, K., & Williams, J.G. (1999). *Visual perception and action in sport*. Routledge.

34. Johnston, K., Wattie, N., Schorer, J., & Baker, J. (2018). Talent identification in sport: A systematic review. *Sports Medicine, 48*, 97-109.

35. Wattie, N., & Baker, N. (2018). An uneven playing field: Talent identification systems and the perpetuation of participation biases in high-performance sport. In R. Dionigi and M. Gard (Eds.), *Sport and physical activity across the lifespan: Critical perspectives* (pp. 117-133). Macmillan.

Chapter 8

1. Ehrmann, J. (2011). *Inside out coaching: How sports can transform lives*. Simon & Schuster.

2. Gavazzi, S.M. (2015). Turning boys into men: The incentive-based system in Urban Meyer's plan to win. *International Sport Coaching Journal, 2*, 298-304.

3. Gould, D., Collins, K., Lauer, L., & Chung, Y. (2007). Coaching life skills through football: A study of award-winning high school coaches. *Journal of Applied Sport Psychology, 19*, 16-37.

4. Dweck, C. (2006). *Mindset: The new psychology of success*. Random House.

5. Fraser-Thomas, J.L., Côté, J., & Deakin, J. (2005). Youth sport programs: An avenue to foster positive youth development. *Physical Education & Sport Pedagogy, 10*, 19-40.

6. Côté, J., & Gilbert, W. (2009). An integrative definition of coaching effectiveness and expertise. *International Journal of Sports Science & Coaching, 4*, 307-323.

7. Lerner, R.M. (2006). Developmental science, developmental systems, and contemporary theories of human development. In W. Damon & R.M. Lerner (Eds.), *Handbook of child psychology: Volume 1—Theoretical models of human development* (6th ed., pp. 1–17). Wiley.

8. Côté, J., Bruner, M.W., Erickson, K., Strachan, L., & Fraser-Thomas, J. (2010). Athlete development and coaching. In J. Lyle & C. Cushion (Eds.), *Sport coaching: Professionalization and practice* (pp. 63-83). Elsevier.

9. Côté, J. (1999). The influence of the family in the development of talent in sport. *The Sport Psychologist, 13*, 395-417.

10. Balyi, I., & Hamilton, A. (1995). The concept of long-term athlete development. *Strength and Conditioning Coach, 3*, 5-6.

11. International Council for Coaching Excellence, Association of Summer Olympic International Federations, & Leeds Beckett University. (2013). *International sport coaching framework* (Version 1.2). Human Kinetics.

12. Steinberg, L. (2014). *Age of opportunity: Lessons from the new science of adolescence*. Houghton Mifflin Harcourt.

13. Camiré, M., & Trudel, P. (2014). Helping youth sport coaches integrate psychological skills in their coaching practice. *Qualitative Research in Sport, Exercise, and Health*, *6*, 617-634.

14. Vealey, R.S. (1988). Future directions in psychological skills training. *The Sport Psychologist*, *2*, 318-336.

15. Rogerson, L.J., & Hrycaiko, D.W. (2002). Enhancing competitive performance of ice-hockey goaltenders using centering and self-talk. *Journal of Applied Sport Psychology*, *14*, 14-26.

16. Thelwell, R.C., & Greenlees, I.A. (2003). Developing competitive endurance performance using mental skills training. *The Sport Psychologist*, *17*, 318-337.

17. Camiré, M. (2014). Youth development in North American high school sport: Review and recommendations. *Quest*, *66*, 495-511.

18. Fournier, J.F., Calmels, C., Durand-Bush, N., & Salmela, J.H. (2005). Effects of a season-long PST programme on gymnastic performance and on psychological skill development. *International Journal of Sport and Exercise Psychology*, *3*, 59-78.

19. Gilbert, J.N., & Lewis, D.K. (2013). Sport psychology with high school student-athletes: UNIFORM and the Game Plan Format. *Journal of Performance Psychology*, *6*, 1-30. www.centerforperformancepsychology.org/assets/resources/pageResources/The-Journal-of-Performance-Psychology-Issue-Six.pdf

20. Gucciardi, D.F., Gordon, S., & Dimmock, J.A. (2009). Evaluation of a mental toughness training programme for youth-aged Australian footballers: I. A quantitative analysis. *Journal of Applied Sport Psychology*, *21*, 307-323.

21. Gucciardi, D.F., Gordon, S., & Dimmock, J.A. (2009). Evaluation of a mental toughness training programme for youth-aged Australian footballers: II. A qualitative analysis. *Journal of Applied Sport Psychology*, *21*, 324-339.

22. Sheard, M., & Golby, J. (2006). Effect of a psychological skills training programme on swimming performance and positive psychological development. *International Journal of Sport and Exercise Psychology*, *4*, 149-169.

23. Thelwell, R.C., Greenlees, I.A., & Weston, N.J.V. (2006). Using psychological skills training to develop soccer performance. *Journal of Applied Sport Psychology*, *18*, 254-270.

24. Zhang, L., Ma, Q., Orlick, T., & Zitzelsberger, L. (1992). The effect of mental-imagery training on performance enhancement with 7-10-year-old children. *The Sport Psychologist*, *6*, 230-241.

25. Harwood, C. (2008). Developmental consulting in a professional football academy: The 5Cs coaching efficacy program. *The Sport Psychologist*, *22*, 109-133.

26. Harwood, C., Barker, J.B., & Anderson, R. (2015). Psychosocial development in youth soccer players: Assessing the effectiveness of the 5Cs intervention program. *The Sport Psychologist*, *29*, 319-334.

27. Burton, D., & Raedeke, T.D. (2008). *Sport psychology for coaches*. Human Kinetics.

28. Gilbert, J.N. (2015). Sport psychology teaching approaches for high school coaches and their student-athletes. *Journal of Physical Education, Recreation and Dance*, *88*, 52-88.

29. Bandura, A. (1997). *Self-efficacy: The exercise of control*. Freeman.

30. Danish, S.J. (2002). Teaching life skills through sport. In M. Gatz (Ed.), *Paradoxes of youth and sport* (pp. 49-60). State University of New York Press.

31. Gould, D., & Carson, C. (2008). Life skills development through sport: Current status and future directions. *International Review of Sport and Exercise Psychology, 1*, 58-78.

32. Doran, G.T. (1981). There's a S.M.A.R.T. way to write management's goals and objectives. *Management Review, 70*(11; AMA FORUM), 35-36.

33. Weinberg, R.S., & Gould, D. (2015). *Foundations of sport and exercise psychology* (6th ed.). Human Kinetics.

34. Lauer, L., Gould, D., Lubbers, P., & Kovacs, M. (Eds.). (2010). *USTA Mental skills and drills handbook*. Coaches Choice.

35. Diment, G.M. (2014). Mental skills training in soccer: A drill-based approach. *Journal of Sport Psychology in Action, 5*, 14-27. doi:10.1080/21520704.2013.865005

36. Voight, M. (2005). Integrating mental-skills training into everyday coaching. *Journal of Physical Education, Recreation & Dance, 76*(3), 38-47, doi:10.1080/07303084.2005.10608222

37. Estes, C. (2004). Promoting student-centered learning in experiential education. *Journal of Experiential Education, 27*(2), 141-160.

38. Danish, S.J., & Nellen, V.C. (1997). New roles for sport psychologists: Teaching life skills through sport to at-risk youth. *Quest, 49*, 100-113.

39. Danish, S., Forneris, T., Hodge, K., & Heke, I. (2004). Enhancing youth development through sport. *World Leisure, 46*, 38-49.

40. Allen, G., Rhind, D., & Koshy, V. (2015). Enablers and barriers for male students transferring life skills from the sports hall into the classroom. *Qualitative Research in Sport, Exercise, and Health, 7*, 53-67.

41. Gilbert, J.N., & Orlick, T. (1996). Evaluation of a life skills program with grade two children. *Elementary School Guidance and Counseling, 31*, 139-151.

42. Holt, N.L., McHugh, T.L.F., Tink, L.N., Kingsley, B.C., Coppola, A.M., Neely, K.C., & McDonald, R. (2013). Developing sport-based after-school programmes using a participatory action research approach. *Qualitative Research in Sport, Exercise, and Health, 5*, 332-355.

43. Garcia-Calvo, T., Sanchez-Oliva, D., Leo, F.M., Amado, D., & Pulido, J.J. (2015, May 26). Effects of an intervention programme with teachers on the development of positive behaviours in Spanish physical education classes. *Physical Education and Sport Pedagogy*. https://www.tandfonline.com/doi/abs/10.1080/17408989.2015.1043256

44. Vella, S.A., Oades, L.G., & Crowe, T.P. (2013). A pilot test of transformational leadership training for sports coaches: Impact on the developmental experiences of adolescent athletes. *International Journal of Sports Science and Coaching, 8*, 513-530.

45. Danish, S.J., Fazio, R., Nellen, V.C., & Owens, S. (2002). Community-based life skills programs: Using sport to teach life skills to adolescents. In J. Van Raalte & B. Brewer (Eds.), *Exploring sport and exercise psychology* (2nd ed., pp. 269–288). APA Books.

46. Danish, S.J., Forneris, T., & Wallace, I. (2005). Sport-based life skills programming in the schools. *Journal of Applied School Psychology, 21*(2), 41-62.

47. Weiss, M.R., Stuntz, C.P., Bhalla, J.A., Bolter, N.D., & Price, M.S. (2013). "More than a game": Impact of The First Tee life skills programme on positive youth development: Project introduction and year 1 findings. *Qualitative Research in Sport, Exercise, and Health, 5*, 214–244.

48. Forneris, T., Danish, S.J., & Scott, D.L. (2007). Setting goals, solving problems, and seeking social support: Developing adolescents' abilities through a life skills program. *Adolescence, 42*, 103-114.

49. Falcão, W.R., Bloom, G.A., & Gilbert, W.D. (2012). Coaches' perceptions of a coach training program designed to promote youth developmental outcomes. *Journal of Applied Sport Psychology, 24*, 429-444.

50. Horn, C.M., Gilbert, J.N., Gilbert, W.D., & Lewis, D.K. (2011). Psychological skill straining with community college athletes: The UNIFORM approach. *The Sport Psychologist, 25*, 321-340.

51. Gilbert, J.N. (2011). Teaching sport psychology to high school student-athletes: The Psychological UNIFORM and the Game Plan Format. *Journal of Sport Psychology in Action, 2*, 1-9.

52. Camiré, M., Trudel, P., & Bernard, D. (2013). A case study of a high school sport program designed to teach athletes life skills and values. *The Sport Psychologist, 27*, 188-200.

53. Camiré, M., Forneris, T., Trudel, P., & Bernard, D. (2011). Strategies for helping coaches facilitate positive youth development through sport. *Journal of Sport Psychology in Action, 2*, 92–99.

54. Greenwald, J.H. (2009). Mental skills training for tennis players: An added skill set for the strength and conditioning coach. *Strength and Conditioning Journal, 31*, 94-97.

55. Camiré, M. (2015). Examining high school teacher-coaches' perspective on relationship building with student-athletes. *International Sport Coaching Journal, 2*, 125-136. doi:10.1123/iscj.2014-0098

56. Erickson, K., & Côté, J. (2016). A season-long examination of the intervention tone of coach-athlete interactions and athlete development in youth sport. *Psychology of Sport and Exercise, 22*, 264-272.

57. Smith, R.E., & Smoll, F.L. (2007). Social-cognitive approach to coaching behaviors. In S. Jowett & D. Lavallee (Eds.), *Social psychology in sport* (pp. 75-89). Human Kinetics.

58. Buceta, J.M. (1993). The sport psychologist/athletic coach dual role: Advantages, difficulties, and ethical considerations. *Journal of Applied Sport Psychology, 5*, 64-77.

59. Jones, L., Evans, L., & Mullen, R. (2007). Multiple roles in an applied setting: Trainee sport psychologist, coach, and researcher. *The Sport Psychologist, 21*, 210-226.

60. Aoyagi, M.W., & Portenga, S.T. (2010). The role of positive ethics and virtues in the context of sport and performance psychology service delivery. *Professional Psychology: Research and Practice, 41*, 253-259.

Chapter 9

1. Drabik, J. (1996). *Children and sports training: How your future champions should exercise to be healthy, fit, and happy.* Stadion.

The author also recommends:

Anderson, O. (1999). Things were so easy, until $v\dot{V}O_2$max and then $Tlimv\dot{V}O_2$max had to come along. *Running Research News, 15*(2), 1-5.

Anderson, O. (2000). Torrid new $v\dot{V}O_2$max sessions keep you at $\dot{V}O_2$max—and are easier to carry out. *Running Research News, 16*(7), 1-4.

Bosch, F., & Klomp, R. (2005). *Running: Biomechanics and exercise physiology applied in practice.* Elsevier Churchill Livingstone.

Dick, F. (2014). *Sports training principles: An introduction to sports science* (6th ed.). Bloomsbury.

Gambetta, V.A. (2007). *Athletic development: The art and science of functional sports conditioning.* Human Kinetics.

Gambetta, V., & Winckler, G. (2001). *Sport-specific speed: The 3S system.* Gambetta Sports Training Systems.

Kurz, T. (1994). *Stretching scientifically: A guide to flexibility training* (3rd ed.). Stadion.

Chapter 10

1. Knudson, D.V., & Morrison, C.S. (2002). *Qualitative analysis of human movement* (2nd ed.). Human Kinetics.

2. Knudson, D., & Morrison, C. (1996). An integrated qualitative analysis of overarm throwing. *Journal of Physical Education, Recreation and Dance, 67*(6), 31-36.

3. Ste-Marie, D.M. (1999). Expert–novice differences in gymnastic judging: An information-processing perspective. *Applied Cognitive Psychology, 13*, 269-281.

4. Giblin, G. (2015). *What a coach can see and an athlete can feel* [Unpublished doctoral dissertation]. Victoria University.

5. Giblin, G., Farrow, D., Reid, M., Ball, B., & Abernethy, B. (2015). Exploring the kinaesthetic sensitivity of skilled performers for implementing movement instructions. *Human Movement Science, 41*, 76-91.

6. Abernethy, B., Masters, R.S.W., & Zachry, T. (2008). Using biomechanical feedback to enhance skill learning and performance. In Y. Hong & R. Bartlett (Eds.), *Routledge handbook of biomechanics and human movement science* (pp. 581-593). Routledge.

7. Schmidt, R.A., & Wrisberg, C.A. (2004). *Motor learning and performance: A problem-based learning approach* (3rd ed.). Human Kinetics.

8. Wulf, G. (2013). Attentional focus and motor learning: A review of 15 years. *International Review of Sport and Exercise Psychology, 6*, 77-104.

9. Masters, R. (2013). Practicing implicit (motor) learning. In D. Farrow, J. Baker, & C. MacMahon (Eds.), *Developing sport expertise: Researchers and coaches put theory into practice* (2nd ed., pp. 154-174). Routledge.

10. Lohse, K. (2015). On attentional control: A dimensional framework for attention in expert performance. In J. Baker & D. Farrow (Eds.), *Routledge handbook of sport expertise* (pp. 38-50). Routledge.

11. Salmoni, A.W., Schmidt, R.A., & Walter, C.B. (1984). Knowledge of results and motor learning: A review and critical reappraisal. *Psychological Bulletin*, *95*(3), 355.

12. Phillips, E., Farrow, D., Ball, K., & Helmer, R (2013). Harnessing and understanding feedback technology in applied settings. *Sports Medicine*, *43*(10), 919-925. doi:10.1007/s40279-013-0072-7

13. Magill, R.A., & Anderson, D.I. (2012). The roles and uses of augmented feedback in motor skill acquisition. In N.J. Hodges & A.M. Williams (Eds.), *Skill acquisition in sport: Research, theory, and practice* (2nd ed., pp. 3-21). Routledge.

14. Davids, K., Araújo, D., Vilar, L., Renshaw, I., & Pinder, R. (2013). An ecological dynamics approach to skill acquisition: Implications for development of talent in sport. *Talent Development & Excellence*, *5*(1), 21-34.

15. Barris, S., Davids, K., & Farrow, D. (2013). Representative learning design in springboard diving: Is dry-land training representative of a pool dive? *European Journal of Sport Science*, *13*(6), 638-645.

16. Pinder, R.A., Renshaw, I., & Davids, K. (2009). Information–movement coupling in developing cricketers under changing ecological practice constraints. *Human Movement Science*, *28*(4), 468-479.

17. Low, J., Williams, A.M., McRobert, A.P., & Ford, P.R. (2013). The microstructure of practice activities engaged in by elite and recreational youth cricket players. *Journal of Sports Sciences*, *31*(11), 1242-1250.

18. Ford, P.R., Yates, I., & Williams, A.M. (2010). An analysis of practice activities and instructional behaviours used by youth soccer coaches during practice: Exploring the link between science and application. *Journal of Sports Sciences*, *28*(5), 483-495.

19. Partington, M., & Cushion, C. (2013). An investigation of the practice activities and coaching behaviors of professional top-level youth soccer coaches. *Scandinavian Journal of Medicine & Science in Sports*, *23*(3), 374-382.

20. Handford, C., Davids, K., Bennett, S., & Button, C. (1997). Skill acquisition in sport: Some applications of an evolving practice ecology. *Journal of Sports Sciences*, *15*(6), 621-640.

21. Patterson, J.T., & Lee, T.D. (2013). Organizing practice. In D. Farrow, J. Baker, & C. MacMahon (Eds.), *Developing sport expertise: Researchers and coaches put theory into practice* (2nd ed., pp. 132-153). Routledge.

22. Hossner, E.-J., Käch, B., & Enz, J. (2016). On the optimal degree of fluctuations in practice for motor learning. *Human Movement Science*, *47*, 231-239.

23. Savelsbergh, G.J.P., Kamper, W., Rabius, J., de Koning, J., & Schöllhorn, W. (2010). New methods to learn to start in speed skating: A differential learning approach. *International Journal of Sport Psychology*, *41*, 415–427.

24. Schöllhorn, W.I., Michelbrink, M., Beckmann, H., Trockel, M., Sechelmann, M., & Davids, K. (2006). Does noise provide a basis for the unification of motor learning theories? *International Journal of Sport Psychology*, *37*, 34–42.

25. Davids, K., Shuttleworth, R., Button, C., Renshaw, I., & Glazier, P. (2003). "Essential noise"—Enhancing variability of informational constraints benefits movement control: A comment on Waddington and Adams. *British Journal of Sports Medicine*, *38*, 601-605.

26. Bernstein, N.A. (1967). *The coordination and regulation of movements.* Pergamon.

27. Guadagnoli, M.A., & Lee, T.D. (2004). Challenge point: A framework for conceptualizing the effects of various practice conditions in motor learning. *Journal of Motor Behavior, 36*(2), 212-224.

28. Guadagnoli, M. (2007). *Practice to learn, play to win.* Ecademy.

29. Pinder, R.A., Davids, K.W., Renshaw, I., & Araújo, D. (2011). Representative learning design and functionality of research and practice in sport. *Journal of Sport and Exercise Psychology, 33*(1), 146-155.

30. Slade, D. (2015). Do the structures used by international hockey coaches for practising field-goal shooting reflect game-centred learning within a representative learning design? *International Journal of Sports Science & Coaching, 10*(4), 655-668.

31. Travassos, B., Duarte, R., Vilar, V., Davids, K., & Araújo, D. (2012). Practice task design in team sports: Representativeness enhanced by increasing opportunities for action. *Journal of Sports Sciences, 30*(13), 1447-1454.

32. Farrow, D., & Raab, M. (2013). A recipe for expert decision-making. In D. Farrow, J. Baker, & C. MacMahon (Eds.), *Developing sport expertise: Researchers and coaches put theory into practice* (2nd ed., pp. 210-230). Routledge.

33. Baker, J., Côté, J., & Abernethy, B. (2003). Sport-specific practice and the development of expert decision-making in team ball sports. *Journal of Applied Sport Psychology, 15*, 12-25.

34. Berry, J., Abernethy, B., & Côté, J. (2008). The contribution of structured activity and deliberate play to the development of expert perceptual and decision-making skill. *Journal of Sport & Exercise Psychology, 30*, 685-708.

35. Davies, M.J., Young, W., Farrow, D., & Bahnert, A. (2013). Comparison of agility demands of small-sided games in elite Australian Football. *International Journal of Sports Physiology and Performance, 8*, 139-147.

36. Farrow, D., Pyne, D., & Gabbett, T. (2008). Skill and physiological demands of open and closed training drills in Australian football. *International Journal of Sports Science and Coaching, 3*(4), 485-495.

37. Klusemann, M.J., Pyne, D.B., Foster, C., & Drinkwater, E.J. (2012). Optimising technical skills and physical loading in small-sided basketball games. *Journal of Sports Sciences, 30*, 1463-1471.

38. Jones, S., & Drust, B. (2007). Physiological and technical demands of 4v4 and 8v8 games in elite youth soccer players. *Kinesiology, 39*, 150-156.

39. Casamichana, D., & Castellano, J. (2010). Time-motion, heart rate, perceptual and motor behaviour demands in small-sides soccer games: Effects of pitch size. *Journal of Sports Sciences, 28*(14), 1615-1623.

Chapter 11

1. International Council for Coach Excellence, Association of Summer Olympic International Federations, & Leeds Beckett University. (2013). *International sport coaching framework* (Version 1.2). Human Kinetics.

2. Duffy, P., Hartley, H., Bales, J., & Crespo, M. (2010). The development of sports coaching as a profession: Challenges and future directions in a global context

[Keynote lecture]. 2010 Canadian Sports Leadership Conference, Ottawa, Canada.

3. Trotman, J., & Kerr, T. (2001). Making the personal professional: Pre-service teacher education and personal histories. *Teachers and Teaching, Theory and Practice, 7*(2), 157-171.

4. Taylor, W.G., & McEwan, I.M. (2012). From interprofessional working to transprofessional possibilities: The new age of sports coaching in the United Kingdom. *Sport Coaching Review, 1*(1), 38-51.

5. Taylor, W.G., & Garratt, D. (2008). Report on the professionalisation of sports coaching in the UK: Definitions and conceptualization. Sports Coach UK.

6. Taylor, W.G., & Garratt, D. (2010). The professionalisation of sports coaching: Relations of power, resistance, and compliance. *Sport Education and Society, 15*(1), 121-139.

7. Taylor, W.G., & Garratt, D. (2013). The professionalisation of coaching. In P. Potrac, W. Gilbert, & J. Dennison (Eds.), *Routledge handbook of sports coaching* (pp. 27-39). Routledge.

8. Taylor, W.G., & Groom, R. (2016). Quality assurance in coach education. In A. Abrahams, A. Cale, & W. Allison (Eds.), *Advances in coach education and development: From research to practice.* Routledge.

9. North, J. (2009). *The UK coaching framework: The coaching workforce 2009-2016.* Coachwise Business Solutions.

10. Gould, D., Carson, S., & Blanton, J. (2013). Coaching life skills. In P. Potrac, W. Gilbert, & J. Dennison (Eds.), *Routledge handbook of sports coaching* (pp. 259-270). Routledge.

11. Sage, G. (1989). Becoming a high school coach: From playing sports to coaching. *Research Quarterly for Exercise and Sport, 60*(1), 81-98.

12. Nash, C.S., Sproule, J., Callan, M., McDonald, K., & Cassidy, T. (2009). Career development of expert coaches. *International Journal of Sports Science & Coaching, 4*(1), 121-138.

13. Dawson, A., & Phillips, P. (2013). Coach career development: Who is responsible? *Sport Management Review, 16*(4), 477-487.

14. SHAPE America. (2006). *Quality coaches, quality sports: National standards for sport coaches* (2nd ed.). Author.

15. Ohio Department of Education. (2017). *Ohio's educator standards.* http://education.ohio.gov/Topics/Teaching/Educator-Equity/Ohio-s-Educator-Standards

16. Ohio Department of Education. (2017). *Renew a license.* http://education.ohio.gov/Topics/Teaching/Licensure/Renew-Certificate-License

17. Gilbert, W., & Trudel, P. (2001). Learning to coach through experience: Reflection in model youth sport coaches. *Journal of Teaching in Physical Education, 21*, 16-34.

18. Kenttä, G., Mellalieu, S., & Roberts, C.M. (2016). Are career termination concerns only for athletes? A case study of the career termination of an elite female coach. *Sport Psychologist, 30*(4), 314-326. http://dx.doi.org/10.1123/tsp.2015-0134

19. Coaches Association of British Columbia. (n.d.). *Coach self-evaluation tool.* http://biathlon.ca/wp-content/uploads/2016/01/Coachselfevaluationtool.pdf

20. Team USA. (n.d.). *Coach effectiveness tool.* www.teamusa.org/~/media/USA_Volleyball/Documents/Education/Resources/IMPACT-Resources/USOC-Coaching-Effectiveness-Tool.pdf?la=en

21. Gilbert, W. (2017). *Coaching better every season: A year-round system for athlete development and program success.* Human Kinetics.

22. Trudel, P., & Gilbert, W. (2006). Coaching and coach education. In D. Kirk, M. O'Sullivan, & D. McDonald (Eds.), *Handbook of physical education* (pp. 516-539). Sage.

23. National Coaching Certification Program. (2017). *Overview of the NCCP model.* www.coach.ca/files/NCCPModel_en_skin.swf

24. Lyle, J. (2002). *Sports coaching concepts: A framework for coaches' behavior.* Routledge.

25. Positive Coaching Alliance. (2016). *11 tips for the first-time coach.* http://devzone.positivecoach.org/resource/article/11-tips-first-time-coach?gclid=CjwKEAiAqozEBRDJrPem0fPKtX0SJAD5sAyHiQLPAw7vxeqtadgG7Ajs58G5-4uX0eof5Z-wuJPv2XRoC1Efw_wcB

26. Morris, E., Arthur-Banning, S., & McDowell, J. (2016). Constraints to millennial generation female athletic coaches pursuing head coaching careers. *International Journal of Sport Management, 17*(3), 336-356.

27. Cunningham, G.B. (2003). Already aware of the glass ceiling: Race-related effects of perceived opportunity on the career choices of college athletes. *Journal of African American Studies, 7*(1), 57-71.

28. Farris, L.G. (2004). Becoming a better coach through reflective practice. *BC Coach's perspective, 6,* 10-11.

29. Gilbert, W. (2016). *Demonstrating core values and clear purpose in coaching.* Human Kinetics Coach Education Center. www.humankinetics.com/AcuCustom/Sitename/DAM/134/PP_Demonstrating_Core_Values_and_Clear_Purpose_in_Coaching.pdf

30. Singh, P., & Surujlal, J. (2006). Factors affecting the job satisfaction of South African sport coaches. *South African Journal for Research in Sport, Physical Education and Recreation, 28*(1), 127-136.

31. Soukup, G.J. (2004). How to find the coaching job you want. *Texas Coach, 48*(8), 26-28.

32. Mackay, M. (2013). *A games approach to teaching basketball skills – Mike MacKay.* YouTube. https://www.youtube.com/watch?v=Hpyg18buShA

33. ESPN. (2014). *Becky Hammon hired to Spurs staff.* www.espn.com/nba/story/_/id/11312366/becky-hammon-hired-san-antonio-spurs

34. Amorose, A.J., & Horn, T.S. (2000). Intrinsic motivation: Relationships with collegiate athletes' gender, scholarship status, and perceptions of their coaches' behavior. *Journal of Sport and Exercise Psychology, 22,* 63-84.

35. Duda, J.L. (1987). Toward a developmental theory of children's motivation in sport. *Journal of Sport Psychology, 9,* 130-145.

36. Carron, A.V., Colman, M.M., Wheeler, J., & Stevens, D. (2002). Cohesion and performance in sport: A meta analysis. *Journal of Sport & Exercise Psychology, 24*(2), 168-188.

37. Vealey, R., & Chase, M. (2016). *Best practice in youth sport*. Human Kinetics.

38. Bates, I. (2007). Coaching experience, coaching performance. In J. Denison (Ed.), *Coaching knowledges*. A & C Black.

39. Ross, D. (2017). *Commissioner of the Ohio High School Athletic Association (OHSAA) at the annual meeting of the Ohio Association of Local School Superintendents (OALSS)*. Columbus, OH.

40. Konukman, F., Agbuğa, B., Erdoğan, D., Zorba, E., Demirhan, G., & Yılmaz, I. (2010). Teacher-coach role conflict in school-based physical education in USA: A literature review and suggestions for the future. *Biomedical Human Kinetics, 2*, 19-24.

41. Coyle, G. (2016). *Longtime Huggins assistant Larry Harrison shares in journey to 800*. West Virginia Illustrated. www.wvillustrated.com/story/34071247/longtime-huggins-assistant-larry-harrison-shares-in-journey-to-800

42. Johnson, K.C. (2016, January 18). Johnny Bach dies at 91; Michael Jordan: "He was more than a coach to me." *Chicago Tribune*. www.chicagotribune.com/sports/basketball/bulls/ct-johnny-bach-bulls-20160118-story.html

43. New Orleans Saints. (2015). *Rob Ryan*. www.neworleanssaints.com/team/coaches/rob-ryan/280d0ea9-4989-4a03-99b8-fa862a2d1349

44. Cassidy, T., Potrac, P., & McKenzie, A. (2006). Evaluating and reflecting upon a coach education initiative: The CoDe of rugby. *The Sport Psychologist, 20*, 145-161.

45. Culver, D.M., & Trudel, P. (2006). Cultivating coaches' communities of practice: Developing potential for learning through interactions. In R. Jones (Ed.), *The sport coach as educator: Reconceptualising sport coaching* (pp. 97-112). Routledge.

46. Stoszkowski, J., & Collins, D. (2014). Communities of practice, social learning, and networks: Exploiting the social side of coach development. *Sport, Education, and Society, 19*(6), 773-788.

47. Raedeke, T., & Kenttä, G. (2013). Coach burnout. In P. Potrac, W. Gilbert, & J. Denison (Eds.), *Routledge handbook of sports coaching* (pp. 424-435). Routledge.

48. Van Valkenberg, K. (2015). *How Urban Meyer found his balance*. ESPN. www.espn.com/college-football/bowls14/story/_/id/12152579/ohio-state-buckeyes-coach-urban-meyer-finds-balance-coaching-again

49. Sheridan, M.P. (2016). Coaching burnout: Challenges and solutions. *Future Focus: Ohio Journal of Physical Education, Recreation, and Dance, Spring/Summer*, 8-11.

50. Lavallee, D. (2005). The effect of a life development intervention on sports coach career transition adjustment. *The Sport Psychologist, 19*, 193-202.

51. Wylleman, P., Alfermann, D., & Lavallee, D. (2004). Career transitions in sport: European perspectives. *Psychology of Sport and Exercise, 5*, 7-20.

52. Standal, O., & Hemmested, L. (2011). Becoming a good coach: Coaching and phronesis. In A. Hardmans & C. Jones (Eds.), *The ethics of sports coaching* (pp. 45-56). Routledge.

53. Green, M., & Houlihan, B. (2005). *Elite sport development: Policy learning and political priorities*. Routledge.

54. Cushion, C., Nelson, L., & Potrac, P. (2013). Enhancing the provision of coach education: The recommendations of UK coaching practitioners. *Physical Education and Sport Pedagogy, 18*(2), 204-218.

55. Cushion, C., Armour, K., & Jones, R. (2003). Coach education and continuing professional development: Experience and learning to coach. *QUEST, 55,* 215-230.

56. Piggott, D. (2012). Coaches' experience of formal education: A critical sociological explanation. *Sport, Education, and Society, 17*(4), 535-554.

57. Morgan, K., Jones, R., Gilbourne, D., & Llewellyn, D. (2013). Innovative approaches in coach education pedagogy. In P. Potrac, W. Gilbert, & J. Dennison (Eds.), *Routledge handbook of sports coaching* (pp. 486-496). Routledge.

58. Cushion, C. (2006). Mentoring: Harnessing the power of experience. In R.L. Jones (Ed.), *Coach as educator: Reconceptualising sports coaching* (pp. 128–144). Routledge.

59. UK Sport. (2015). Elite Coaching Apprenticeship Programme. www.uksport.gov.uk/our-work/coaching/elite-coaching-apprenticeship-programme

Chapter 12

1. Mallett, C.J., & Lara-Bercial, S. (2016). Serial winning coaches: People, vision, and environment. In M. Raab, P. Wylleman, R. Seiler, A.-M. Elbe, & G. Hatzigeorgiadis (Eds.), *Sport and exercise psychology research: From theory to practice* (pp. 289-322). Elsevier.

2. Rynne, S.B., & Mallett, C.J. (2014). Coaches' learning and sustainability in high-performance sport. *Reflective Practice, 15*(1), 12-26.

3. Werthner, P., & Trudel, P. (2009). Investigating the idiosyncratic learning paths of high-performance Canadian coaches. *International Journal of Sports Science & Coaching, 4*(3), 433-449.

4. Jarvis, P. (2006). *Towards a comprehensive theory of human learning.* Routledge.

5. Ambrose, S.A., Bridges, M.W., DiPietro, M., Lovett, M.C., & Norman, M.K. (2010). How learning works: 7 research-based principles for smart teaching. Jossey-Bass.

6. Trudel, P., Gilbert, W., & Rodrigue, F. (2016). The journey from competent to innovator: Using Appreciative Inquiry to enhance high-performance coaching. *International Journal of Appreciative Inquiry, 18*(2), 40-46.

7. Callary, B., Werthner, P., & Trudel, P. (2011). Shaping the way five women coaches develop: Their primary and secondary socialization. *Journal of Coaching Education, 4,* 76–125.

8. Gilbert, W., Côté, J., & Mallett, C. (2006). Developmental paths and activities of successful sport coaches. *International Journal of Sport Science & Coaching, 1*(1), 69-76.

9. Trudel, P., Gilbert, W., & Werthner, P. (2010). Coach education effectiveness. In J. Lyle & C. Cushion (Eds.), *Sports coaching: Professionalization and practice* (pp. 135-152). Elsevier.

10. Tao, Y.C., Rynne, S.B., & Mallett, C.J. (2019). Blending and becoming: Migrant Chinese high-performance coaches' learning journey in Australia. *Physical Education and Sport Pedagogy, 24*(6), 582-597. doi:10.1080/17408989.2019.1641191

11. International Council for Coach Excellence, Association of Summer Olympic International Federations, & Leeds Beckett University. (2013). *International sport coaching framework* (Version 1.2). Human Kinetics.

12. Gilbert, W., & Côté, J. (2013). Defining coaching effectiveness: A focus on coaches' knowledge. In P. Potrac, W. Gilbert, & J. Denison (Eds.), *Routledge handbook of sports coaching* (pp. 147-159). Routledge.

13. Lynch, M., & Mallett, C. (2006). Becoming a successful high-performance track and field coach. *Modern Athlete and Coach, 22*(2), 15-20.

14. Trudel, P., & Gilbert, W. (2013). The role of deliberate practice in becoming an expert coach: Part 3—Creating optimal settings. *Olympic Coach Magazine, 24*(2), 15-28.

15. Moon, J.A. (2001). *Short courses and workshops: Improving the impact of learning, training, and professional development.* Kogan Page.

16. Mallett, C.J., & Dickens, S. (2009). Authenticity in formal coach education: Online postgraduate studies in sports coaching at The University of Queensland. *International Journal of Coaching Science, 3*(2), 79–90.

17. Mallett, C.J., Rynne, S.B., & Billett, S. (2016). Valued learning experiences of early career and experienced high-performance coaches. *Physical Education and Sport Pedagogy, 21*(1), 89-104.

18. Rynne, S.B., Mallett, C.J., & Tinning, R. (2010). Workplace learning of high-performance sports coaches. *Sport, Education, and Society, 15*(3), 315-330.

19. Trudel, P., & Gilbert, W. (2006). Coaching and coach education. In D. Kirk, D. Macdonald, & M. O'Sullivan (Eds.), *Handbook of physical education* (pp. 516-539). Sage.

20. Moon, J.A. (2006). *Learning journals: A handbook for reflective practice and professional development* (2nd ed.). Routledge.

21. Occhino, J., Mallett, C.J., & Rynne, S.B. (2013). Dynamic social networks in high-performance football coaching. *Physical Education and Sport Pedagogy, 18*(1), 90-102.

22. Wenger, E., McDermott, R., & Snyder, W.M. (2002). *Cultivating communities of practice: A guide to managing knowledge.* Harvard Business School Press.

23. Bertram, R., Culver, D., & Gilbert, W. (2016). Creating value in a sport coach community of practice: A collaborative inquiry. *International Sport Coaching Journal, 3*(1), 2-16.

24. Culver, D.M., & Trudel, P. (2006). Cultivating coaches' communities of practice: Developing the potential for learning through interactions. In R. Jones (Ed.), *The sports coach as educator: Re-conceptualising sports coaching* (pp. 97-112). Routledge.

25. Culver, D.M., & Trudel, P. (2008). Clarifying the communities of practice concept in sport. *International Journal of Sports Science and Coaching, 3*(1), 1-10.

26. Mallett, C. (2010). Becoming a high-performance coach: Pathways and communities. In J. Lyle and C. Cushion (Eds.), *Sports coaching: Profession and practice* (pp. 119-135). Elsevier.

27. Trudel, P., & Gilbert, W. (2004). Communities of practice as an approach to foster ice hockey coach development. *Safety in Ice Hockey, 4*, 167-179.

28. Gilbert, W., & Trudel, P. (2006). The coach as a reflective practitioner. In R. Jones (Ed.), *The sports coach as educator: Re-conceptualising sports coaching* (pp. 113-127). Routledge.

Appendix

1. World Anti-Doping Agency. (2015, January 1). *World anti-doping code 2015.* https://www.wada-ama.org/sites/default/files/resources/files/wada-2015-world-anti-doping-code.pdf

APPENDIX

Governing Rules and Laws: The World Anti-Doping Code

Anti-doping policy has formally recognized the potential influence of coaches on behaviors related to doping among sportspeople. More pointedly, anti-doping rules apply to coaches as athlete support personnel, a category that includes "any coach, trainer, manager, agent, team staff, official, medical, paramedical personnel, parent, or any other Person working with, treating, or assisting an Athlete participating in or preparing for sports Competition."[1, p. 136]

Since January 2015, the World Anti-Doping Code—the global policy outlining rules and regulations associated with the management of drug use in sport—has placed greater responsibility on athlete support personnel to recognize the role they play in supporting athletes and the influence they can exert. Therefore, it is vital for coaches to understand the code and its implications for them and their athletes. In fact, they are prescribed anti-doping roles and responsibilities in an effort to "protect the athletes' fundamental right to participate in doping-free sport and thus promote health, fairness, and equality for athletes worldwide."[1, p. 11] Specifically, under Article 21.2 of the code,[1, p. 116] the following responsibilities are prescribed for every coach:

- "To be knowledgeable of and comply with all anti-doping policies and rules adopted pursuant to the *Code* and which are applicable to them or the *Athletes* whom they support.
- To cooperate with the *Athlete Testing* program.
- To use his or her influence on *Athlete* values and behavior to foster anti-doping attitudes.
- To disclose to his or her *National Anti-Doping Organization* and International Federation any decision by a non-*Signatory* finding

that he or she committed an anti-doping rule violation within the previous ten years.

- To cooperate with *Anti-Doping Organizations* investigating anti-doping rule violations.
- [To] . . . not *Use* or *Possess* any *Prohibited Substance* or *Prohibited Method* without valid justification."

To clarify, coaches are subject to sanctions if they are found to commit an anti-doping rule violation (ADRV). Under the Code, the following violations pertain to coaches:

- Tampering or attempted tampering with any part of doping control
- Possession of a prohibited substance or method
- Trafficking or attempted trafficking in any prohibited substance or method
- Administration or attempted administration of a prohibited substance or method to an athlete
- Complicity assisting, encouraging, aiding, abetting, conspiring, covering up, or any other type of complicity involving an anti-doping rule violation or attempted violation by another person
- Prohibited association (associating with a person such as a coach, doctor, or physiotherapist who has been found guilty of a criminal or disciplinary offense equivalent to a doping violation)

INDEX

ABOUT THE EDITORS

Dan Gould, PhD, is the director of the Institute for the Study of Youth Sports and professor in the department of kinesiology at Michigan State University. Gould's current research focuses on the psychology of coaching, the role coaches have in teaching life skills to young athletes, and the development of youth leaders through the sport captaincy experience. In addition to his research interests, Gould has dedicated much of his career to applied sport psychology efforts as a mental skills training consultant, coaching educator, and author.

Gould has given over 1,000 coaching education clinic presentations and developed numerous coaching and coaching education programs aimed at coaches ranging from the youth level to the Olympic level. He has written a number of books, including the *USTA Mental Skills and Drills Handbook*, *Sport Psychology for Young Athletes*, and *Foundations of Sport and Exercise Psychology*, the most widely used text in the field.

Cliff Mallett, PhD, is a professor of sport psychology and coaching in the School of Human Movement and Nutrition Sciences at the University of Queensland (Australia) and an honorary professor at the Technical University of Munich (Germany).

Mallett is an Olympic and World Championship medal winning coach. He is internationally recognized as a leading researcher in sport psychology, coaching, and coach development. His research interests are varied but focus on motivation, mental toughness, and leadership as it pertains to coaching in high-performance sport.

Mallett has been cochair and chair of the research committee for the International Council for Coaching Excellence (2009-2019). He served as associate editor for the *International Sport Coaching Journal* for several years.

ABOUT THE AUTHORS

Sue Backhouse is a professor and the director of research in the Carnegie School of Sport at Leeds Beckett University in the United Kingdom. Her research interests include sporting integrity and athlete welfare, with a focus on doping in sport.

Joe Baker is a professor in the School of Kinesiology and Health Science at York University in Canada. His research examines the varying factors affecting skill acquisition and maintenance across the life span. He is internationally recognized as a leader in the science of athlete development and is the author or editor of 10 books and hundreds of peer-reviewed articles.

John Bales is president of the International Council for Coaching Excellence. His interests in coaching include coach education systems and policies, coach and coach developer training and assessment, and coaching values and philosophy.

Martin Camiré is an associate professor in the School of Human Kinetics at the University of Ottawa in Canada. Dr. Camiré is interested in examining how positive youth development can be facilitated in the context of sport. Dr. Camiré also studies the role played by coaches in facilitating the development of life skills in youth sport participants.

Karen Collins is the chair of the department of kinesiology at the University of New Hampshire (UNH). She is an expert in coaching philosophy, coach development and education, and leadership development. At UNH, she has also served as the sport studies program coordinator, the CHHS faculty fellow for teaching excellence, and a sport psychology consultant for the department of athletics.

Bob Crudgington is an associate lecturer and researcher in sports coaching at the University of Queensland. He is highly experienced in elite sport: He was the head coach of the medal-winning Australian softball team in the Atlanta and Sydney Olympics and was high-performance manager for Diving Australia in the Athens Olympics. His current interests include designing hybrid, authentic learning experiences for emerging high-performance coaches.

Kristen Dieffenbach is an associate professor of athletic coaching education at West Virginia University and the director of the Center for Applied Coaching and Sport Sciences. She is also currently the president of the United States Center for Coaching Excellence. Her research interests include professionalism and ethics in coaching and the support of the sport coaching profession.

Andy Driska is an assistant professor in the department of kinesiology at Michigan State University. He directs the online sport coaching and leadership master's program, and he lectures in sport psychology and skill development. Through the Institute for the Study of Youth Sports, he researches coach learning programs and their intersection with information technology. He has coached competitive swimming for 20 years.

Karl Erickson is an assistant professor in the Institute for the Study of Youth Sports within the department of kinesiology at Michigan State University. Dr. Erickson's research focuses on how coaches can facilitate positive youth development through sport, with a specific emphasis on coach–athlete interactions and relationships.

Damian Farrow is a professor of skill acquisition in the Institute for Health and Sport at Victoria University. He is also the coaching and innovations manager for the Australian Football League umpiring department. His research and practical interest focus on development of sport expertise with a particular focus on practice methodology and decision-making skill.

Vern Gambetta is the director and founder of the GAIN Network. Vern's coaching experience of more than 50 years spans all levels of competition and many sports. Vern has authored over 100 articles and seven books on sports training and coaching. He received his bachelor's degree from Fresno State University and his teaching credential, with a coaching minor, from University of California at Santa Barbara. Vern attended Stanford University and obtained his master's degree in education with an emphasis in physical education.

Jenelle N. Gilbert is a professor and the graduate program coordinator in the kinesiology department at California State University at Fresno. Her Mental Toughness UNIFORM curriculum, designed to teach mental skills to adolescent athletes via sport, is her primary research focus, along with coach development and positive youth development through sport.

Wade Gilbert is a professor in the department of kinesiology at California State University at Fresno. He is an internationally renowned coaching consultant and sport scientist. He served as the inaugural editor in chief for the *International Sport Coaching Journal* and has authored many influential coaching resources, including the highly acclaimed book *Coaching Better Every Season* and *United States Olympic and Paralympic Committee Quality Coaching Framework*.

Sergio Lara-Bercial is a reader in sport coaching at Leeds Beckett University in the United Kingdom. He is also the strategy and development manager for the International Council for Coaching Excellence. His areas of interest include coaching policy and systems, coach development and high-performance coaching, and positive youth development through sport.

Laurie Patterson is a senior lecturer in sport and exercise psychology within the Carnegie School of Sport at Leeds Beckett University in the United Kingdom. Her work focuses on understanding doping and clean sport behaviors across a range of stakeholder groups in order to inform effective practice, programs, and policy. A large proportion of Patterson's research investigates coaches' anti-doping roles and factors that influence this.

Steven Rynne is an associate professor and program convenor for sports coaching with the School of Human Movement and Nutrition Sciences at the University of Queensland in Australia. His ongoing research focus is on pedagogy, and his primary interests relate to high-performance coach learning and indigenous sports.

Mike Sheridan has more than 30 years of experience as an administrator, teacher, and head coach at the college and high school levels. His areas of interest include youth sport development, applied sport psychology, and coaching effectiveness. Sheridan is an elementary physical education teacher in the Tri-Valley (Ohio) School District.

William Taylor is an honorary research fellow at Leeds Beckett University in the United Kingdom. His primary research interests are the social and political elements of coaching and the professionalization of coaching. He has coached and developed coach education programs for 30 years.

Pierre Trudel is an emeritus professor at the University of Ottawa in Canada. His research interests are coach development and organizational learning. He is a consultant for many sport organizations, developing programs and acting as a personal learning coach for high-performance coaches.

Nick Wattie is an assistant professor in the faculty of health sciences at Ontario Tech University. His research examines sport expertise, skill acquisition, constraints on talent identification and development in sport, and the health outcomes associated with sport participation. He is coeditor of the *Routledge Handbook of Talent Identification and Development in Sport*.

ABOUT THE ICCE

The **International Council for Coaching Excellence (ICCE)** is a not-for-profit organization based at Leeds Beckett University whose mission is to lead and develop sport coaching globally. In pursuit of that mission, ICCE has developed an international sport coaching framework and built a global coaching community to strengthen the position of coaching as a profession. ICCE partners and markets include national representative bodies responsible for coach development, international federations, institutions that deliver coach education or represent coaches, individuals who design and deliver coach education, coaches, and the international sport community at large.

ICCE president **John Bales** and ICCE manager for strategy and development **Sergio Lara-Bercial** lent their experience and expertise to this project, not only as chapter contributors but also as selectors of leading coach educators to be part of this ambitious collaboration.